MAGIC
THE GATHERING

THE VISUAL GUIDE

Senior Editor Cefn Ridout
Senior Designer Clive Savage
Senior Production Editor Jennifer Murray
Senior Production Controller Mary Slater
Managing Editor Emma Grange
Managing Art Editor Vicky Short
Publishing Director Mark Searle

Packaged for DK by Amazing 15
Editor Martin Eden
Designers Martin Stiff, Marcus Scudamore

Cover Kieran Yanner

First published in Great Britain in 2022 by Dorling Kindersley Limited
One Embassy Gardens, 8 Viaduct Gardens, London SW11 7BW
A Penguin Random House Company

The authorised representative in the EEA is
Dorling Kindersley Verlag GmbH. Arnulfstr. 124, 80636 Munich, Germany

Page design copyright © 2022 Dorling Kindersley Limited
DK, a Division of Penguin Random House LLC
22 23 24 25 26 10 9 8 7 6 5 4 3 2 1
001–328145–Dec/2022

For the curious
www.dk.com

THE VISUAL GUIDE

Written by
Jay Annelli

CONTENTS

FOREWORD

Over the course of its decades of history, *Magic: the Gathering* has defined the modern trading card game. First released in 1993 at the Origins Game Fair in Dallas, Texas, the game was an instant hit, selling out at the convention and immediately requiring a reprinting. Thirty years and over 25,000 cards later, *Magic* remains a vibrant property full of dozens of unique fantasy worlds, most of which you'll find in these pages.

A major part of *Magic*'s appeal has been the art and lore of the card game. With each subsequent set release following its debut, *Magic* has continued to expand its roster of planes, characters, and lore through novels, comic books, web fiction, and video games. But it didn't come together all at once. Realizing they had a hit on their hands, Wizards

of the Coast spent a couple of years working with other publishers to release novels and comic books tangentially related to the sets they were developing. But in 1996, everything changed. Seizing on the idea of a multiyear epic story arc, Wizards of the Coast took over story development internally and began working on the Weatherlight saga.

Over the course of four years, a single cohesive story was told through cards, novels, and comic books. Despite some rocky patches, it was a hit with fans, reaching them on every level, from casual card player to dedicated lore fan. After years on Dominaria, however, it was clear that *Magic* needed to spend more time on new planes. The multiyear story arcs were scaled back in favor of self-contained stories for each of the new planes visited. But it was clear something was still missing.

The self-contained stories lacked a hook to keep people interested in the story long-term. *Magic* had often relied on godlike beings called planeswalkers to drive the story, but those kinds of characters were difficult to write and design cards for. So a solution was proposed: what if the planeswalkers were more like regular people? In 2006 came Time Spiral block, a hugely nostalgic group of sets that introduced a crisis with multiversal consequences. To save the Multiverse and fix their mistakes, those godlike planeswalkers were forced to depower.

Wizards of the Coast used this opportunity to skip ahead in their internal timeline and introduce a new batch of characters who could jump between settings and keep the story going. These characters, like mind mage Jace Beleren and pyromancer Chandra Nalaar, proved to be hugely popular, and a few years later, a team of the more heroic planeswalkers was formed: the Gatewatch. After barely foiling the plans of elder dragon planeswalker Nicol Bolas, the last couple of years have seen an insidious new evil thread its way through many of the sets, building to an epic climax in 2023 against the machine horrors of New Phyrexia.

In advance of that major conclusion, *Magic: the Gathering The Visual Guide* offers a look at the planes and characters that make *Magic* special, and perhaps a few hints at what's to come in *Magic*'s future ...

JAY ANNELLI, *MAGIC: THE GATHERING* LOREMASTER

INTRODUCTION

THE MAGIC OF THE MULTIVERSE

A MULTIVERSE OF MAGIC

The Multiverse is a vast system of planes, each of which is home to a world full of unique people, creatures, magic, and metaphysics. Although similar elements exist between planes, they are distinct worlds, not different versions of each other. On one plane, people may live on a planet orbiting a sun. On other planes, the sun may rise and set by the will of the gods over a flat world whose edges end in waterfalls into nothingness. The denizens of a world where the gods are present and tangible may be shocked to learn that other worlds have never heard of their version of divinity.

THE BLIND ETERNITIES

Dividing the planes are the Blind Eternities, an unknowable maelstrom of aether that fills the abstract void between worlds. The Blind Eternities are traversable only by those whose souls have been touched by aether, granting them a planeswalker's spark. Even then, it remains a perilous journey, as the Eternities threaten to rip apart a careless planeswalker.

THE COLORS OF MAGIC

The lifeblood of every plane are the five colors of magic, which exist in balance with one another. Every living creature in the Multiverse has an affinity for one or more of the colors of magic, but only mages have the ability to turn that affinity into magical power. Although most mages are aware that people may have an inclination toward one type of magic over another, generally only the most academic wizards concern themselves with theories about the colors of magic. A person's affinity for a color is determined by their personality and environment.

 WHITE is the color of order, associated with plains, laws, and civilizations. A white mage is concerned for the greater good, and white magic usually manifests ways to protect, to heal, and to punish the wicked.

 BLUE is the color of curiosity, associated with islands, water, and sky. A blue mage is motivated by the pursuit of knowledge, and blue magic usually manifests in telepathy, illusions, and the ability to impose control over oneself and one's environment.

 BLACK is the color of ambition, associated with swamps, death, and decay. A black mage is motivated by the pursuit of power, and black magic usually manifests in ways to dominate and to manipulate death itself.

 RED is the color of passion, associated with mountains, chaos, and change. A red mage is motivated by impulse and channels their emotions into magical power. Red magic usually manifests in destructive ways, like pyromancy.

 GREEN is the color of nature. A green mage is motivated to preserve balance, harmony, and the natural state of things. Green magic usually manifests in ways to control natural forces and creatures.

THE PLANESWALKER SPARK

Only a few sentient beings, called embers, are born with the potential to become a planeswalker. Fewer still will ever ignite their spark, which happens during the most extreme experiences, from a near-death experience to a moment of transcendent joy. If only the Multiverse was a kind enough place that the latter was more common, but unfortunately most planeswalkers find their spark igniting during moments of trauma, then being ripped away from their plane and thrust into the Blind Eternities without warning. Those who survive the experience quickly become skilled in navigating the planes and find ways to blend in on foreign planes to avoid attention. Some even become heroes, seeing their spark as a duty to others, while others merely see new worlds to conquer. The one thing all planeswalkers have in common is the ability to wield magic.

A first-year mage student learns geography at Strixhaven University.

A HISTORY OF THE MULTIVERSE

THE MENDING ERA The following events are dated based on their proximity to the Mending. Most dates are approximate.

–15,000 ME

DOMINARIA—THE ELDER DRAGON WAR

Nicol Bolas, a supremely powerful elder dragon, begins a war to eliminate his rivals and rule the plane of Dominaria. Only a handful of his kin survive his purge, including his twin, Ugin. The war ends when his planeswalker spark ignites, and he sets about conquering the Multiverse instead.

–10,017 ME

RAVNICA—THE GUILDPACT

The sphinx planeswalker Azor brings an end to an era of seemingly eternal war on Ravnica. The leaders of 10 warring factions become signatories to Azor's Guildpact, a magically binding charter that unifies the factions into guilds.

Elder dragon Arcades Sabboth oversees his kingdom on Dominaria.

–9500 ME

DOMINARIA—THE THRAN-PHYREXIA WAR

The Thran, an arrogant, technologically advanced civilization of humans, rises as the superior power on Dominaria. Manipulated by a tyrant named Yawgmoth, a civil war erupts and the Thran civilization disappears almost overnight. Yawgmoth's faction, the Phyrexians, depart for his machine paradise.

–6000 ME

ZENDIKAR—THE SEALING OF THE ELDRAZI

The spirit dragon Ugin, Nicol Bolas's twin, recruits Sorin Markov, a vampire planeswalker, and Nahiri the Lithomancer to help him build a prison for the interplanar Eldrazi. After 40 years of work, the Hedron Network is complete, and the Eldrazi are lured to and imprisoned on Nahiri's home of Zendikar.

–4437 ME

DOMINARIA—THE BROTHERS' WAR

The artificer brothers Urza and Mishra lead opposing sides in a continental war that devastates Dominaria, with the Phyrexians pulling the strings of the conflict. When Urza is faced with his brother, now a horrifying amalgam of flesh and metal in service of Phyrexia, he detonates a super weapon that ignites his spark and lays waste to the continent.

–1273 ME

KAMIGAWA—THE KAMI WAR

Lord Konda of Eiganjo attempts to extend his reign by stealing the divinity of the supreme kami, O-Kagachi. Enraged, the spirit realm wages war on the material realm for 20 years, until Konda's daughter Michiko and O-Kagachi's offspring Kyodai put an end to the fighting.

A solemn monument to Eladmri, an elven hero of the Phyrexian Invasion who died fighting for the freedom of all people.

–1221 ME

IXALAN/TARKIR—FATE REFORGED

An ill-fated attempt to trap Nicol Bolas leaves Azor stranded on Ixalan and Ugin dying on Tarkir. It is only the intervention of a time-displaced Sarkhan Vol that saves Ugin from death, placing him in hibernation.

–940 ME

ZENDIKAR/INNISTRAD—SORIN'S BETRAYAL

After millennia in hibernation guarding the Eldrazi's prison, Nahiri awakes to find the Eldrazi's influence had seeped from their prison. She puts a stop to cultists who are intent on releasing the Eldrazi titans and departs the plane to find out why her old partners did not answer her summons for aid. She does not return.

–295 ME

PHYREXIA/DOMINARIA—THE PHYREXIAN INVASION

Phyrexia returns to Dominaria for a full-scale invasion. Urza, with the crew of the skyship Weatherlight, unleashes the Legacy Weapon to defeat Yawgmoth and Phyrexia. Karn, a golem created by Urza, inherits his creator's spark.

–100 ME

MIRRODIN—THE MIRRODIN CRISIS

Memnarch, the warden of Karn's metallic plane of Argentum, is infected and corrupted by Phyrexian oil, which drives him to remake the plane. He renames the plane Mirrodin and steals living beings from across the Multiverse in the hopes of acquiring a spark like Karn, his creator.

–17 ME

RAVNICA—THE BROKEN GUILDPACT

After 10,000 years, guild rule has transformed Ravnica into a plane-encompassing metropolis. The leader of House Dimir, however, shatters the Guildpact, throwing the plane into disarray.

0 ME

THE MENDING

Teferi, a student of Urza, discovers that Dominaria is riddled with devastating time rifts that threaten the entire Multiverse. The only means to heal the rifts is by using planeswalker sparks. As the last rift is sealed, the nature of the spark is changed forever, as planeswalkers become less powerful.

56 ME

RAVNICA—AGENTS OF ARTIFICE

Jace Beleren, a young but powerful mind mage, is recruited by the nefarious Tezzeret for his interplanar crime syndicate. Jace slowly discovers he doesn't have the stomach for the dirty work and flees from Tezzeret with fellow planeswalker Liliana Vess. Liliana manipulates Jace on behalf of Nicol Bolas, forcing Jace to confront and defeat Tezzeret.

56 ME

REGATHA—THE PURIFYING FIRE

Gideon Jura, a heroic planeswalker, is hired to track down Chandra Nalaar after a theft goes wrong, but the two end up becoming friends, and when Chandra destroys the corrupt organization chasing her, Gideon follows. Unknown to Chandra, she is being mentored by ancient pyromancer Jaya Ballard under an assumed name.

56 ME

ALARA—SHARDS OF ALARA

Nicol Bolas plans to use the Maelstrom of magic unleashed by the Conflux of Alara to restore some of the power he lost in the Mending. One of his schemes results in the death of leonin chief Jazal Goldmane. Jazal's brother, the planeswalker Ajani Goldmane, manages to prevent the destruction of Alara with the aid of the knight Elspeth Tirel.

56 ME

SHANDALAR—THE CURSE OF THE CHAIN VEIL

Liliana Vess hunts down the mysterious Chain Veil at the behest of one of her demonic masters, Kothophed. With the power of the Veil, Liliana is able to kill the demon, and she sets out to kill the rest of the demons to whom she owes her soul. Garruk Wildspeaker is cursed in a confrontation with the necromancer.

Nicol Bolas interrogates his minion, the dragon shaman Sarkhan Vol, about his mission to Zendikar.

57 ME

MIRRODIN/NEW PHYREXIA— SCARS OF MIRRODIN

After decades spent gestating in Mirrodin's core, New Phyrexia emerges onto the surface of Mirrodin. Koth recruits Elspeth Tirel and Venser to help him battle this threat. They journey into Mirrodin's core and Venser sacrifices himself to free the golem planeswalker Karn and cleanse him of Phyrexian corruption.

57 ME

ZENDIKAR—RISE OF THE ELDRAZI

Jace, Chandra, and Sarkhan Vol battle at the Eye of Ugin on Zendikar, unlocking the Eldrazi prison. Sorin returns to Zendikar and enlists the aid of Nissa Revane, an elven planeswalker from Zendikar, to reseal the prison, but Nissa doesn't trust the vampire and destroys the prison instead, freeing the Eldrazi titans.

58 ME

INNISTRAD—INNISTRAD

Liliana destroys the Helvault in order to kill another of the demonic masters to whom she owes her soul. Unbeknownst to her, she also frees Nahiri, who had been sealed away for a millennia by Sorin after a confrontation.

59 ME

RAVNICA—RETURN TO RAVNICA

Jace and Ral Zarek stumble across a Ravnican failsafe left behind by Azor. Racing against time, Jace uses his powers to unite the guilds, and he becomes the Living Guildpact. Vraska, a gorgon assassin, fails to assassinate him.

59 ME

THEROS—GODSEND

Elspeth retreats from a losing battle on New Phyrexia and journeys to Theros. She becomes the champion of Heliod, but the jealous god does not care to share the spotlight and kills Elspeth once her task is complete.

59 ME

TARKIR—DRAGONS OF TARKIR

Ugin's voice in Sarkhan's head directs him to the dead elder dragon's bones. Sarkhan is transported back to the moment Bolas killed Ugin and saves the spirit dragon by placing him in a hedron cocoon. When Sarkhan returns to the present, the plane has been altered forever.

59 ME

ZENDIKAR—BATTLE FOR ZENDIKAR

Gideon gathers Jace, Chandra, and Nissa to put a stop to the Eldrazi titans. Together, they're able to combine their powers and destroy two of the titans. Realizing they have the power to stop interplanar threats together, they form the Gatewatch.

59 ME

INNISTRAD—SHADOWS OVER INNISTRAD

Jace travels to Innistrad to find the world driven mad by the influence of Emrakul. The Gatewatch arrives to drive back the final Eldrazi titan, but they lack the power to destroy her. With the help of Liliana and moonfolk planeswalker Tamiyo, they're able to seal the titan in Innistrad's moon. In the aftermath, Liliana joins the Gatewatch for her own ends.

60 ME

KALADESH—THE PLANAR BRIDGE

Chandra returns home to Kaladesh and discovers Tezzeret plotting a coup. The Gatewatch help kickstart a revolution, and they push back against the authoritarian Consulate. Tezzeret acquires the invention he'd been searching for—the Planar Bridge, an artifact capable of transporting inorganic matter between planes—and escapes the revolt. Ajani, also on Tezzeret's trail, joins the Gatewatch.

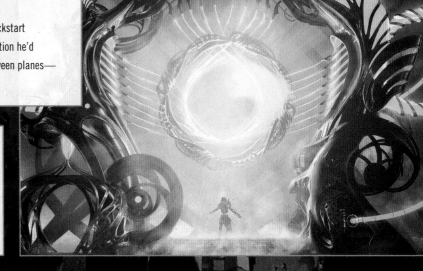

60 ME

AMONKHET—HOUR OF DEVASTATION

The Gatewatch learns Nicol Bolas may be on Amonkhet, which is also the home of Liliana's third demon. To their horror, Bolas has turned the place into a charnel house for a zombie army. When Bolas returns to claim his army, the Gatewatch are brutally defeated.

Nicol Bolas casts the elderspell on Ravnica, using his Eternal army to harvest planeswalker sparks and to restore his godhood.

60 ME

IXALAN—THE IMMORTAL SUN

Jace awakes on Ixalan with no memories. He is rescued from a deserted island by Vraska, and without the baggage of the past, the two fall in love. When Jace's memory is restored, he realizes Bolas hired Vraska to steal the Immortal Sun, and they vow to sabotage the dragon's plan.

60 ME

DOMINARIA—RETURN TO DOMINARIA

The rest of the Gatewatch rendezvous on Dominaria, where Liliana's fourth demon has taken control of the evil Cabal and threatens the plane. Working with a new crew of Weatherlight heroes, they stop the demon, but Liliana discovers Bolas was behind her demon deals all along, and he claims her as his thrall. Teferi regains his spark and joins the Gatewatch.

60 ME

RAVNICA—WAR OF THE SPARK

Bolas's endgame comes to fruition as he lures planeswalkers from across the Multiverse to Ravnica. He traps them with the Immortal Sun and summons his zombie army through the Planar Bridge, then casts the elderspell to harvest planeswalker sparks. The Gatewatch fight back, and thanks to Ugin's plans in the background, Bolas is defeated, desparked, and believed dead. Ugin imprisons the weakened Bolas on his own Meditation Realm.

60 ME

ELDRAINE—THRONE OF ELDRAINE

Rowan and Will Kenrith journey to find their missing father, the High King of Eldraine. King Kenrith was kidnapped by the planeswalker Oko in an effort to subvert the realm. Will and Rowan befriend Oko's ensorcelled servant Garruk and break him free of his curse. Together, they run Oko off the plane.

61 ME

THEROS—THEROS: BEYOND DEATH

Elspeth is visited by the nightmare weaver Ashiok in the Underworld, who shakes her from the illusion of paradise that she'd been trapped in. She ventures through the Underworld, spreading the tale of Heliod's betrayal, and with the help of Erebos, god of the dead, traps Heliod in the Underworld. As a boon, Erebos grants a return to life.

61 ME

IKORIA—IKORIA: LAIR OF THE BEHEMOTHS

In the wake of the War of the Spark, Vivien Reid, a ranger from a dead plane, investigates a disturbance on Ikoria, where she meets the monster bonder Lukka. Lukka intends to take back his home by force, and Vivien only barely stops him.

61 ME

ZENDIKAR—ZENDIKAR RISING

The millennia-old planeswalker Nahiri plans to stop the wild elemental upheaval on Zendikar—known as the Roil—by using dangerous ancient Kor technology. Nissa comes to Jace for aid, but his attempts to broker a peace between them earn him the resentment of both.

61 ME

KALDHEIM—KALDHEIM

Kaya, ghost-assassin and newest member of the Gatewatch, is hired to hunt a monster on Kaldheim, but gets sidetracked by cruel trickster Tibalt. As she stops a war between the realms, the monster—a Phyrexian Praetor named Vorinclex—takes sap from the plane's World Tree and escapes through a portal.

61 ME

ARCAVIOS—STRIXHAVEN: SCHOOL OF MAGES

Liliana becomes a professor at Strixhaven in the wake of her role during the War of the Spark. When she discovers the Oriq plotting against the school, she recruits young students Rowan and Will to help her stop them. Rowan channels the power of the Strixhaven snarl, a locus of magic energy, to stop the Oriq Leader.

Kaya battles Vorinclex on Kaldheim, as the Phyrexian hunts for a sample of the World Tree.

61 ME

INNISTRAD—INNISTRAD: MIDNIGHT HUNT & CRIMSON VOW

The day and night cycle on Innistrad threatens to usher in an eternal night. The Gatewatch is forced to battle the vampires and werewolves of the plane to help activate the Celestus, which restores the balance.

61 ME

KAMIGAWA—KAMIGAWA: NEON DYNASTY

Kaito, a ninja from the high-tech world of Kamigawa, is searching for the plane's lost emperor and discovers Tezzeret and Phyrexian Jin-Gitaxias experimenting on the Kami, spirits of Kamigawa. With Tamiyo's help, Kaito finds the emperor, who has been traveling the Multiverse as the Wanderer. Unknown to the others, Tamiyo is captured by Jin-Gitaxias and forcibly converted into a Phyrexian.

62 ME

NEW CAPENNA—STREETS OF NEW CAPENNA

Elspeth returns to her home plane of New Capenna and discovers it's nothing like she remembers. She and Vivien Reid get involved in a war between crime lords over the magical Halo, an angelic essence that was used to stave off a Phyrexian Invasion in the past. Tezzeret and the Praetor Urabrask reveal that Elesh Norn, the supreme leader of New Phyrexia, has a plan for the Multiverse and they offer to help undermine it.

62 ME

DOMINARIA—DOMINARIA UNITED

Karn discovers the final praetor, Sheoldred, secretly subverting the nations of Dominaria in preparation for a new invasion. As Sheoldred's forces attack, Karn, Teferi, Jaya, and Ajani build a coalition to fight them. Ajani is revealed as a sleeper agent during a major battle, killing Jaya and kidnapping Karn.

62 ME

DOMINARIA—THE BROTHERS' WAR

Rebuilding after their devastating loss, Teferi leads an effort to scry into the past with a time machine and construct a powerful weapon called a Sylex to defeat New Phyrexia.

PEOPLE OF THE MULTIVERSE

Whether through co-evolution, peregrination, or other mysterious means, many planes of the Multiverse are populated by the same handful of peoples. Some show marked differences in their physiology between planes, while others, like humans, almost always appear the same.

GOBLINS
Goblins are passionate and chaotic creatures, often underestimated by other beings in the Multiverse who mistake their zeal for life for stupidity. Goblins vary wildly in morphology across the Multiverse, but they all share a short stature and excitable disposition.

ELVES
Elves are similar to humans in size, shape, skin tone, and hair color, but they have distinctive pointed ears, and they tend to be significantly longer-lived. Elven cultures across the Multiverse normally have a deep respect for the natural world.

HUMANS
Humans are the most populous creatures in the Multiverse, appearing on almost every populated plane. They feature an array of different skin tones and hair colors and can be found living and thriving in any environment and in varied cultures.

KOR
Kor are very similar to humans in appearance, but with skin tones and hair in hues of white, gray, and blue. Kor men often exhibit dangling barbels around their chin.

VEDALKEN
Vedalken are hairless, blue-skinned humanoids with exceptional mental acumen. Vedalken across the Multiverse may be found with differences in appendages or digits, with some possessing four arms and others having six fingers instead of five.

DRAGONS

While dragons have a similar appearance across the Multiverse, their intelligence varies greatly—some having an intellect the equivalent of very large wild animals, while others are brilliant beyond human comprehension. All are incredibly powerful apex predators and carry within them the primal essence of the Ur-Dragon, the avatar of dragonkind.

VIASHINO

Viashino are bipedal lizard peoples with scales that come in shades of green, brown, and red. They're most at home in arid climates but can be found in many different biomes.

AVEN

Aven are humanoid in shape but possess avian features like wings and beaks. There are many different types of aven, with different species possessing the features of different types of birds.

MERFOLK

Merfolk are amphibious humanoids that possess fishlike features. Merfolk across the Multiverse usually have their own distinctive fin shapes and possess either legs or flippers.

DEMONS

Demons, in contrast to angels, are diabolic manifestations of black mana, embodiments of chaos and power. On every plane, they make bargains with foolish mortals to exchange power for a price—usually one that will benefit the demon in the end.

LEONIN

Leonin are humanoids with feline features, often larger than other humanoids and with fur patterns similar to lions, panthers, and tigers. Leonin society often revolves around close-knit communities called prides, led by a chief called a Kha.

ANGELS

Angels throughout the Multiverse are divine manifestations of white mana, embodiments of order and justice. They are often the subject of worship by humans, although their actual intervention in the day-to-day lives of mortals varies considerably across planes.

RHOX AND LOXODON

Rhox and Loxodon are humanoid rhinoceroses and elephants, respectively. Both are significantly larger than other humanoids and live in small familial social groups. Due to their size, they can be mistaken for warriors, but they often make excellent scholars, ascetics, and healers.

THE MULTIVERSE AND ITS PLANESWALKERS

ALARA

Long ago, Alara was split into five shards, each becoming its own plane which lacked two colors of magic. Over time, these shards evolved in dramatically different ways until they were no longer recognizable to each other. After centuries apart, the shards collided and reforged into a unified Alara.

THE MAELSTROM
The reunification of Alara created a nexus of magical power known as the Maelstrom.

THE SHARDS OF ALARA

In a time lost to history, an ancient planeswalker drained Alara's mana to the point that the fabric of reality itself began to fracture. In this event, known as the Sundering, great empires crumbled and fell as Alara shattered and the archangel Asha sacrificed herself to keep the demon dragon Malfegor's hordes at bay. The five shards split apart, and each found itself without two of the five colors of Magic.

The pieces of the shattered plane became known as Bant, Naya, Jund, Grixis, and Esper. On Bant, the knightly kingdoms of Alara thrived without the influence of chaos and decay. A highly defined society developed, and any wars became ritualized and were rarely lethal. On Naya, the over-abundance of life-giving magic caused its rainforests and beasts to grow to epic proportions, the latter worshipped by the elves as

near-divinities. Elsewhere on Naya, the leonin civilization crumbled from civil war. On Jund, a volcanic jungle landscape was created from the lack of order and control magic, and survival of the fittest became the norm. Grixis became a festering hellscape populated by the undead, due to the lack of life magic. On Esper, the absence of chaotic magic created a mathematically precise stormscape where mages held sway.

That all changed with the Conflux. The agents of elder dragon Nicol Bolas accelerated the process of reunification by destroying ancient magical obelisks to stabilize the shards. Bolas's agents sowed discord between the shards, inciting a war that unleashed fearsome magical power. Bolas intended to consume the power of the ensuing Maelstrom before destroying the plane, but he was stopped by planeswalker Ajani Goldmane, who drew forth a soul duplicate of Bolas, which ran the dragon off.

THE CONFLUX WAR
Malfegor, long denied his conquest, led the hordes of Grixis into Bant, where he was killed by Elspeth Tirel.

ALARA UNBROKEN

Years later, travel between the former shards has become commonplace, and a new equilibrium has been found. Leonin have begun joining knightly orders. Esper artificers travel the wilds of Jund for rare materials. The living of Grixis find refuge in lands not plagued by the undead.

SIGILS

Sigils are both badges of distinction and magical talismans. Every kingdom, city, monastery, and even angel has their own unique sigil, which they bestow on those who earn their support. The more sigils one has, the greater their status among the Sigiled. Sigils can carry a range of powerful magic, from healing wounds to granting incredible strength and endurance in battle. In the reunited Alara, some sigils even carry darker magic, unseen since the Sundering.

> ## "Their war forgotten, the nations of Bant stood united in the face of a common threat."

BANT

Bant's five kingdoms are led by a noble caste called the Blessed. Below the Blessed are the Sighted, the clerics, and the Sigiled, those whose acts have raised their status from common origins. The common folk are called the Mortar, while the Unbeholden are those who have lost all status as criminals or otherwise do not fit into Bant society.

KEY DATA

DEMONYM Alaran

TERRAIN Coastal Savannah (Bant), Tropical Rainforest (Naya), Volcanic Jungle (Jund), Festering Swamp (Grixis), Archipelago (Esper)

KEY LOCATIONS Bant, Naya, Jund, Grixis, Esper

CREATURES Angel, Aven, Cyclops, Demon, Devil, Dragon, Elf, Giant, Goblin, Homunculus, Human, Leonin, Minotaur, Ogre, Rhox, Sphinx, Thallid, Vampire, Vedalken, Viashino

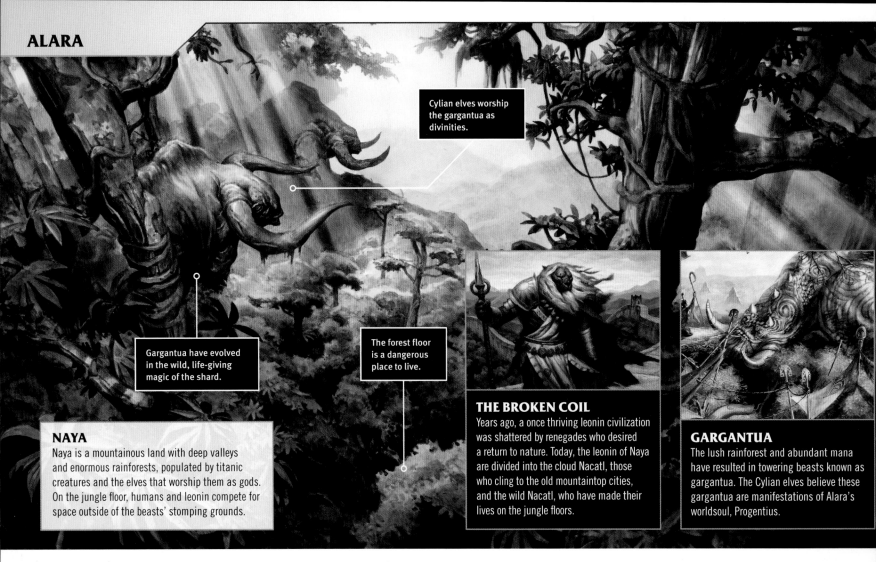

Cylian elves worship the gargantua as divinities.

Gargantua have evolved in the wild, life-giving magic of the shard.

The forest floor is a dangerous place to live.

NAYA

Naya is a mountainous land with deep valleys and enormous rainforests, populated by titanic creatures and the elves that worship them as gods. On the jungle floor, humans and leonin compete for space outside of the beasts' stomping grounds.

THE BROKEN COIL

Years ago, a once thriving leonin civilization was shattered by renegades who desired a return to nature. Today, the leonin of Naya are divided into the cloud Nacatl, those who cling to the old mountaintop cities, and the wild Nacatl, who have made their lives on the jungle floors.

GARGANTUA

The lush rainforest and abundant mana have resulted in towering beasts known as gargantua. The Cylian elves believe these gargantua are manifestations of Alara's worldsoul, Progentius.

Dragons rule the skies.

Harsh volcanic activity is as deadly as a predator.

JUND

Dragons rule the skies on Jund as the undisputed apex predators of the volcanic landscape. On the jungle floor, tribes of humans and viashino compete for dominance against a hostile ecosystem. At the bottom of the food chain, goblins worship the dragons and see it as an honor to become a dragon's meal.

The jungle canopy conceals potential prey from dragons.

THRASHES

The crocodilian viashino of Jund live together in hunting bands called thrashes. They survive through ambush tactics, with lightning raids on human villages or by laying bait and concealing themselves until their prey stumbles into their trap.

BATTLE-TOKEN BRAIDS

The finest hunters and warriors of the human clans are marked by their braids, which are interwoven with trophies from great victories. Status within the clan is determined by braids, and few earn more than a handful of them.

ESPER

Esper is a storm-wracked archipelago of mathematical precision, dominated by wizards and artificers. The aloof sphinx rule the humans and vedalkens of the plane, but in practice both societies are largely left to themselves.

Etherium bodies are the highest marks of status in Esper society.

Etherium's rarity has led to a minimalist filigree style.

Despite its delicate appearance, Etherium is an incredibly strong metal.

THE SECRET OF ETHERIUM

Once, all the Etherium that existed on Esper was created by the sphinx planeswalker Crucius. When Crucius went missing, the mages could only thin the existing supply and salvage every scrap of the precious metal. When Alara was reunified, a young artificer named Breya was the first to rediscover Sangrite, a secret ingredient that Esper mages had lacked for centuries, formed from dragon's blood and found only in Jund.

The landscape itself is eternally rotting.

THE DREGSCAPE

Ancient enchantments have slowed decay on Grixis to a crawl, creating a landscape of living death that lingers for centuries.

GRIXIS

The denizens of Grixis once competed for the life energy of Vis to sustain them in undeath, but with the entire plane now open to them once more, they raid the lands of the living and feast like never before.

THE BALANCE OF POWER

The demon dragon Malfegor was once overlord to all on Grixis. With the abundance of life now on Grixis since his death, the old powers have toppled and chaos reigns, as demons, lich lords, and vampires war with each other as much as with the living.

AJANI GOLDMANE

Ajani Goldmane is respected throughout the Multiverse for his diplomacy and compassion. One of the few beings to face the elder dragon Nicol Bolas alone in battle and live to tell the tale, Ajani has earned the awe and respect of those who have heard of his exploits.

MENTOR OF HEROES

Ajani Goldmane was born to a wild Nacatl pride on the shard of Alara. Shunned from a young age due to his albino fur, his brother Jazal was his inspiration and strength. Ajani's proudest moment was when his brother ascended to kha, or chieftain, of their pride. When Jazal was murdered by an agent of Nicol Bolas, Ajani's spark ignited and he pursued a quest of vengeance to find the killers.

On Bant, he found the knight Elspeth Tirel to be a loyal companion and confidante. Ajani tracked down his brother's killer and, learning that they themselves were coerced, showed the depths of his compassion by forgiving them. Ajani hunted down and stood against the elder dragon himself and, using his newly discovered soul magic and a sliver of power from the Maelstrom, he created an avatar of Bolas's soul. The elder dragon fled, leaving Ajani as one of the few beings in the Multiverse to challenge him and live.

Ajani began traveling the Multiverse, seeking out other prides of leonin and learning their ways. After discovering his old friend Elspeth Tirel had gone missing, he sought her out on Theros, helping her defeat the renegade god Xenagos. In the aftermath, Ajani watched in horror as sun god Heliod betrayed Elspeth and slew her. Devastated, he carried her body back to the mortal world and spread the word of Heliod's betrayal.

When Ajani finally left Theros, he visited his friend Tamiyo on Kamigawa to grieve for his departed friend. There, he learned that Tezzeret was in the employ of Nicol Bolas. Dedicating himself to foiling Bolas's plans once more, he followed Tezzeret to Kaladesh, where he met the Gatewatch and helped thwart Tezzeret's plans. With his new allies, he was instrumental in rallying the planeswalkers against Nicol Bolas in the War of the Spark.

THE STORY-CIRCLE
Ajani has befriended like-minded planeswalkers Tamiyo and Narset and formed the story-circle, a small group of planeswalkers who gather to share their stories of the Multiverse.

"If you can't save yourself, you fight to give someone else a chance."

—AJANI GOLDMANE

Ajani wears Elspeth's cloak to honor his lost friend.

Ajani lost his eye to the dangers of Naya.

KEY DATA

SPECIES Leonin

STATUS Planeswalker

SIGNATURE MAGIC Ajani is a healer and can draw out the hidden potential of his allies

AGE Mid-40s

PLANE OF ORIGIN Naya, Alara

AFFILIATION The Gatewatch (former), New Phyrexia (current)

BASE Naya, Alara (former), New Phyrexia (current)

HAIR White

EYES Pale blue

HEIGHT 6 ft 3 in

ALLIES The Gatewatch, Narset, Sarkhan, Elspeth Tirel (all former), Tamiyo

FOES The Gatewatch (current)

Ajani's albino fur made him a pariah.

AGENT OF PHYREXIA

In the years that followed the War of the Spark, Ajani's close friend Tamiyo was abducted and converted by Phyrexia. She led Ajani into an ambush, where he was turned into a Phyrexian sleeper agent. His body and mind were broken by Phyrexian torture and he was reshaped into a herald of New Phyrexia. The Gatewatch hopes to be able to save their friend one day.

Ajani's double-headed ax incorporates his brother's ax head.

TEZZERET

Tezzeret has earned a reputation for cruelty and ruthlessness. Despite his short fuse, Tezzeret is a brilliant planner and artificer who designs schemes with clockwork precision. Although Tezzeret has been forced to serve far greater powers over the years, he always plays the long game to escape and survive.

ETHERIUM-ENHANCED ARTIFICER
Tezzeret's body has been enhanced by Etherium that boosts his magical abilities.

TEZZERET THE SCHEMER

Tezzeret grew up in the slums of Tidehollow on Esper, and his name is local slang for a type of improvised knife. Tezzeret earned his name through his ruthlessness, ascending through Esper society—from being a lowly scrapper to becoming an artificer in the vaunted Seekers of Carmot. When the Seekers betrayed him, Tezzeret's spark ignited, and he landed on the shard of Grixis, where he first encountered Nicol Bolas.

After years in the dragon's service, Tezzeret broke free and usurped control of the dragon's crime syndicate, the Infinite Consortium. Bolas used Liliana Vess to manipulate Tezzeret's protégé, a young Jace Beleren, into conflict with his former mentor. Tezzeret and Jace's final battle left the Schemer brain dead and ripe for Bolas to reassert his control. Enslaved to the elder dragon again, Tezzeret was forced to scour the Multiverse for artifacts that could aid his

master's end game. On Kaladesh, Tezzeret found the Planar Bridge, the first working portal between planes in decades. This was the missing piece for his master's endgame. Tezzeret incorporated the Bridge into his Etherium body and used it to transport the pieces of Bolas's final plan to Ravnica.

While playing the sniveling servant, Tezzeret ensured the Gatewatch would find clues to Bolas's plans, and when the planeswalkers (assembled during the War of the Spark) fought him, Tezzeret threw the fight and departed, gambling on the others defeating the elder dragon. Not long after, the Planar Bridge began to degrade and poison Tezzeret. Looking for a new metal body, Tezzeret turned to the New Phyrexians, not realizing the scope of their ambitions. As he carried out Elesh Norn's will in exchange for the promise of a new body of indestructible Darksteel, he also aided the rebel praetor Urabrask and tipped off the Gatewatch once more through intermediaries.

> ## "As long as I pull the strings, you will dance."
> —TEZZERET

Tezzeret is pursued for his crimes on Kamigawa.

REBELLIOUS THRALL
Even while serving greater powers, Tezzeret only ever works in his own self-interest, serving first Nicol Bolas and then New Phyrexia as a means to an end, all the while working to undermine his so-called masters at every opportunity.

THE INFINITE CONSORTIUM
Tezzeret's Infinite Consortium once had cells on planes across the Multiverse. On Kamigawa, Tezzeret has earned the wrath of every native planeswalker—from the Wandering Emperor to the normally peaceful moonfolk researcher Tamiyo—for crimes committed there.

Stylized Bolas horns are tattooed on his forehead.

KEY DATA

SPECIES Human

STATUS Planeswalker

SIGNATURE MAGIC Tezzeret is a master artificer with the power to shape metal

AGE Early 40s

PLANE OF ORIGIN Esper, Alara

AFFILIATION New Phyrexia (current), Nicol Bolas (former), The Infinite Consortium (former)

BASE Tezzeret maintains safehouses and workshops across the Multiverse

HAIR Gray

EYES Brown

HEIGHT 5 ft 10 in

ALLIES None

FOES The Gatewatch, Kaito Shizuki, The Wanderer, Tamiyo, Nicol Bolas

The Planar Bridge has been incorporated into the Etherium structure.

When necessary, Tezzeret will conceal his Etherium enhancements.

Tezzeret has replaced his right arm and sections of his torso with Etherium.

AMONKHET

The harsh desert plane of Amonkhet was once home to an oasis-city, Naktamun. The city was destroyed by the coming of their god-pharaoh in the Hour of Devastation, and the people of Naktamun have begun to rebuild their civilization from the ashes.

THE GOD TRIALS

The people of Naktamun spent their lives preparing to undergo five trials decreed by the gods. In the Trial of Solidarity, they worked together to recover one of Oketra the True's arrows from a small army. The Trial of Knowledge tested their intellectual capacity by putting them up against their greatest fears in an illusory labyrinth created by Kefnet the Mindful. The Trial of Strength tested their physical prowess by poisoning them and having them fight through the menagerie of Rhonas the Indomitable to recover the antidote. The Trial of Ambition tested their willingness to sacrifice others to progress, eliminating all but the most ruthless participants. In the final Trial of Zeal, they fought in a gladiatorial arena, and upon proving themselves worthy, they were ritually slain by Hazoret the Fervent.

In Amonkhet's ever-shifting sands, nothing stays buried for long.

Initiates are raised together from birth in groups called Crops.

MUMMIES
Those who fail the god trials are mummified and put to work serving the city.

KEY DATA

DEMONYM Amonkheti

TERRAIN Desert marked by infrequent oasis

KEY LOCATIONS Naktamun, The Luxa River

KEY FACTIONS The Eternals, Hazoret's Survivors

COMMON SPECIES Aven, Human, Khenra, Minotaur, Naga, Sphinx

THE CURSE OF WANDERING
The Curse of Wandering ensures that all those who die rise again.

CARTOUCHES
Initiates are given cartouches made of the magical stone lazotep for every trial they complete. Those who acquire five cartouches are known as the Worthy, and they carry them upon death into the necropolis.

The Hekma keeps out the horrors of the desert.

THE HEKMA
Naktamun is protected by a magical barrier called the Hekma, drawn from the waters of the oasis, which keeps the horrors of the desert from entering the city. The Hekma fell during the Hour of Devastation, but Hazoret has found a way to restore it.

OKETRA THE TRUE
The cat-headed god of solidarity, Oketra brought unity to Naktamun. Her viziers attended to the running of the city and the raising and teaching of its people.

KEFNET THE MINDFUL
The ibis-headed god of knowledge, Kefnet was responsible for maintaining the Hekma. He instilled the desire for wisdom and knowledge in his people.

BONTU THE GLORIFIED
The crocodile-headed god of ambition, Bontu taught her people to strive for greatness. She instilled the belief that greatness would be rewarded in the afterlife.

HAZORET THE FERVENT
The jackal-headed god of zeal, Hazoret, symbolizes the fires of passion and the hearth. She is the final judge of the Worthy and sends them on their passage to the afterlife.

RHONAS THE INDOMITABLE
The cobra-headed god of strength, Rhonas instilled in his people that self-reliance, willpower, and physical prowess would serve them when all other tools failed.

KHENRA
Khenra are jackal-like humanoids unique to Amonkhet. They are almost always born as twins. The Khenra share a deep bond with their twin, one of the few familial relationships encouraged in Naktamun.

NAGA
The snakelike Naga are a rarity in the Multiverse. The Amonkhet variety possess cobralike hoods and an affinity for Rhonas.

AVEN
The aven of Amonkhet have ibis or falcon heads with a winged human body.

Catouches retain skills obtained in life.

COMING OF THE SECOND SUN

Nicol Bolas foretold his return in a series of prophecies called the Hours. The people of Amonkhet would know the Hours were at hand when the second sun took its place between the massive stylized Bolas horns on the horizon.

HOUR OF DEVASTATION

Little is known about Amonkhet before the coming of Nicol Bolas. Sixty years ago, in the waning days of his power, Bolas came to Amonkhet and usurped the gods, corrupting three of them and twisting the rest for his purposes. He slaughtered all but the youngest generation, who were then raised to believe Bolas had always been their god-pharaoh. The gods, believing they had always done so, began training their people for the God Trials, a series of deadly tests designed to cull the weak and create an army of Eternals, Lazotep-infused undead warriors.

When Nicol Bolas returned to claim his army, the corrupted gods arose. One by one, the gods were killed by the Scorpion God, until only Hazoret and Bontu remained. Hazoret, with the aid of her champions, was able to slay the Scorpion God and escape with as many survivors as she could. Bontu was revealed to be a traitor to the other gods and was herself killed by Bolas.

ETERNALS

Those who succeeded at the five trials were dubbed the Worthy and were slain by Hazoret at the culmination of the final trial. Their bodies and cartouches were then sent down the Luxa River to the necropolis, where in secret they were Eternalized—their bodies mummified and encased in the mysterious mineral Lazotep.

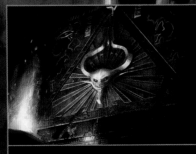

THE GOD-PHARAOH

People and gods alike believed Nicol Bolas to be their god-pharaoh.

Eternals are encased in Lazotep in order to survive the Planar Bridge.

HAZORET THE SURVIVOR

The only god to survive Bolas's purge was Hazoret. With the help of Samut and her childhood friend Djeru, Hazoret was able to overcome the elder dragon's mind control and defeat the Scorpion God. She escaped Naktamun with the survivors of the Hour of Devastation and kept them safe in the desert until the Eternals were summoned to Ravnica for Bolas's invasion. With the Eternals gone, Hazoret and her people returned to Naktamun to rebuild, raising the Hekma once more with the now-aimless Scarab and Locust Gods trapped outside.

THE GOD-ETERNALS

The final step in Bolas's plan for Amonkhet was for the gods—who had outlived their usefulness—to be slain and converted into the titans of his Eternal army. Each of the gods became a nigh-indestructible weapon of destruction in the claws of the elder dragon.

THE INSECT GODS

The true names of the three corrupted gods have been lost to time. All that is known is that the Scarab God was tasked with creating the Eternal Army from the Worthy dead, while the Locust God was responsible for destroying the Hekma. The Scorpion God was created only to slay the other gods, and without the intervention of the Gatewatch and planeswalker Samut, would have succeeded.

BASRI KET

Basri Ket is a selfless paladin who always puts others before himself. Having been off-plane during the Hour of Devastation, he returned home to find it in ruins. Basri now carries an arrow of the fallen Oketra and does his best to honor her memory through service.

Basri has fashioned the god Oketra's arrow into a spear.

Basri wields a golden aura of sand.

HONORED OF OKETRA

Basri Ket was an initiate of Amonkhet like any other, ignorant to the dark truth of the God Trials. A true devotee of Oketra, his greatest goal was to make her proud during the Trial of Solidarity. Using his power over the sands to shield his crop, Basri claimed Oketra's arrow at the end of the trial without suffering any casualties. In that pure moment of joy, his spark ignited. Believing it to be a calling from the gods, Basri began to spread Oketra's teachings while living by her example. But when he finally returned home, he found Naktamun in ruins.

Basri refused to give in to despair. Although almost everything he believed was a lie, he knew in his heart that Oketra's teachings were still true. He fashioned one of Oketra's arrows into a spear and vowed to keep her memory alive. Now, across the Multiverse, he can be found taking a stand for others, and with his skills and charisma, he's never lacking for allies in his quest.

> ## "As long as we survive, we can rebuild."
> —BASRI KET

OKETRA'S ARROW
Basri wields a spear fashioned from Oketra's divine arrow.

KEY DATA

SPECIES Human

STATUS Planeswalker

SIGNATURE MAGIC Basri controls a golden aura of sand that allows him to absorb the injuries of his allies

AGE Early 20s

PLANE OF ORIGIN Amonkhet

BASE Naktamun, Amonkhet

HAIR Black

EYES Dark brown

HEIGHT 6 ft

ALLIES Samut, Hazoret

FOES Nicol Bolas

SAMUT

Samut learned the dark secret of Amonkhet at a young age and devoted her life to revealing the truth and freeing her people. With the help of the Gatewatch, she succeeded, only to watch her home crumble around her. With renewed purpose, Samut has dedicated her life to helping her people rebuild.

Samut fights with twin khopesh, the swords of Amonkhet.

Samut creates bursts of speed by building up magical power.

KEY DATA

SPECIES Human

STATUS Planeswalker

SIGNATURE MAGIC Samut can channel her magic into bursts of supernatural speed

AGE Early 20s

PLANE OF ORIGIN Amonkhet

BASE Naktamun, Amonkhet

HAIR Brown

EYES Brown

HEIGHT 5 ft 8 in

ALLIES Basri Ket, Djeru, Hazoret

FOES Nicol Bolas

DJERU, WITH EYES OPEN
Samut's closest friend is the warrior Djeru. He was once a fervent believer in the god-pharaoh and the final initiate deemed Worthy by Hazoret before the God Trials were revealed to be a lie.

VOICE OF DISSENT

As a youth, Samut snuck out of Naktamun and passed through the Hekma with two of her cropmates, Nakht and Djeru. Out in the shifting sands, they discovered a ruin that hinted that the god-pharaoh was not originally part of Amonkhet. When her friend Nakht died in the horrors of the desert, Samut dedicated herself to uncovering the truth, while Djeru believed they had erred and dedicated himself to the God Trials. Samut became known as a dissident and was imprisoned for questioning the god-pharaoh, only to be rescued by a group known as the Gatewatch. Together, they saved Djeru just as the fated Hours arrived and the god-pharaoh, Nicol Bolas, returned.

Unable to stop the destruction and the death of their gods, Samut and Djeru teamed up with Hazoret to defeat the corrupted Scorpion God. In the aftermath, Hazoret's gratitude caused Samut's spark to ignite, but she quickly returned to help the survivors escape the city. When the Planar Beacon called planeswalkers to Ravnica, Samut was among those who stood against Nicol Bolas in the War of the Spark. Believing it her duty to release the Eternals from undeath in servitude of Bolas, Samut used her awesome speed to lay them to rest.

> **"I'll fight no more just for the honor of dying. The afterlife will have to wait."**
>
> —SAMUT

ARCAVIOS

Arcavios is best known as the home of Strixhaven University, the premier center of magical learning across the Multiverse. Strixhaven was founded 700 years ago by five elder dragons, and the five colleges of Strixhaven bear the names of these founders: Silverquill, Prismari, Witherbloom, Lorehold, and Quandrix.

THE THREE AGES

Arcavios' history began with the Dawning Age. It is believed the world was formed from the merger of two planes, but the mana of the planes overlapped in an unusual way. Opposing forces joined together in what came to be called dichotomies, resulting in mana snarls. From the most powerful of these snarls, five elder dragons were born, becoming living representations of their respective dichotomies. The Dawning Age ended with the emergence of the humanoid people of Arcavios around 7,000 years ago. They warred against each other for millennia in the Blood Age, until the elder dragons founded Strixhaven University to train mages for peace. The Mystic Age was born as these mages put an end to the seemingly unending era of war.

THE ORACLE
The Oracle is a lifetime appointment by the founder dragons to be the ultimate authority in ensuring that magic is used to help people and not for evil ends. Only the wisest and most powerful of archmages are considered for this position.

STRIXHAVEN UNIVERSITY
Strixhaven University is home to five colleges with different fields of study, administrated by a director. Each college is led by two deans, each of whom is responsible for one half of the college's programs, and serve as contradictory advisors for their students. The school's central campus is home to the Biblioplex, which is said to contain the largest collection of magical knowledge in the Multiverse.

Mage athletes compete to steal rival college's mascots.

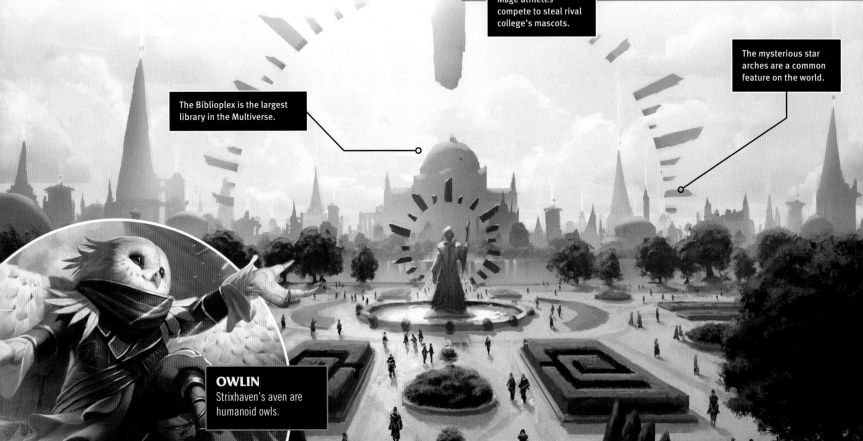

The Biblioplex is the largest library in the Multiverse.

The mysterious star arches are a common feature on the world.

OWLIN
Strixhaven's aven are humanoid owls.

SILVERQUILL COLLEGE

Silverquill's founder, Shadrix Silverquill, is a master of light and shadow focused through communication. Known as the college of eloquence, Silverquill teaches students to wield magics to help and to harm through their words. The college seeks to produce leaders that will go out into the world and lead by example.

To a Silverquill, language is the most powerful weapon there is. The fundamental dichotomy among the Silverquill is whether it should be used to uplift and inspire friends or to weaken and break foes. The white-aligned among the Silverquill use their power to shine a light on the evils of society, while the black-aligned among them use it to point out painful truths and bring down their rivals.

Strixhaven's five colleges encourage natural rivalries among the students, but some bonds transcend all barriers.

INKLINGS
Silverquill shadow magic can craft living inky voids called Inklings as a familiar.

KEY DATA

DEMONYM Arcavian

TERRAIN Arcavios is made up of two linked continents, Orrithia (the Vastlands) and Galathul

KEY LOCATIONS Strixhaven University

KEY FACTIONS Silverquill College, Prismari College, Witherbloom College, Lorehold College, Quandrix College, the Dragonsguard, the Oriq

COMMON SPECIES Aven, Bearfolk, Djinn, Dragon, Dryad, Dwarf, Elf, Burrog (Frogfolk), Giant, Goblin, Kor, Loxodon, Merfolk, Minotaur, Orc, Treefolk, Troll, Turtlefolk, Vampire

THE ORIQ
Opposing Strixhaven and the founder dragons are the Oriq, a secret society of mages who study the magic forbidden by Strixhaven. They seek to infiltrate Strixhaven and recruit disaffected students, preying on youthful arrogance and insecurity. Their goal is to topple the University and negate the founder dragons' influence on the world.

The Oriq's primary weapons are Mage Hunters, horrifying creatures from the continent of Galathul that can sense magic.

ELEMENTALS
Prismari's mascots are works of art sculpted of living elemental energy.

PRISMARI COLLEGE

Prismari's founder, Galazeth Prismari, has mastered elemental energies through artistic expression. Prismari College seeks to inspire wonder in students, so that they believe magic is beautiful and should never be purely practical. Prismari students express themselves through elemental art, with which they gain a deeper understanding of magic and themselves.

To a Prismari, art is the purest expression of magic. The fundamental dichotomy among the Prismari is whether art is best when honed by years of practice and study, or if it is best when it is a pure expression of emotional intensity. Most Prismari are elementalists of some kind, and the difference in philosophy is apparent in their work. For blue-aligned Prismari, creating the perfect piece requires skill and diligence, often resulting in complex and thought-provoking works. For red-aligned Prismari, perfection is less important than the purity of expression and inspiration, creating powerful works which often have clear meanings.

PESTS
Witherbloom mages use irritating salamanderlike creatures aptly named pests as mediums for channeling life magic.

WITHERBLOOM COLLEGE

Witherbloom's founder, Beledros Witherbloom, has mastered the entwined forces of life and death. Witherbloom College educates on the importance of both for the natural cycle. Witherbloom students learn to manipulate the energies of life and death to heal or decay, using this power to safeguard the natural cycle.

To a Witherbloom, life is the most powerful kind of magic. The fundamental dichotomy between the Witherbloom is whether to use it to preserve or expand one's own power. For green-aligned Witherbloom, life energy is used to blossom and grow, and often defend ecosystems. For a black-aligned Witherbloom, life energy is used to command power over death or create curses or foul potions.

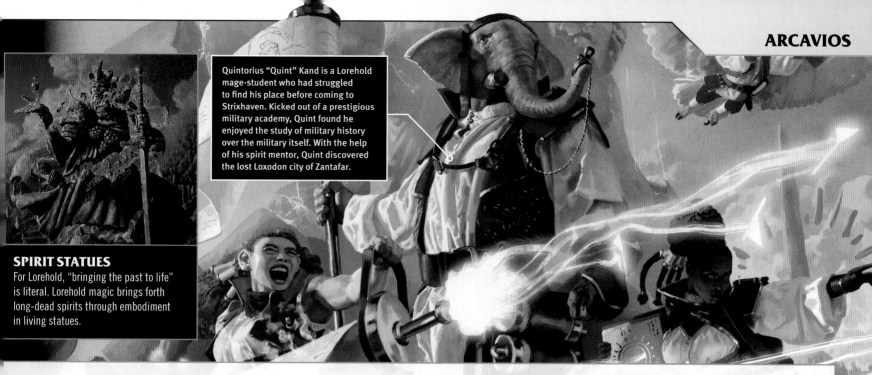

SPIRIT STATUES
For Lorehold, "bringing the past to life" is literal. Lorehold magic brings forth long-dead spirits through embodiment in living statues.

Quintorius "Quint" Kand is a Lorehold mage-student who had struggled to find his place before coming to Strixhaven. Kicked out of a prestigious military academy, Quint found he enjoyed the study of military history over the military itself. With the help of his spirit mentor, Quint discovered the lost Loxodon city of Zantafar.

LOREHOLD COLLEGE

Lorehold's founder, Velomachus Lorehold, has mastered the magic of order and chaos. Lorehold College uses this magic as a lens into the past, learning from it to predict the future. Lorehold students learn to bring the past to life through magic and study so that its lessons will never be forgotten.

To a Lorehold, history holds the answer to questions in the present, and those truths are just waiting to be uncovered. The fundamental dichotomy between the Lorehold is whether the past is simply a chaos of conflict and coincidence, or if it is a gradual, unswerving progression toward order. For red-aligned Lorehold, the past is all about the untrammeled spirit of adventure in discovery. For a white-aligned Lorehold, uncovering the past is careful, delicate work that cannot be rushed without losing the essential and underlying truths that are being searched for.

FRACTALS
Lorehold's mascots are Fractals, abstract life forms representing the formulaic underpinnings of life.

QUANDRIX COLLEGE

Quandrix's founder, Tanazir Quandrix, has mastered the magics that govern reality and abstraction. Quandrix College uses this magic to gain a fundamental understanding of the nature of existence. The fundamental dichotomy among the Quandrix is whether or not mathematics is an abstraction of reality, or simply a logical extrapolation of the true nature of reality. They all agree, however, that they're the ones who should study it. For a green-aligned Quandrix, magic is about bringing mathematical possibility to life in physical form. In practice, this often means creating exponential growth in objects or physically manifesting fractals. For the blue-aligned mages, magic is all about exploring abstraction and possibilities.

DOMINARIA

History lives alongside the people of Dominaria as ancient megaliths dominate the horizon of a plane that has seen more cataclysms than any other. However, Dominaria is nothing if not resilient in the face of extinction—a threat they've faced again and again—and each time they pick up the pieces and build anew.

ARGIVIAN RECKONING

Dates on Dominaria use the Argivian Reckoning (AR), in which 0 AR is the birth of the infamous planeswalker Urza.

MYTHOHISTORY (BETWEEN –20,000 AR AND –15,000 AR)

Legend says that at the dawn of history on Dominaria, the primordial being known as the Ur-Dragon soared through the Blind Eternities, brushing past the plane and spawning the forerunners of all dragonkind on Dominaria, the elder dragons. After a few millennia, war between the elder dragons broke out, and all but a handful were wiped out of existence. Five of their progeny became the embodiments of the draconic lifecycle and ruled as the Primeval Dragons, but their reign was cut short by a group of wizards called the Numena, who captured or killed them and stole their powers. The Numena themselves turned on one another, with the three survivors becoming near-divinity before disappearing themselves.

THE FALL OF THE THRAN (–5,000 AR)

The millennia-long reign of the Thran, a culture of human artificers, came to a sudden end with an apocalyptic civil war. The faction of the Thran led by the tyrant Yawgmoth fled through a portal to the plane of Phyrexia. There, Yawgmoth spent millennia turning the Thran into machine horrors known as Phyrexians.

SIVITRI SCARAZAM
After the fall of the Thran Empire, the planeswalker Sivitri Scarazam invaded Dominaria with a horde of dragons, but her dragons were wiped out through poison and she was forced to flee.

DEATH OF THE ELDERS
The ravages of the Elder Dragon War left just a handful alive during the Time of Legends. Of those, the most vicious elder dragons, Palladia-Mors and Vaevictis Asmadi, fell to infighting. The remaining elder dragons, Chromium Rhuell, his mate Piru, and Arcades Sabboth were slain by planeswalkers in the following centuries, leaving only planeswalkers Nicol Bolas and Ugin as the survivors.

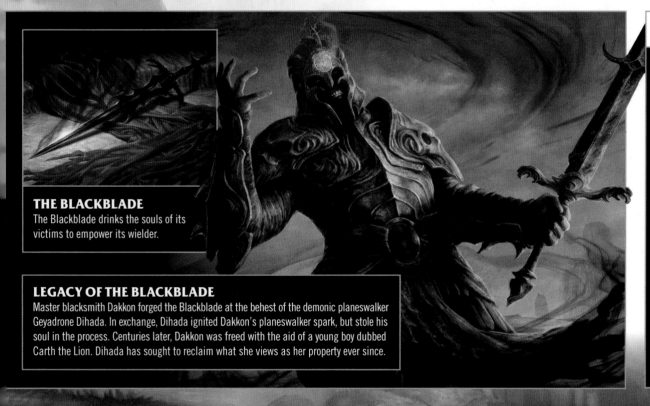

THE BLACKBLADE
The Blackblade drinks the souls of its victims to empower its wielder.

LEGACY OF THE BLACKBLADE
Master blacksmith Dakkon forged the Blackblade at the behest of the demonic planeswalker Geyadrone Dihada. In exchange, Dihada ignited Dakkon's planeswalker spark, but stole his soul in the process. Centuries later, Dakkon was freed with the aid of a young boy dubbed Carth the Lion. Dihada has sought to reclaim what she views as her property ever since.

KEY DATA

DEMONYM Dominarian

TERRAIN A massive planet with every biome and climate

KEY LOCATIONS New Argive, New Benalia, Keld, Yavimaya, Llanowar, Shiv, Keld, Zhalfir, Vodalia

KEY FACTIONS The Church of Serra, The Cabal, The Tolarian Academies, The Coalition

COMMON SPECIES Aven, Centaur, Cephalid, Djinn, Dragon, Dryad, Dwarf, Efreet, Elf, Faerie, Giant, Goblin, Gorgon, Harpy, Homarid, Homunculus, Human, Imp, Kithkin, Kobold, Kor, Leonin, Merfolk, Minotaur, Nantuko, Orc, Ouphe, Rhox, Satyr, Sphinx, Thallid, Treefolk, Troll, Vampire, Viashino, Werewolf

THE TIME OF LEGENDS (BETWEEN −5000 AR AND 0 AR)
When the Thran themselves disappeared almost overnight after a brief but devastating civil war, the age that followed became known as the Time of Legends, an era of great heroes and even greater deeds.

THE CARTHALION LINEAGE
Carth the Lion founded House Carthalion, whose fortunes have waxed and waned over the millennia. House Carthalion became entangled with many great events in Dominaria's history. The most notable Carthalion in the ages since its creation has been Jared Carthalion, a planeswalker who defends Dominaria to this day.

NICOL BOLAS

Feared across the Multiverse, the draconic tyrant Nicol Bolas wielded magic at a scale that few beings can comprehend. Having been severed from his near-divinity, he will stop at nothing to reclaim his lost power. The elder dragon's only weakness is his own arrogance.

THE GOD-EMPEROR

Nicol Bolas was once the god-emperor of a dominion stretching across the Multiverse. He ruled as such for millennia, slaying any creature that might pose a threat to his regime, from demonic leviathans to his own twin, Ugin. His regime came to an abrupt end centuries ago, when his champion on Dominaria, Tetsuo Umezawa, laid a cunning trap for the elder dragon. But death was not the end for Bolas. His spirit lingered in one of the many time rifts that had formed on Dominaria, and he was revived during Teferi's crusade to seal the time rifts just prior to the Mending.

Alive again, but with his power fading, Bolas enacted a plan to regain what he had lost. Setting his schemes into motion across the Multiverse, Bolas retreated to the Meditation Realm to pull the strings of his agents behind the scenes. His plans began to come to fruition 60 years later, when the reunifying Alara supplied him with the power he would need for his end game.

With his pieces assembled, Bolas launched an invasion of Ravnica with his army of Eternals. When the Ravnican planeswalkers activated the Planar Beacon to call for aid, Bolas activated the Immortal Sun, trapping all the arriving planeswalkers. The invasion was merely bait to capture enough

planeswalkers to cast the Elderspell, terrifying magic that would harvest the planeswalkers' sparks and reawaken Bolas's near-divinity.

The plan failed as his pawns turned on him at crucial moments, and a revived Ugin pulled strings of his own behind the scenes. Bolas himself lost his spark, and as his power faded, Ugin dragged him back to the Meditation Realm, now his eternal prison.

"As I desire, so it shall be."

—NICOL BOLAS

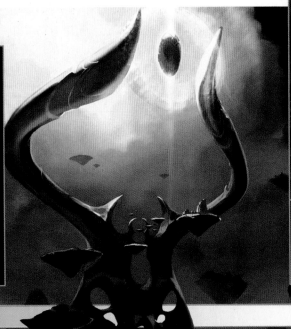

THE SPIRIT-GEM
After slaying his brother Ugin on the Meditation Realm, Bolas discovered a golden egglike artifact that was metaphysically linked to the realm. Claiming it as his own, he wore it for millennia as both an object of power and a symbol of his supremacy. The gem would ultimately be his undoing, as the revived Ugin's link to the Meditation Realm allowed him to spy on Bolas's plans.

THE SPIRIT DRAGON'S TWIN
Nicol Bolas hatched as a twin of the elder dragon Ugin. Ugin is the only being who has seen Bolas at his weakest and the only being who can put the lie to Bolas's self-aggrandizement. Bolas's jealousy at Ugin's growing powers has led to a vicious rivalry over the millennia.

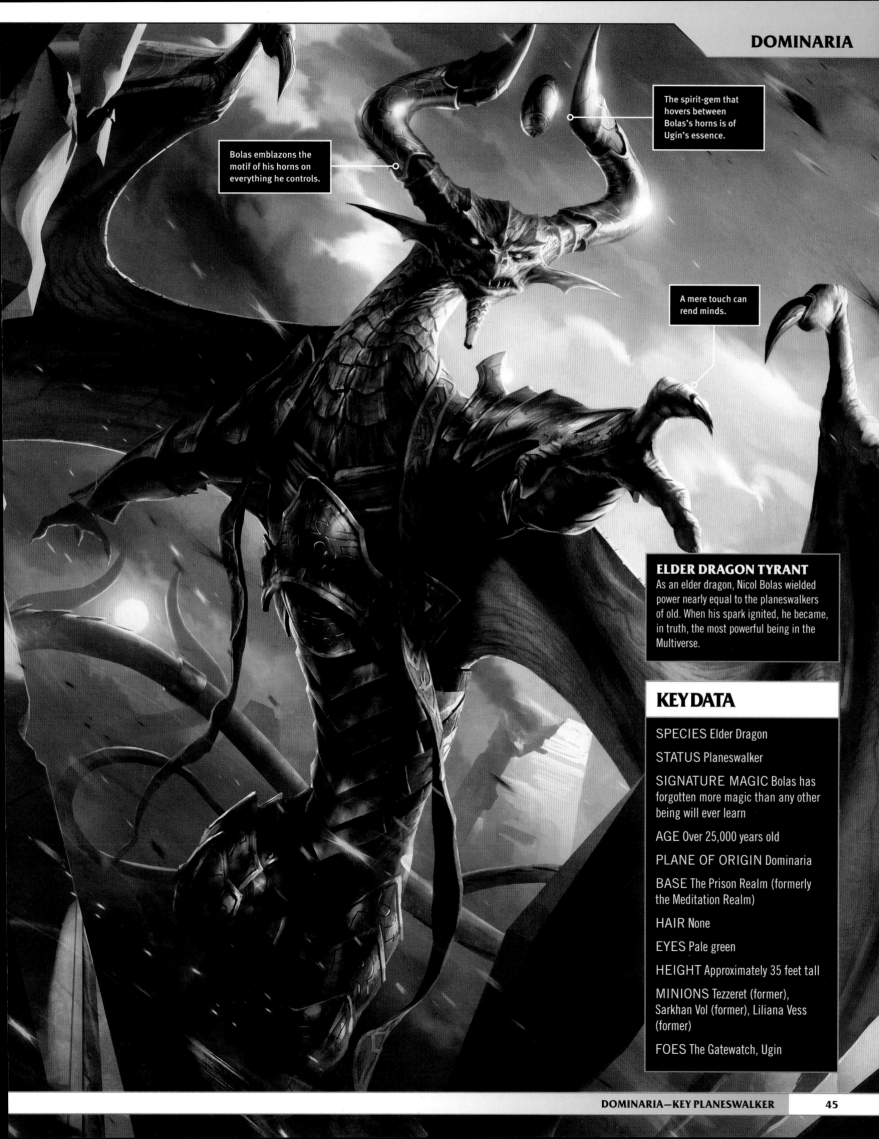

The spirit-gem that hovers between Bolas's horns is of Ugin's essence.

Bolas emblazons the motif of his horns on everything he controls.

A mere touch can rend minds.

ELDER DRAGON TYRANT

As an elder dragon, Nicol Bolas wielded power nearly equal to the planeswalkers of old. When his spark ignited, he became, in truth, the most powerful being in the Multiverse.

KEY DATA

SPECIES Elder Dragon

STATUS Planeswalker

SIGNATURE MAGIC Bolas has forgotten more magic than any other being will ever learn

AGE Over 25,000 years old

PLANE OF ORIGIN Dominaria

BASE The Prison Realm (formerly the Meditation Realm)

HAIR None

EYES Pale green

HEIGHT Approximately 35 feet tall

MINIONS Tezzeret (former), Sarkhan Vol (former), Liliana Vess (former)

FOES The Gatewatch, Ugin

UGIN

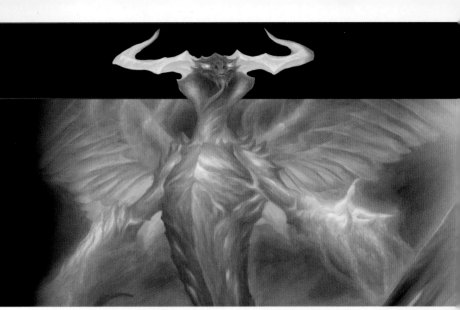

The elder dragon Ugin is the antithesis of his twin, Nicol Bolas. Where Bolas seeks to dominate, Ugin seeks to understand. Where Bolas seeks to control, Ugin seeks harmony. Ugin has manipulated history and fate as much as his nefarious sibling, but rarely for his own self-interest.

THE SPIRIT DRAGON

Ugin seeks to bring the Multiverse into a cosmic balance, careful not to destroy what he doesn't understand. After millennia of conflict with his twin, Ugin is careful to wield his power and influence behind the scenes. His pursuit of the greater good can sometimes be just as myopic and destructive as his brother's actions, and he refuses to see the damage he can wreak on the short-lived mortals he often views as beneath his notice.

Ugin's first conflict with Bolas left him dead on the Meditation Realm, where he was soon revived by the realm's energies as the spirit dragon, a living being of flesh but with a deep connection to the ethereal. He found a new home on the plane of Tarkir, which responded so strongly to his presence that primordial dragon storms began birthing dragons into the plane. Upon discovering the Eldrazi, Ugin resolved to study the bizarre beings that lived in the Blind Eternities but fed on the mana of planes. To end the Eldrazi's destruction, Ugin partnered with vampiric planeswalker Sorin Markov and his protégé, the lithomancer Nahiri, to bind them with the Hedron Network, a vast metaphysical prison of stone monoliths created through the combination of their powers.

Eventually, Ugin could no longer tolerate his brother's evil. He partnered with the sphinx planeswalker Azor to trap Bolas on Ixalan, but the plan backfired. Bolas appeared to Ugin before he was ready, and seemingly killed his brother. If not for the time-displaced planeswalker Sarkhan Vol, Ugin would have died. Instead, he recovered in a cocoon of hedrons, reemerging a millennia later to counteract his brother's plans. Working behind the scenes, Ugin created opportunities to defeat his brother during Bolas's endgame to restore his godhood. When his plans succeeded, Ugin abducted his depowered brother and hid him away in the Meditation Realm

"Our stories define our reality."

—UGIN

THE MEDITATION REALM
An ethereal subplane on Dominaria, the Meditation Realm was discovered by Ugin and later claimed by Nicol Bolas. Once accessible through a form of astral projection, it was split off into its own pocket plane during the Mending.

Ugin wields ethereal magic.

CRUX OF FATE

Before Sarkhan Vol's intervention, Ugin's fate was very different. In the original timeline of Tarkir, Ugin perished, leaving behind only his bones and an ethereal voice that drove Sarkhan to find and save him in the past. Even Ugin doesn't know how he accomplished this.

KEY DATA

SPECIES Elder Dragon

STATUS Planeswalker

SIGNATURE MAGIC Ugin wields magic beyond the conventional five colors

AGE Over 25,000 years old

PLANE OF ORIGIN Dominaria

BASE Tarkir

HAIR None

EYES Silver-teal glow

HEIGHT Approximately 35 feet tall

ALLIES Azor, Sorin Markov, Nahiri, Sarkhan Vol, Narset

FOES Nicol Bolas

THE GHOSTFIRE DRAGON

Ugin has reached a level of transcendent enlightenment and is able to channel power beyond the five colors of magic.

THE BROTHERS WAR

Millennia after the necro-machine horrors of Phyrexia were sealed away, two brothers accidentally unleashed the Phyrexians on an unsuspecting Dominaria. Propelled by sibling jealousy turned to enmity, the brothers fought a vicious war between their nations that devastated the continent of Terisiare, culminating in the detonation of an ancient weapon of mass destruction.

Mishra's flesh was replaced by a mechanical endoskeleton by the Disciples of Gix.

Mishra's designs are sleek but harsh, glowing with inner fire.

THE ANTIQUITIES WAR (0 AR—64 AR)

The brothers Urza and Mishra were orphaned at a young age and apprenticed to the archaeologist Tocasia. They spent their early life digging for ancient Thran relics, and together they unlocked the Thran's secrets. In an ancient ruin, they discovered a mighty powerstone that split in half when they touched it. Each brother claimed half, but coveted the other's stone. When their rivalry culminated in the accidental death of Tocasia, the bond between the two was shattered. Mishra fled into the desert, where he was captured by Fallaji tribes, while Urza left for the nation of Yotia.

Tensions over disputed land between the Yotians and the Fallaji tribes led to a series of escalating clashes. As the brothers proved their worth through their mastery of artifice, they quickly found themselves in positions of power. The conflict continued to escalate, with each brother building

ever stronger machines. Slowly, the entire continent became embroiled in their conflict, until no corner of the land was untouched by their war—or their insatiable hunger for more raw materials for their war machines.

Unknown to either brother, the powerstone they had claimed long ago had unlocked the portal to Phyrexia. Through the portal came Gix, a Phyrexian praetor. He suborned a small monastery and sent them out as evangels to spy and convert in the name of Phyrexia. Within a few decades, Gix had converted even Mishra himself. As the war turned to the last unspoiled land, the island of Argoth, Gix revealed himself and the corrupted Mishra, seizing control of the war machines of both sides. Left with no other options, Urza unleashed a devastating super weapon called the Sylex. Argoth was destroyed, and Urza ascended as a planeswalker.

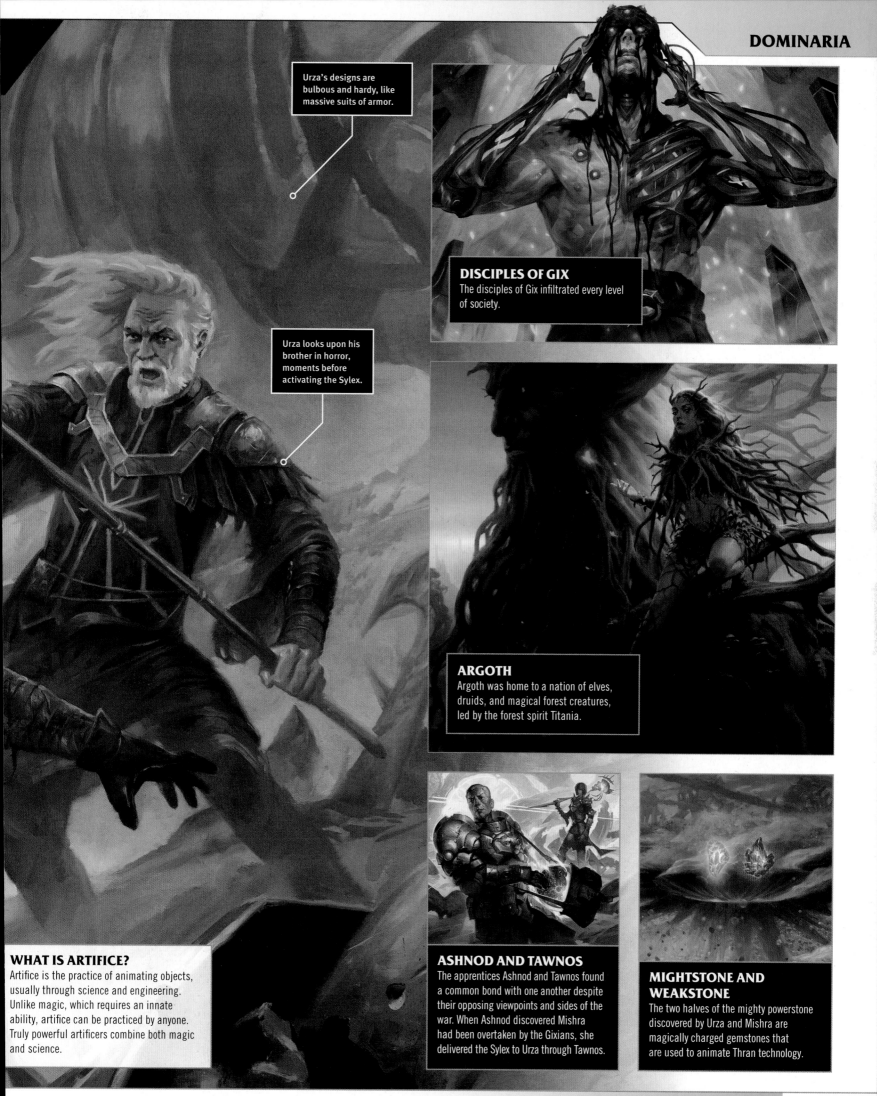

Urza's designs are bulbous and hardy, like massive suits of armor.

Urza looks upon his brother in horror, moments before activating the Sylex.

DISCIPLES OF GIX
The disciples of Gix infiltrated every level of society.

ARGOTH
Argoth was home to a nation of elves, druids, and magical forest creatures, led by the forest spirit Titania.

WHAT IS ARTIFICE?
Artifice is the practice of animating objects, usually through science and engineering. Unlike magic, which requires an innate ability, artifice can be practiced by anyone. Truly powerful artificers combine both magic and science.

ASHNOD AND TAWNOS
The apprentices Ashnod and Tawnos found a common bond with one another despite their opposing viewpoints and sides of the war. When Ashnod discovered Mishra had been overtaken by the Gixians, she delivered the Sylex to Urza through Tawnos.

MIGHTSTONE AND WEAKSTONE
The two halves of the mighty powerstone discovered by Urza and Mishra are magically charged gemstones that are used to animate Thran technology.

THE ICE AGE

The Sylex Blast devastated Terisiare. An already barren land was driven into a dark as the world cooled, empires fell, and finally a grim Ice Age descended. For millennia, most of the plane was covered in a magical winter that threatened to wipe out all life if left unchecked.

TIME OF ICE (450 AR—2934 AR)

In the centuries between the Sylex Blast and the Ice Age, the old nations of Terisiare fell and were replaced by feuding city-states in an era known as the Dark Age. In the wake of the brothers Ursa and Mishra's seemingly magical machines, magic and artifice were outlawed. Mages were forced to study in secret or be hunted. With the climate cooling, civilizations crumbled as resources grew scarce. Finally, as the Ice Age dawned, those that remained were divided into two warring peoples—the nomadic Balduvians and the kingdom of Kjeldor.

The great necromancer Lim-Dûl played the two nations against one another as he created a zombie horde to topple both civilizations. It was only with the intervention of the ageless archmage Jodah and his young protégé, the pyromancer Jaya Ballard, that the Kjeldorans and Balduvians united against Lim-Dûl and defeated him. After their victory, Jodah and Jaya helped the planeswalker Freyalise end the Ice Age. Decades later, Lim-Dûl's spirit attempted to seize control of Jaya Ballard, but with Jodah's help, her planeswalker spark ignited and the necromancer was defeated once more.

NEW ARGIVE
As the ice thawed, a new nation was founded by the previously warring peoples of the Ice Age—New Argive.

HOMARIDS
A crustacean civilization that lives in deep sea trenches.

JAYA BALLARD
A young thief with an impressive talent for fire magic, Jaya impressed the ageless Jodah with her ingenuity, and they've been friends ever since.

JODAH
Jodah always acted with compassion for regular people and had great contempt for planeswalkers who deemed those people beneath their notice.

YAVIMAYA
The sentient forest of Yavimaya was born from the wreckage of Argoth. After the ice receded, Yavimaya became a lush forest-island.

VODALIA
The ecosystems of the oceans were hit hard by the Ice Age, causing a mass migration of the homarid civilization that pushed the Vodalian merfolk out of their home and across the ocean. This event caused the merfolk to adopt a militaristic bent, and today the merfolk empire is the largest on Dominaria ... but their lack of legs precludes them from surface territory.

THE FLOOD AGES

The era following the great thawing of the Ice Age is known as the Flood Ages, and the land healed in the wake of the planeswalker Freyalise's Worldspell. Dominaria was resurgent—new heroes and villains emerged across the plane, and new epic legends were forged.

THE LEGEND OF JEDIT OJANEN (3334 AR)

Jedit Ojanen was a leonin from the land of Efrava in Jamuraa. After his father disappeared while adventuring beyond the borders of their desert oasis home, Jedit, who had inherited his father's intrepid spirit, embarked on a journey to discover his father's fate. Out in the world, he joined the Robaran Mercenaries, a band of good-hearted rogues who helped him defeat his father's murderer, the villainous wizard Johan. Centuries later, Efrava was destroyed in one of Dominaria's many cataclysms, with the Efravan leonin becoming the name of their nomadic pride.

THE DEATH OF THE GOD-EMPEROR (3607 AR)

After the Ice Age, Nicol Bolas had usurped the island nation of Madara, off the western coast of Jamuraa, as part of his interplanar empire. It was here that he would meet his end for the first time.

Few mortals cross an elder dragon and live to tell the tale, but Tetsuo Umezawa was just such a man. Hailing from the Umezawa clan, founded by a transplant from Kamigawa centuries earlier, Tetsuo had worked his way into becoming the god-emperor Nicol Bolas's champion. But Tetsuo could not stomach the elder dragon's endless cruelty and laid a trap for him.

Taking advantage of Bolas's arrogance, Tetsuo lured him into the Meditation Realm for a duel. When Bolas projected his spirit into the realm, Tetsuo destroyed the dragon's body, killing him. Upon Bolas's revival centuries later during the Great Mending, he vowed to exterminate the entire Umezawa lineage.

ZAR OJANEN
Zar Ojanen is a modern-day descendant of Jedit Ojanen.

TETSUKO UMEZAWA
Tetsuo's descendant Tetsuko has been one step ahead of Bolas since his revival.

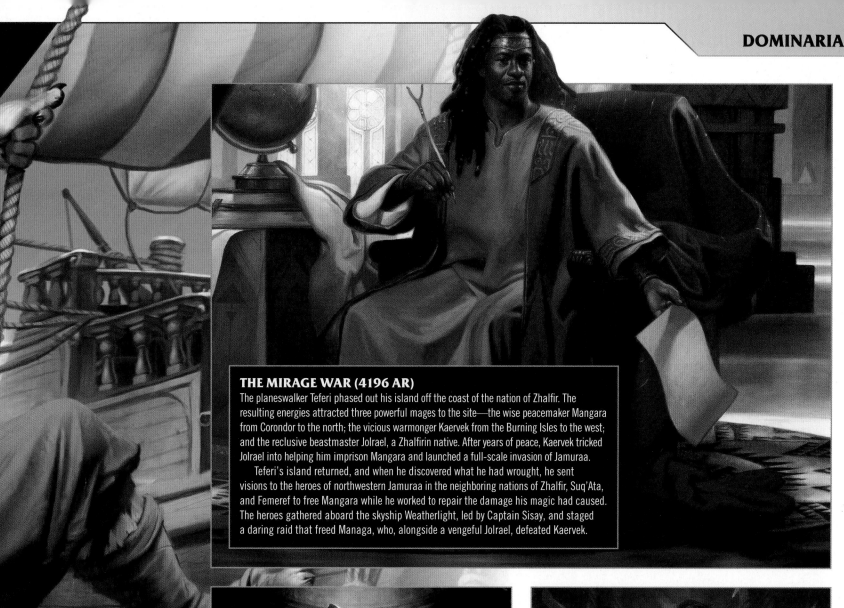

THE MIRAGE WAR (4196 AR)

The planeswalker Teferi phased out his island off the coast of the nation of Zhalfir. The resulting energies attracted three powerful mages to the site—the wise peacemaker Mangara from Corondor to the north; the vicious warmonger Kaervek from the Burning Isles to the west; and the reclusive beastmaster Jolrael, a Zhalfirin native. After years of peace, Kaervek tricked Jolrael into helping him imprison Mangara and launched a full-scale invasion of Jamuraa.

Teferi's island returned, and when he discovered what he had wrought, he sent visions to the heroes of northwestern Jamuraa in the neighboring nations of Zhalfir, Suq'Ata, and Femeref to free Mangara while he worked to repair the damage his magic had caused. The heroes gathered aboard the skyship Weatherlight, led by Captain Sisay, and staged a daring raid that freed Managa, who, alongside a vengeful Jolrael, defeated Kaervek.

THE PLANESWALKER WAR (4196 AR)

Just to the north of Zhalfir, the contested island continent of Corodor was waging its own war. A small group of planeswalkers arrived at the activation of an artifact called the Mox Beacon. Although Teferi was too busy with his own crisis to aid his allies, the planeswalker Jared Carthalion led a small group of heroes to victory. Little is known about the events of this war, but it was here that the diabolical Geyadrone Dihada returned to Dominaria.

GEYADRONE DIHADA

The demonic, shape-shifting planeswalker Dihada has plotted since the Time of Legends to acquire the souls of powerful individuals. She commissioned Dakkon to create the Blackblade during the Time of Legends, and even millennia later wished to reacquire Dakkon as her thrall. To that end, in the modern era she has seized control of Corondor to force Jared Carthalion into a conflict that may bring Dakkon back into her grasp.

JARED CARTHALION

Known as the Shadowmage, Jared Carthalion has been defeating evil planeswalkers since he was just a teenager. An old man by modern times, he still wields his trusty sword, Foecleaver, in defense of the innocent. He one day hopes to free his home kingdom on Corondor, but he won't be baited into a conflict by Dihada before he is ready.

THE PHYREXIAN INVASION

The Sylex Blast and the Ice Age delayed Phyrexia's long-awaited return to Dominaria. Urza, now a planeswalker, had spent millennia fighting a cold war against Phyrexia across the Multiverse. When the Ice Age ended, he finally returned to defend his home plane.

The horrors of Phyrexia were twisted by Yawgmoth into necro-machine abominations.

Urza's partner at the Tolarian Academy was the master wizard Barrin.

THE TOLARIAN ACADEMY

The original Tolarian Academy was founded by the planeswalker Urza as the front line in an ongoing cold war against Phyrexia. Recruiting and training only the best and brightest children, the Academy trained its students in magic and artifice and put them to work on cutting-edge research in war machine design, temporal modifications, and genetic manipulation to produce the greatest weapons to fight Phyrexia.

Urza's first attempt to defeat Phyrexia involved traveling in time to stop them before they could begin. His time machine used a sentient silver golem to probe into the past, but met with limited success. Urza entrusted the golem to his best students, Teferi and Jhoira. Jhoira named the golem Karn and became Karn's first friend. When a Phyrexian incursion led by a sleeper agent left Jhoira dead, Karn broke time using the machine to travel to the past and save her life. This event left Teferi and Jhoira changed forever.

While the original Academy was destroyed in the Phyrexian Invasion, the campuses of the Tolarian Academies of today carry on its legacy as the most prestigious magical institute on the plane.

SQUEE

The Weatherlight's cabin boy was killed and resurrected by Yawgmoth in an attempt to sway Urza's champion, Gerrard Capashen, to join the Phyrexians. The resurrection took a little too well, and Squee now resurrects whenever he is killed ... a useful trait for a goblin.

THE WEATHERLIGHT

Built with living wood from the forest of Yavimaya and Thran metal, Urza's ultimate weapon against Phyrexia was the skyship Weatherlight. The Weatherlight's crew uncovered Phyrexia's imminent invasion plans and led the defense of the plane. The crew are now legends, holding near-mythical status among modern Dominarians.

LLANOWAR AND KAVU

Kavu are primordial creatures unleashed by the goddess Gaea to fight Phyrexia. The elves of Yavimaya and their cousins in the forests of Llanowar have taken to wrangling them as mounts. Where Yavimaya is wild, Llanowar is ordered—home to many elven kingdoms, although both groups of elves worship Gaea and Freyalise.

FINAL STAGES OF INVASION (4205 AR)

As the peoples of Dominaria finally felt that they had a fighting chance against Phyrexia, the true might of the machine hells was unleashed when the Phyrexians merged their staging ground, a plane called Rath, with Dominaria. Against the full armies of Phyrexia, the Dominarian coalition was quickly overrun, and all remaining forces regrouped for the final battle at ground zero of the invasion—the Phyrexian Stronghold in the swamp-ridden island of Urborg.

Any remaining hope for victory vanished as Yawgmoth himself returned to Dominaria, having achieved the near-omnipotence he had long desired. But with the Phyrexian's god exposed, Urza still had one remaining gambit—combine the artifacts known as the Legacy into the focal point for his last-ditch Legacy Weapon. The unfettered power of this final attack, fueled by Urza's own life force, slew Yawgmoth but also destroyed Urza, Gerrard, and the Weatherlight. Fused with his creator's powerstone eyes, Karn ascended as a planeswalker.

KARN

The silver golem Karn is unique among planeswalkers as an artificial being who ascended with the spark of another. Created to be a weapon, Karn instead chose a life of peaceful scholarship. Unfortunately, Urza's legacy thrusts Karn into conflict again and again to protect his friends, including against the New Phyrexians.

SILVER GOLEM
Karn is a golem built to withstand the rigors of time travel and battle Phyrexians.

SCION OF URZA

Karn was constructed by Urza as a probe for his time travel experiments. Gifted with sentience and then abandoned by his creator, it was the care of Urza's student Jhoira that taught Karn what it meant to be human. When Jhoira was killed by a Phyrexian sleeper agent, Karn used Urza's time machine and shattered time on Tolaria to go back and save her. Over the years, Urza used Karn as a bargaining chip on many occasions, treating the golem as an asset to be traded instead of as a person, while secretly placing the golem as a protector for his various interests. One such interest was over the young Gerrard Capashen, a boy engineered by Urza to be a great hero.

Karn's role as a guardian for young Gerrard led him to join the Weatherlight crew. When Yawgmoth himself descended on Dominaria during the Phyrexian Invasion, Urza revealed Karn's true purpose as a piece of the Legacy Weapon.

Karn survived the Legacy Weapon's blast, but inherited his creator's planeswalker spark in the process. Gifted with phenomenal powers, Karn chose to create Mirrodin, a metal world in his image, but left it infected by mistake with Phyrexian oil.

Centuries later, after sealing one of the many time rifts on Dominaria by sacrificing his spark, Karn felt the Phyrexian infection within himself and flung himself to Mirrodin. What he found was a plane teeming with Phyrexians beneath the surface. He was captured and made their new god, only to be rescued by planeswalkers Venser, Elspeth Tirel, and Koth. His mind cleared of infection and his spark reignited, Karn began searching for the secrets of Urza's Sylex as a means to destroy New Phyrexia once and for all. Unfortunately, as he defended Dominaria from a New Phyrexian invasion, he was betrayed by Ajani Goldmane, who had been turned into a Phyrexian Sleeper Agent. Karn was abducted and returned to New Phyrexia, to be held as a prize by its new ruler, Elesh Norn.

Urza inscribed this Thran glyph in Karn during his creation.

VOW OF PACIFISM

As Gerrard Capashen's protector, Karn was tricked into killing an innocent man. Karn's perfect recall meant the pain of killing an innocent would never fade, and he took a vow of pacifism so that he would never repeat his mistake. He kept this vow for years, until the Phyrexian Invasion forced him to become a weapon once more or lose everything he had cared about.

XANTCHA'S HEARTSTONE

Phyrexians were grown in vats and implanted with powerstones, called Heartstones, that absorbed their souls. When constructing Karn, Urza used the heartstone of his old friend Xantcha, a Phyrexian newt who betrayed the Phyrexians. Xantcha died destroying the Phyrexian Gix once and for all.

KEY DATA

SPECIES Golem

STATUS Planeswalker

SIGNATURE MAGIC Karn is a master artificer who can shape metal to his whim

AGE Over 1,200 years old

PLANE OF ORIGIN Dominaria

BASE Dominaria

HAIR None

EYES Amber

HEIGHT Approximately 7 feet tall

ALLIES Elspeth, Koth, Teferi and the Gatewatch

FOES Nicol Bolas, New Phyrexia

VENSER

The young artificer was the first of the new breed of planeswalker. Venser gave up his life, and his spark, to cure Karn.

THE GREAT MENDING

Millennia of cataclysms wreaked havoc on the fabric of Dominaria's reality. Time rifts began to form across the plane, linked to terrible magic unleashed throughout Dominaria's history. Worse, these rifts threatened the entire Multiverse with collapse. To stop the crisis, the very nature of the planeswalker spark had to change.

THE MENDING OF DOMINARIA (4500 AR)

During the Phyrexian Invasion, Teferi saved the nation of Zhalfir and the island continent of Shiv from the Phyrexian Invasion by phasing them out of the timeline entirely. The time rifts that formed in the wake of this magic threw off his calculations, and he returned centuries later than he intended. The landscape had changed too much by that time, and returning the phased-out lands would destroy them. Teferi found a solution in a new kind of planeswalker, one with sparks connected to these time rifts. Connecting his own spark with the Shivan rift, he was able to heal it. The effort extinguished Teferi's spark, leaving him without the power to return Zhalfir to its proper place.

THE CABAL

A century after the Phyrexian Invasion, the Cabal held sway on Otaria. While ostensibly a criminal enterprise, it was in truth a cult dedicated to one of the ancient Numena. Centuries later, the Cabal's power waned in the intervening years, until a handful of remaining cultists attempted to summon their dead god once more. Instead, they freed a long-sealed elder demon named Belzenlok, who quickly assumed control and began to rebuild the Cabal as a death cult in his own honor.

RADHA AND THE KELDONS

For generations, the people of Keld were known as reavers and mercenaries. Linked to the power of their sacred mountain, Keldon warhosts were feared across Dominaria. But when the Phyrexian Invasion devastated their homeland and brought forth a twisted parody of their end of days prophecies, they were left aimless and fractured.

Radha, the granddaughter of a great Keldon hero named Astor and an elf of the Skyshroud Forest, felt out of place among the other elves. She longed to lead a Keldon warhost like her grandfather, and when Teferi came to investigate her nascent planeswalker spark, she would get her wish. Although her spark was burned out sealing Time Rifts, Radha unified the Keldons and reforged their nation into something new.

THE CHURCH OF SERRA

While Benalia had long prohibited worship of the goddess Serra and her angels, their role in defending the plane engendered good will, and the Church of Serra became the predominant faith in Benalia. Benalian weapons and armor incorporated the stained-glass motifs of the church, and the church found a new home in the rebuilt Dominaria.

JHOIRA AND SHIV

The volcanic landscape of Shiv hid many ancient secrets. Populated by the nomadic Ghitu and their goblin, dragon, and lizardlike viashino neighbors, the Shivans have united into a single nation of their varied peoples. Shiv is home to the Mana Rig, a Thran megastructure that produces powerstones and unique Thran steel.

NEW BENALIA

The legendary Weatherlight hero, Gerrard Capashen, hailed from the martial nation of Benalia. Although Benalia was decimated in the invasion, they were able to rally around the savior of Dominaria being one of their own. New Benalia emerged from the ruins and with the help of the Church of Serra has rebuilt and expanded.

TEFERI

Teferi has been embroiled in the greatest events in Dominaria's history. Trained by the infamous Urza and a master of time magic, Teferi's power was matched only by his arrogance. He was forced to reckon with his legacy when his arrogance cost him his spark and his homeland.

NIAMBI
Niambi is an unflappable cleric in her homeland of Femeref. She has learned from her father's experience that other people are the only thing that truly matters. She's heard all the stories of the great Teferi Planeswalker, but to her he's still her doting, funny father.

MASTER OF TIME
Teferi is a master of temporal manipulation, a fascination born of a youthful accident.

MAGE OF ZHALFIR

Teferi was a child prodigy at the Tolarian Academy, his brilliance only matched by his appetite for mischief. He tormented Karn with juvenile pranks, but that ended when time itself was sundered on Tolaria. Teferi's robe caught fire and he became trapped in a bubble of slow time, nearly frozen until Karn and fellow student Jhoira could free him decades later. His experience of chronal displacement stimulated a lifelong fascination with the subject and, before long, Teferi returned home to the nation of Zhalfir to continue his experiments with time.

When the Phyrexian Invasion began, Urza came to Teferi asking for help. Teferi had learned during his tenure at the Tolarian Academy that Urza ultimately couldn't be trusted to have the best interests of Zhalfir in mind, so he instead phased Zhalfir and Jhoira's homeland of Shiv out of harm's way. When he returned, he found the invasion over by centuries and the plane dying—and it was his fault. Teferi sacrificed his spark to return Shiv to its proper place, but without it, Zhalfir was beyond his reach.

A mortal once more (although aging at a glacial pace), Teferi wandered Dominaria until he met Subira.

Subira saw through Teferi's ancient mystique to the deeply empathetic man underneath. Together, they started a family, with Teferi raising their daughter, Niambi, while Subira traveled with her merchant caravan. After millennia, Teferi finally gained perspective. When the Gatewatch came seeking help to defeat the elder demon Belzenlok and Nicol Bolas, it was with great reluctance that Teferi left his old life. But Niambi, now an adult and parent herself, wished nothing more than for Teferi to follow his calling again. With Jhoira's help, Teferi's spark reignited and he joined the Gatewatch.

"The wind whispers, 'come home,' but I cannot."

—TEFERI

Teferi's robes are that of a royal mage of Zhalfir.

Teferi's staff has served him well for millennia.

KEY DATA

SPECIES Human

STATUS Planeswalker

SIGNATURE MAGIC Teferi manipulates time itself, slowing or accelerating pockets of it

AGE Over 1,200 years old

PLANE OF ORIGIN Dominaria

AFFILIATION The Gatewatch

BASE Femeref, Dominaria

HAIR Black and gray

EYES Dark brown

HEIGHT Approximately 6 feet tall

ALLIES The Gatewatch, Karn, Wrenn, Jared Carthalion

FOES Nicol Bolas, New Phyrexia

LOST ZHALFIR
Although Teferi is grieved by the loss of Zhalfir, the reality is far more tragic. Zhalfir isn't truly lost, merely displaced, and Teferi lacks the power to return it. As a planeswalker once more, Teferi is always keeping an eye out for artifacts and relics—such as those left behind by his mentor Urza—that may help him return Zhalfir to its rightful place.

DOMINARIA UNITED

The New Phyrexians were thought to be confined to the plane that was once Mirrodin, but in secret they infiltrated Dominaria. Capturing and converting people across the plane, a new breed of sleeper agents heralded their return. Only Karn's early warning saved the plane from catastrophe.

Radha is the Grand Warlord of Keld.

Danitha is the leader of House Capashen of New Benalia.

SHEOLDRED'S INFILTRATION (4562 AR)

Most planeswalkers believed the New Phyrexians were contained on their own plane, but Karn suspected otherwise. Investigating how to activate his recovered Sylex, he discovered the praetor Sheoldred hidden in a secret base with an army of sleeper agents at her disposal. His worst fears confirmed, he was trapped by a cave-in while the Phyrexians commenced their infiltration of the plane. By the time his old ally Ajani Goldmane found and freed him, the Phyrexians were ready to reveal themselves.

Karn and Ajani reunited with old allies Teferi, Jodah, and Jaya, just in time for sleeper agents across the plane to launch their attack. They split up to recruit the nations of the plane for a coalition against the Phyrexians and made their stand against Sheoldred's forces at the Mana Rig, a Thran relic weaponized by Jhoira during the first invasion. During the battle, Ajani was revealed as a sleeper agent, killing Jaya Ballard and destroying the Sylex. Ajani and Sheoldred kidnapped Karn and brought him to New Phyrexia.

THE NEW COALITION

The scars of the Phyrexian Invasion remained ingrained in most of the peoples of Dominaria, and when faced with the New Phyrexians, old feuds were put aside. Coordinated by Jhoira, the Coalition fights back against the Phyrexians.

ERTAI AND THE RUINS OF OLD PHYREXIA

Unable to move a large amount of troops between planes, Sheoldred relied on the wreckage of the Phyrexian Invasion to supplement her army. Returning to the Stronghold on Urborg, Sheoldred resurrected Ertai, a member of the Weatherlight crew who was captured and converted by Phyrexia. Ertai became one of Sheoldred's top lieutenants, happy to have a chance for revenge against Dominaria, and one annoying goblin in particular.

BRAIDS

A legendary dementia caster of the original Cabal, Braids was resurrected after the death of Belzenlok and quickly assumed control.

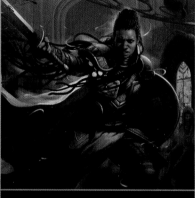

SHANNA SISAY

A descendant of the legendary Captain Sisay of the Weatherlight, Shanna was Jhoira's first mate of a restored Weatherlight before becoming captain herself. Shanna's efforts alerted and united much of Dominaria, before the ship was lost to Phyrexian corruption.

WEATHERBLIGHT

Once a beacon of hope, the Weatherlight became a flagship of invasion.

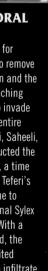

RONA, DISCIPLE OF GIX

Like the Disciples of Gix of old, the traitor Rona willingly joined Phyrexia.

THE TEMPORAL ANCHOR

Sheoldred's goal for Dominaria was to remove the threat of Karn and the Sylex before launching their true plan to invade and convert the entire Multiverse. Teferi, Saheeli, and Kaya constructed the Temporal Anchor, a time machine to send Teferi's spirit back in time to observe the original Sylex and its secrets. With a new Sylex in hand, the Gatewatch recruited planeswalkers to infiltrate and destroy New Phyrexia.

LILIANA VESS

Liliana Vess has always strived to determine her own fate. Those who have attempted to control her, from her parents to ancient demons and malign elder dragons, have come to regret it. As the most powerful necromancer in the Multiverse, there's very little that can stop Liliana from getting what she wants.

UNTOUCHED BY DEATH

As a young Benalian noble, Liliana trained as a healer but secretly dabbled in darker arts. When her brother was afflicted by a magical illness in battle, Liliana desperately searched for the plants to save him, only to find the grove had been burned. At the behest of the mysterious Raven Man, Liliana used her burgeoning necromantic powers on the plants, but the cure mistakenly cursed her brother with undeath. Liliana's spark ignited, and she has spent the rest of her life running from death. After the Mending stripped her of her power and old age came, she asked Nicol Bolas to broker demonic contracts on her behalf to restore her power and agelessness.

Bound to four demons, Liliana sought the means to escape her debt. She bargained with Bolas for help to free her from the contracts in exchange for returning an organization usurped by Tezzeret. However, Jace Beleren ensured that the scheme fell through. Forced to repay her debt, one of her demons sent Liliana after the mysterious Chain Veil, which amplified her power enough to defeat the demons who owned her soul.

But she couldn't do it all alone. Joining Jace and the Gatewatch, Liliana found herself actually enjoying her time with would-be heroes like Gideon Jura, people she initially sought only to use. Liliana slew her final demonic debtor, only for Bolas to reveal that her debt defaulted to him. Forced to serve the elder dragon against her new friends, Liliana decided she'd had enough and attacked Bolas, using his own Eternals to steal his spark and seemingly kill him. The price for such a betrayal was death, and as the magic began to kill Liliana, Gideon arrived to take up the contract himself.

> ## "You bound me with a contract only your death could end—and you thought *me* the fool?"
>
> —LILIANA VESS

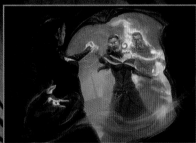

PROFESSOR ONYX
Liliana fled Ravnica in the aftermath of the War of the Spark, as most of the planeswalkers present there viewed her as a willing accomplice. She went into hiding, assuming names on various planes before settling in as Professor Onyx at Strixhaven. Although she grudgingly realized she enjoyed mentoring young mages and ensuring they learned from her mistakes, she grew tired of concealing her true self and took her real name once more—consequences be damned.

THE RAVEN MAN
A recurring figure in Liliana's life, the Raven Man was manipulating Liliana for an unknown purpose. When she returned to Dominaria during the New Phyrexian invasion, she discovered the Raven Man's real identity—he was the ancient necromancer Lim-Dûl.

Liliana's tiara was taken from an angel she destroyed.

Liliana's demonic contracts were etched into her skin and glow when she uses her magic.

THE CHAIN VEIL
An ancient artifact of the mysterious Onakke ogres of Shandalar, the Chain Veil contains many unlocked secrets.

DEFIANT NECROMANCER
Liliana Vess is an ageless and stylish necromancer of unparalleled power.

KEY DATA

SPECIES Human

STATUS Planeswalker

SIGNATURE MAGIC Liliana is a necromancer who controls the forces of death

AGE Over 200 years old

PLANE OF ORIGIN Dominaria

AFFILIATION The Gatewatch

BASE Arcavios, Strixhaven

HAIR Black

EYES Violet

HEIGHT 5 ft 10 in

ALLIES The Gatewatch

FOES Nicol Bolas, Tezzeret, Garruk, New Phyrexia

ELDRAINE

Eldraine is a world of virtuous knights and storybook magic. The plane is divided between the Realm, where five noble courts keep order, and the Wilds, where the fae creatures follow their whims. Humanity's best defense against the capricious—if whimsical—Wilds are the virtuous knights of the Realm.

ONCE UPON A TIME

Long ago, Eldraine was ruled by the elves, their kingdoms spanning the length of the plane. Fae magic suffused the world, and humanity there was subjugated under elven rule. On the mesa that would become Castle Ardenvale, the defenders of humanity finally took a stand against their elven oppressors. Throwing off their shackles, they pushed the elves back into the forests and cleared large swaths of land that would be free of fae magic.

Today, the Realm consists of five courts united by a High King. The High King or Queen is chosen once in a generation by the Questing Beast to undergo the High Quest and prove their worth. This generation, an unprecedented two candidates were chosen, Algenus and Linden of canton Kenrith. During the High Quest, Algenus went missing, and Linden went in search of him, returning from the Wilds with Algenus and infant twins in tow.

Algenus went on to finish the High Quest, and he and Linden fell in love. Linden raised the twins as her own, but never revealed the dark truth to them: a witch had ensorcelled Algenus with a love spell and attempted to sacrifice their children for power. Linden used the magic of her Questing Blade to revive the children.

This dark truth would come back to haunt the Kenrith twins, Will and Rowan, upon their 18th birthday. Their father, now High King, had gone missing. Their journey to find their father led them to cross paths with the mysterious Oko and his enthralled servant, Garruk. The twins freed Garruk from Oko's grasp and the deadly curse infecting him, and together they saved their father from Oko's plot to reignite a war between the Realm and the Wilds. In the process, however, they learned the truth of their birth, and their emotional distress caused their shared planeswalker spark to ignite.

THE QUESTING BEAST
The Questing Beast chooses those worthy of being High King or Queen.

HIGH KING KENRITH AND QUEEN LINDEN
The current High King is Algenus Kenrith. Together with Queen Linden, they rule from Castle Ardenvale. Although not High Queen, Linden holds knighthoods at three courts.

King Kenrith was transformed into a stag by the planeswalker Oko.

Indrelon, the magic mirror, requires a secret in exchange for a vision.

THE FIVE KNIGHTLY VIRTUES

The five courts each focused on one of the five knightly virtues: Loyalty, Knowledge, Persistence, Courage, and Strength. An aspirant may be knighted at any of the courts, and some knights prove themselves by attaining multiple knighthoods. At Castle Ardenvale, a knight must prove themselves in the Circle of Loyalty, a magical flame that senses selfishness and pride. At Castle Vantress, one must bring the magic mirror Indrelon a piece of knowledge they do not possess. At Castle Locthwain, one must prove their persistence to its ageless queen, Ayara. At Castle Embereth, one must prove their courage by plunging their blade into the molten surface of the Irencrag. The Irencrag judges the truly courageous and allows them to pull their blade back out, sometimes granting it extraordinary powers and a legendary name. Finally, at Castle Garenbrig, one must impress King Yorvo with a feat of strength. As the last remaining giant in the Realm, Yorvo is not easily impressed.

KEY DATA

DEMONYM Eldrainian

TERRAIN An enchanted forest held back by human civilization

KEY LOCATIONS The Realm, The Wilds

KEY FACTIONS Ardenvale, Vantress, Locthwain, Embereth, Garenbrig

COMMON SPECIES Elf, Faerie, Giant, Goblin, Human, Merfolk, Ogre, Troll

WILL KENRITH

Will Kenrith is a contemplative and studious young man. Always one to take his time to ensure a task is done right, Will often finds himself pulled along by his more impulsive twin sister, Rowan. Sharing a spark with a sibling isn't easy, but Will's patience helps make it work.

SCHOLAR OF FROST

The Kenrith twins are the children of the High King of Eldraine and a witch of the Wilds, who had ensorcelled their father and used the twins as a ritual sacrifice. They were found and rescued by their stepmother Linden, who used the magic of her Questing Blade to revive them, ending her chances at the High Quest. This strange revival has caused the twins to share a single spark. Will is always engrossed in a book or mastering his spellcraft, and it's Rowan that pushes him outside of his comfort zone and helps him grow … and socialize. Will struck up an unusual friendship with the beastmaster Garruk during their joint effort to free Will's father from the duplicitous planeswalker Oko.

After first departing Eldraine, the twins spent time improving their teamwork at Valor's Reach on Kylem. When the enigmatic planeswalker Kasmina reached out to them with an invitation to attend the prestigious Strixhaven University, Will leapt at the chance. He threw himself into his work, excited for the chance to expand his repertoire of spells, but Rowan's disregard for her own schoolwork led to tension between them. Their teamwork faltered, and spell combinations that once came naturally began backfiring. Slowly but surely, a division was formed between them, even as they worked side by side to stop the villainous Oriq and the summoned Blood Avatar.

Will's quick thinking meshed with Rowan's raw power to bring down the Blood Avatar.

Will has an intrinsic aptitude for ice magic.

Will lost his leg in the battle with the Blood Avatar, but his ice mastery has allowed him to create a frosty prosthetic.

KEY DATA

SPECIES Human

STATUS Planeswalker

SIGNATURE MAGIC Will manifests and shapes magical ice

AGE Early 20s

PLANE OF ORIGIN Eldraine

BASE Castle Ardenvale, Eldraine

HAIR Blond

EYES Blue

HEIGHT 5 ft 10 in

ALLIES Rowan Kenrith, Garruk, Liliana Vess, Kasmina

FOES Oko, Lukka

ROWAN KENRITH

Rowan Kenrith is a courageous but impulsive young woman. Always ready to leap into the next challenge, her hot-headed nature is tempered by her twin brother's cool demeanor. Rowan's restless nature often dictates where and when the twins travel in their journeys across the Multiverse.

Rowan prefers action to careful spellcraft.

Rowan is capable of channeling vast amounts of power.

FEARLESS SPARKMAGE

Like her brother, Rowan is truly devoted to Linden, who she views as her real mother, regardless of birth. When she learned the true horror of her birth, her shock caused the twins' shared spark to ignite. For a time, she poured her energy into competitions at Valor's Reach on Kylem, which proved a good distraction. But when Kasmina invited the twins to Strixhaven, Rowan found herself frustrated with the more sedate pace and relentless tide of schoolwork.

Rowan chose instead to spend her time with friends and at Mage Tower matches, neglecting her studies. Over the school year, her relationship with Will grew more and more strained, as their once finely honed teamwork started to falter. This culminated in a final battle against the Oriq, where Will was wounded. Rowan drew upon the power of the Strixhaven Snarl to defeat the Oriq leader and his summoned Blood Avatar. The taste of power was incredibly alluring to Rowan, who felt like her time at Strixhaven had come to an end, although she stayed for her brother.

Will gasped as Rowan drew from the raw power of the Strixhaven Snarl. For a moment, she was luminous, transcendent, terrible.

KEY DATA

SPECIES Human

STATUS Planeswalker

SIGNATURE MAGIC Rowan manifests sparks and lightning

AGE Early 20s

PLANE OF ORIGIN Eldraine

BASE Castle Ardenvale, Eldraine

HAIR Blonde

EYES Blue

HEIGHT 5 ft 9 in

ALLIES Will Kenrith, Garruk, Liliana Vess, Kasmina

FOES Oko, Lukka

HAZEL AND EREC KENRITH
The younger children of Algenus and Linden, Hazel and Erec adore their older siblings and want to follow in their footsteps one day.

THE WILDS

The Wilds are an unruly landscape, governed by strange rules and whimsical creatures. The enchanted region is as beautiful as it is hauntingly dangerous. The Wilds are inhabited by a diverse array of creatures collectively known as the fae, or the fair folk, all of whom have a fundamental disdain for human culture.

FAERIES

Faeries on Eldraine are among the most diverse in the Multiverse. The fae typically fall into three varieties, although more may yet be undiscovered or unrevealed in the Wilds. Meddling fae are the size of people and emit a divine glow. They take the role of storybook guides, often helping those they view as worthy and hindering the wicked. Thieving fae are small mischief-makers, stealing shiny trinkets or causing chaos among humans. Prankster fae are about the size of human children, and their name belies the cruelty of their deeds, often—for their own enjoyment—leading humans to harm.

RANKLE

Rankle is a well-known prankster fae who is known for his cruel streak, even among his own kind.

THE GREAT HENGE

King Yorvo and Castle Garenbrig guard the Great Henge, an ancient portal into the deep Wilds.

DWARVES

The dwarves of Eldraine are welcome in the Realm, having a long-standing and amicable relationship with humanity. Most dwarves prefer their independence and live in small, tight-knit clans centered around a trade. They value hard work and place great emphasis on the things they make with their own hands. A few, like the Thane Torbran, spend time at Embereth proving their courage.

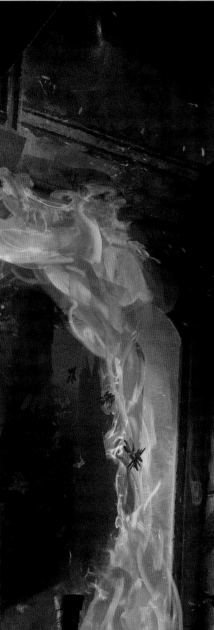

GIANTS

Few giants remain in the Realm, although the most notable is King Yorvo, who has ruled his lands since ancient times. Giants range from 10 to 15 feet in height and have stone skin often growing with green moss instead of hair. While giants are welcome in the Realm, only the handful who view the knightly virtues as a worthy cause do so—for the others, there is too much resentment over the past to remain. These other giants have departed for the deep Wilds, and a few are even rumored to rule kingdoms in the clouds.

ELVES

Many of the ancient elven courts still thrive deep in the forest, rarely seen by humanity. The few elves humans may still encounter are seldom friendly, many being elvish rangers mounted on giant foxes, but rarely does bloodshed erupt unless they are strongly provoked.

REDCAPS

Goblins on Eldraine are known as redcaps for their distinctive red hair, said to be stained so by the blood of their enemies. Goblins are the most common threat to the Realm, attacking villages in lightning-fast raids and then fading back into the forest.

THE CAULDRON OF ETERNITY

Lost centuries ago, the Cauldron of Eternity is sought by Queen Ayara and the knights of Lochthwain. It is believed that the Cauldron will only appear to one who is worthy.

WITCHES

Humans who practice magic outside the laws of the Realm are known as witches. While not all witches are evil, folktales on Eldraine revolve around stories of evil witches bestowing curses on those who wrong them or stealing away children for nefarious deeds.

QUEEN AYARA

The most famous elf on Eldraine is Queen Ayara of Locthwain, the sole remaining elven noble to remain in the Realm. Ayara is shunned by the rest of her kind, who resent the rise of humanity.

MERFOLK

Merfolk on Eldraine are known as hoarders of knowledge, the opposite of Vantress's virtue of Knowledge in the service of others. Little is known about them, as they mostly keep to themselves in the plane's rivers and lakes.

FIORA

Fiora is a beautiful plane experiencing a renaissance of fashion and technology. The pinnacle of this is Paliano, which has been elevated on massive pillars into the clouds themselves. Despite Fiora's beauty, conspiracies lurk around every corner as the denizens of the high city vie for power and control.

BETRAYAL AND CONSPIRACY

Fiora is a plane of vast natural beauty, cutthroat politics, and precarious alliances. Powerful city-states are divided by a vast wilderness and treacherous seas, but the true danger comes from within. Fioran politics are a tangled web of lies, betrayals, and conspiracies, and only the most ruthless survive the competition. Nowhere is this more apparent than in the city of Paliano, where repeated political upheaval has left rulership up for grabs. Brago, once a minor lord known for his reforms in Paliano's legislature, worked his way into a position of leadership before being declared king.

Just a few short years into his reign, Brago was diagnosed with a terminal illness. To extend his reign, he turned to the Custodi, a secretive cabal of healers and mages. But his health continued to decline, and so he called upon his old friend Selvala to help bring his suffering to an end. With a heavy heart, Selvala helped her friend pass on … only to realize she had been betrayed. Brago rose again as a ghost, to the surprise of even the Custodi, and his friend was arrested for assassinating the king. Believing himself beyond the reach of mortal assassins, Brago began what he believed would be an eternal reign.

Marchesa, the noblewoman and crime lord known as the Dusk Rose, was not satisfied with this outcome. She hired Kaya, a planeswalker with the ability to shift into a ghost form and kill spirits, to assassinate the king … for real this time. Upon the king's true death, Marchesa stepped into the vacuum with well-placed bribes and dubious papers of inheritance. Marchesa's rule was met with an outcry from the populace, igniting civil unrest in the city.

On Fiora, no matter is settled until King Brago offers an opinion.

The High City of Paliano is a city in the clouds.

PALIANO, THE HIGH CITY
The city-state of Paliano is literally elevated into the clouds, creating sharp divisions in social classes between the residents of the High City and those of the Low City. Located along the prosperous Corru River which leads to the sea, whoever controls Paliano controls the wealth of the city.

KING BRAGO

The so-called King Eternal, Brago spent his life climbing the political ranks as a zealous reformer. With the support of the legislature, he was declared king. When his reign seemed destined to be cut short by illness, Brago used the Custodi to bind his spirit to the land of the living, and he became an eternal tyrant.

QUEEN MARCHESA

The Dusk Rose has a reputation for murderous ruthlessness, controlling all crime in the city of Paliano. Not content to be merely the queenpin of crime, she plotted to replace Brago as Queen. Her sudden ascent inflamed the city, as former guard captain Adriana turned to rebellion under her reign, a dissent she's still trying to quell.

LEOVOLD, EMISSARY OF TREST

Paliano's primary rival is the elvish port city of Trest. Leovold, Trest's emissary to Paliano, is a careful and subtle manipulator who spies on Paliano's power brokers.

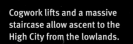

Cogwork lifts and a massive staircase allow ascent to the High City from the lowlands.

The lowlands spread for miles around the High City.

DACK FAYDEN

Once known as the greatest thief in the Multiverse, Dack Fayden was born outside Paliano. His hometown was destroyed by a villainous planeswalker while he was off-world, initiating Dack's journey as a reluctant hero. Dack's journey ended during Nicol Bolas's invasion of Ravnica, where his spark was harvested by one of Bolas's Eternals.

KEY DATA

DEMONYM Fioran

TERRAIN Fiora is a plane of vast wilderness and seafaring civilizations

KEY LOCATIONS The High City of Paliano, The City of Trest

KEY FACTIONS The Monarchy, The Academy, The Custodi, Trest

COMMON SPECIES Elf, Goblin, Homunculus, Human, Ogre, Vampire

DARETTI

Daretti is a brilliant artificer who overcame adversity, only to find his work stolen by his peers. When one of his projects was destroyed by sabotage, his spark ignited, despite it nearly killing him. Although embittered by the experience, he still finds joy in invention and discovering fresh ideas.

GOBLIN ARTIFICER
Daretti is a short but sturdy goblin with an incredible intellect and uncommon skill as an artificer.

Daretti still wears vestiges of his garments as a professor.

Manipulator arms and constructs are built into the chair to handle any task.

Daretti's cogwork conveyance is capable of moving through any terrain.

INGENIOUS ICONOCLAST

Despite the multitude of goblins living often hazardous lives throughout the Multiverse, goblin planeswalkers remain an uncommon sight. Goblins with Daretti's massive intellect are rarer still. Growing up as a poor goblin in Paliano's Lowlands, Daretti used scraps to create devices that experienced artificers could only dream of. Despite prejudices against goblinkind, Daretti earned tenure and a professorial position at the prestigious Academy at High Paliano, where he was a pioneer in the field of artifice. The Academy was not immune to the treacherous politics of the city, and many of his colleagues saw him as both a threat and embarrassment, with his best ideas often denigrated by his fellow professors.

It was in this climate that one of Daretti's projects malfunctioned and exploded. Daretti was believed to have perished in the blast, and the Academy elite breathed a sigh of relief. Many of his former colleagues grew rich and famous by stealing the work they had previously scoffed at. In truth, however, Daretti's spark had ignited in the blast and he was carried across the Multiverse. Daretti spent years traveling among the Multiverse's wonders before finally deciding to return home and address his former colleagues' treachery.

And so Daretti plotted revenge. Partnering with fellow goblin Grenzo, they instigated fear and mistrust of cogwork in the populace, resulting in the exile of Daretti's former protégé Muzzio and the closure of the Academy. When Marchesa ascended to the throne, Grenzo instigated a goblin riot as a cover while he and Daretti eliminated the professors who had wronged him.

> **"Look at these appendages, such a mess. The power requirements alone must have cost a small fortune. Garbage."**

COGCHAIR
After the explosion that ignited his spark, Daretti lost the use of his legs. Undaunted, Daretti devised an intimidating cogwork conveyance. Equipped with massive cogwheels and a variety of manipulator arms, the conveyance is adept at manipulating artifacts, maneuvering over rough terrain, or engaging in combat when necessary.

GRENZO

The goblin underclass in Paliano is led by the former dungeon warden, Grenzo. Too often overlooked by the rich and powerful, Grenzo used their biases to his advantage. He controls a network of goblins and passages throughout the secret routes of the dungeons and sewers of the city. Upon the crime queen Marchesa's ascent, Grenzo used the upheaval to lead a goblin riot in the city, backed by Daretti.

MUZZIO

Daretti's field of expertise is in cogwork devices, like most of the artificers of the Academy at High Paliano. There, he mentored the young genius Muzzio. Despite rumors that he was the one who sabotaged Daretti's project, Muzzio possesses knowledge of other planes that could only have come from being in contact with Daretti.

KEY DATA

SPECIES Goblin

STATUS Planeswalker

SIGNATURE MAGIC Daretti is an artificer with a keen eye

AGE Early 50s

PLANE OF ORIGIN Fiora

AFFILIATION None

BASE Paliano, Fiora

HAIR Auburn

EYES Brown

HEIGHT 6 ft in cogchair

ALLIES Grenzo

FOES The Academy at High Paliano

IKORIA

I koria is a world ruled by monsters, where human civilization ekes out a living in a handful of heavily defended sanctuaries. The struggle for survival on Ikoria has created a militant attitude among human settlements, but hope exists in the form of mysterious bonders—humans who are able to forge a metaphysical connection to the monsters.

Drannith uses crystals as an early warning system.

Dirigibles are the primary means of long travel for humans.

CRYSTALS
Magical crystals litter the landscape, resonating with the monsters' power.

Bonders take on the characteristics of their bonded monsters.

THE BASTIONS OF HUMANITY

The largest and most well-defended sanctuary is Drannith, which is centered around the biggest crystal ever discovered—the Argalith. The city is protected from even the largest monster attacks by its four concentric walls and the Drannith Defense Force (known as the Coppercoats). Drannith is one of the more authoritarian sanctuaries, with the Coppercoat General also being the city's leader. With the death of General Kudro at the hands of the planeswalker bonder Lukka, Kudro's daughter Jirina has assumed nominal control of the city.

The sanctuary of Lavabrink is nestled between a volcanic shelf and a lake of magma, making use of a curtain of falling lava to protect the city from monster attacks. Skysail, a floating city made up of hundreds of different skyships, takes a different approach—the city avoids all terrestrial monster attacks and can divide like a flock of sparrows to evade flying predators.

BONDERS
A growing number of people have found themselves forming a metaphysical bond—called an eludha—with monsters. These bonders use their connection to influence—but not control—their bonded monster. Centuries of fear have led to bonders being ostracized from most sanctuaries.

LUKKA

When Lukka bonded with a monstrous cat that slew his special forces platoon, he didn't understand what was happening to him at first. A loyal Coppercoat, he was shocked to learn that his most senior officer, General Kudro, was planning to have him executed. His fiancée, Kudro's daughter Jirina, helped him escape the city, where he met planeswalker Vivien Reid. Unlike the other bonders he met on his journey, Lukka viewed the bond only as a weapon, one that he intended to use to return home one day.

Investigating the recent wave of overly aggressive monster activity, Vivien and Lukka journeyed to the Ozolith, a mysterious new crystal formation. Tapping into its magic, Lukka's bonding powers were amplified and he decided to lead an army of monsters back to Drannith. The monster army only made things worse, however, and Lukka ended up killing General Kudro, only to be stopped by a united force of bonders and Coppercoats, led by his ex-fiancée Jirina.

In the process, Lukka drew too deeply from the Ozolith, shattering the crystal and igniting his planeswalker spark. Lukka now travels the Multiverse in search of a new purpose … and to find a way to force his home to accept him again.

MONSTER HUNTERS

A monster hunter is a broad term for a wide variety of rangers, poachers, bounty hunters, and mercenaries who make a living killing monsters outside the sanctuaries. These ruthless hunters specialize in taking down a variety of monsters, usually without heed as to whether or not a monster actually posed a threat.

JIRINA KUDRO

The current leader of Drannith seized power from her tyrannical father upon his death. Saddened by what had happened to her estranged fiancé, Lukka, Jirina immediately relaxed the city's stance on bonders and allowed them and their monsters into the first ring of the city.

THE OZOLITH

Brimming with power, the Ozolith was controlled by a mysterious figure.

KEY DATA

DEMONYM Ikorian

TERRAIN An island-continent wracked with crystal growths

KEY LOCATIONS Drannith, Lavabrink, Skysail, Indatha, Ketria, Raugrin, Savai, Zagoth

KEY FACTIONS Drannith, Lavabrink, Skysail, Bonders, Monster Hunters

COMMON SPECIES Beast, Cat, Dinosaur, Elemental, Human, Nightmare

MONSTERS AND CRYSTALS

The unique evolution of monsters on Ikoria is due to the influence of magical crystals. These crystals create mutations in the monsters, causing them to grow or blend their characteristics with other monster clades. Strangely, these crystals have no effect on humans, who struggle to survive in a world dominated by ever-evolving monsters.

MONSTER CLADES

Ikorian monsters generally belong to one or more of five monster groups called clades, but because of the unique crystals of the plane, their evolution is rapid and often defies natural classification. Each clade has an apex monster, a hybrid representing the strongest the clade has to offer with the characteristics of three clades.

CAT ELEMENTAL

NIGHTMARE ELEMENTAL

ELEMENTAL
Elementals hail from the lush, crystal-infused rainforest valleys of Ketria. At first glance, it is not clear if they are natural animals infused with elemental energy or elemental beings in the form of animals—and at a certain point, it doesn't matter. Unlike other monster clades, elementals are not aggressive—however, their elemental nature can often lead to sudden and unpredictable disasters.

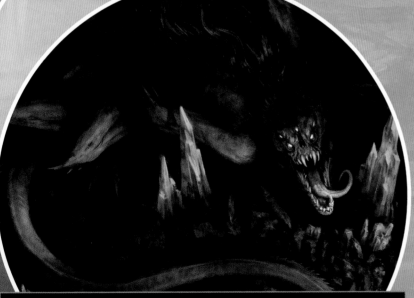

The Ozolith's appearance spawned a new era of wild mutation on Ikoria. Some creatures hunted different prey, lived in new habitats, and thrived on mutation itself.

NIGHTMARE
Nightmares from the Indatha wetlands seem to feed on fear. More than any other clade, they don't seem to conform to a natural physiology. Most nightmares have an unnerving number of extra eyes or appendages. They are far more dangerous than the other clades, which, for the most part, follow the instincts of natural creatures.

NIGHTMARE BEAST

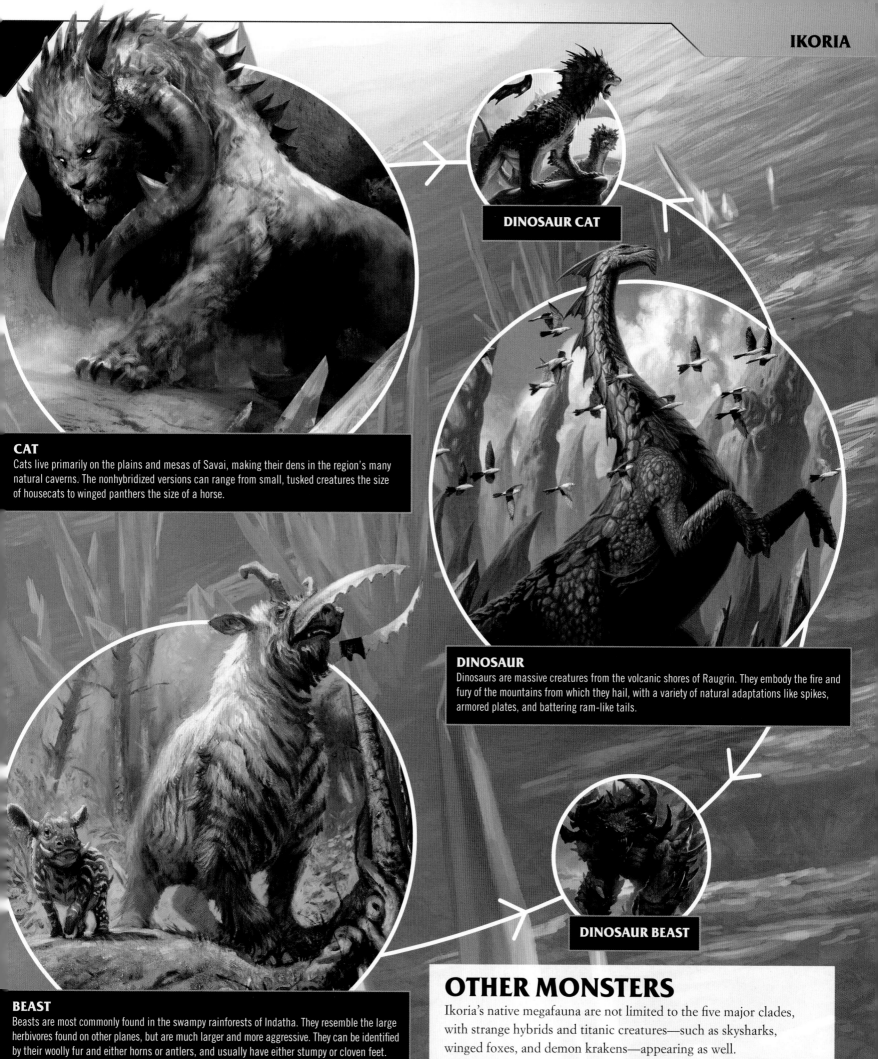

DINOSAUR CAT

CAT
Cats live primarily on the plains and mesas of Savai, making their dens in the region's many natural caverns. The nonhybridized versions can range from small, tusked creatures the size of housecats to winged panthers the size of a horse.

DINOSAUR
Dinosaurs are massive creatures from the volcanic shores of Raugrin. They embody the fire and fury of the mountains from which they hail, with a variety of natural adaptations like spikes, armored plates, and battering ram-like tails.

DINOSAUR BEAST

BEAST
Beasts are most commonly found in the swampy rainforests of Indatha. They resemble the large herbivores found on other planes, but are much larger and more aggressive. They can be identified by their woolly fur and either horns or antlers, and usually have either stumpy or cloven feet.

OTHER MONSTERS

Ikoria's native megafauna are not limited to the five major clades, with strange hybrids and titanic creatures—such as skysharks, winged foxes, and demon krakens—appearing as well.

INNISTRAD

Creatures of the night stalk humanity on Innistrad, where life is fleeting and bumps in the night cannot be safely ignored. As the power of the Church that once protected them wanes, the people of Innistrad band together to fight off the darkness.

The silver moon is metaphysically linked to the creatures of the night.

BORN FROM BLOOD

Life on Innistrad has always been precarious. Demons and the undead have plagued the living since time immemorial. But when the alchemist Edgar Markov, at the behest of a demon, created a "cure" for the famine sweeping through his lands, vampires were born. While undergoing the vampiric ritual, Edgar's grandson, Sorin Markov, became a planeswalker and took on the responsibility of protecting the plane—including from his own kind. To that end, he created Avacyn, an angelic protector who quickly became the focus of the central faith. The Church of Avacyn was formed around her, allowing humanity to channel her power. For millennia, Avacyn protected humanity, keeping the monsters that would feed on humanity in check—while never destroying them completely.

THE HELVAULT
Using the limited Lithomancy he learned from Nahiri, Sorin tore a small chunk from Innistrad's moon, which is made of a mystical silver. He fashioned it into the Helvault, a prison for beings who threatened the plane.

THE SIEGE OF THRABEN

The first event to disrupt Innistrad's delicate balance was the disappearance of Avacyn. Locked in battle with the demon Griselbrand, Avacyn attempted to seal him into the Helvault, only to be sealed alongside him in a sudden reversal. Mikaeus, the pontiff of the Church known as the Lunarch, ordered this to be kept secret. Then came the necromancer twins Gisa and Geralf Cecani, whose zombie hordes surged as the Church's magic waned.

The Cecani twins marched their army straight to the capital, Thraben, and nearly succeeded in razing the city but were stopped by the cunning and desperation of a young soldier named Thalia. In the aftermath, Liliana Vess arrived looking for Griselbrand, one of her demonic masters. Armed with the power of the Chain Veil, she gave Thalia a choice—she could save her men or protect the Helvault. Thalia chose her people, and the Helvault was destroyed. Avacyn was freed, but so too were all the demons she had imprisoned in the Helvault … along with the planeswalker Nahiri.

THE TRAVAILS

When the Helvault was destroyed, Sorin's past came back to haunt him. His former protégé Nahiri, bent on revenge, upended the careful balance of the plane by luring the Eldrazi titan Emrakul there. Emrakul's influence corrupted Avacyn, and she turned on humanity. In the end, Sorin was forced to destroy her. Without Avacyn protecting the plane, Emrakul manifested fully and began laying waste to Innistrad. Only the intervention of the Gatewatch, which left the titan imprisoned in the moon, averted total annihilation. With Avacyn gone, the Church's power waned, and humanity turned toward other faiths and powers, both new and old, to protect themselves. The years of upheaval when Avacyn perished are today collectively referred to as the Travails.

THE HARVESTTIDE FESTIVAL

Two years after the Travails, nights on Innistrad began overtaking the days. The witches of the Dawnhart Coven sought to employ an ancient orrery called the Celestus to restore the balance using a secret ritual. Before they could do this, the festival was attacked by werewolves and the key to the ritual was stolen by Olivia Voldaren, a vampire lord. With the help of the Gatewatch, the key was reclaimed and balance restored.

KEY DATA

DEMONYM Innistradi

TERRAIN Chilly moors marked by shadowed mountains, dark woods, and quiet coastlands

KEY LOCATIONS Gavony, Nephalia, Stensia, Kessig

KEY FACTIONS The Church of Avacyn, the Vampiric Houses, the Howlpacks

COMMON SPECIES Angel, Demon, Devil, Homunculus, Human, Vampire, Werewolf

Avacyn, the Angel of Hope, was unmade by her creator, Sorin Markov, after being corrupted by the Eldrazi titan Emraukl.

THE CHURCH OF AVACYN

The Church of Avacyn is both religion and government on Innistrad, with the reigning Lunarch Council being housed in the town of Ollenbock after Thraben was overrun by zombies. Founded to follow the will of the Archangel Avacyn, the Church provides refuge and relative safety for the populace. Avacynian magic, practiced by the clerics of the Church and the warrior-priests called cathars, is the most effective weapon in the fight against creatures of the night. Weapons of blessed moonsilver can cut through unholy creatures better than steel. The Church makes no promises about an afterlife other than the Blessed Sleep, the chance for humanity to rest peacefully after death and not be resurrected as a zombie or ghost. Once, the Church worshipped four archangels, but three were killed during the Travails.

Avacyn lives on in the hearts and minds of Innistrad's people.

FOUR PROVINCES

Innistrad is divided into four regions, with human settlements facing different threats in each. On the plains of Gavony lies the former capital city of Thraben, overrun with ghouls after the battle with Emrakul. Humanity is most populous in the parishes of Gavony, although the undead and the ghoulcallers who raise them are a persistent issue. The shores of Nephalia are a hub of trade, but the silver beaches hold a restless tide of vengeful spirits, called the Nebelgast. The rocky peaks of Stensia are home to most of the major vampire families and the ashmouth, a portal to hell from which spawn demons and devils. Kessig is relatively newly settled, but nature spirits make the woods dangerous here, and werewolves hide among regular people.

Weapons made of blessed moonsilver are prized in the fight against the night.

THE SIGARDIAN SECT

When Avacyn and the other angels turned on humanity, warped by the influence of Emrakul, only one archangel remained true: Sigarda. The Sigardian sect has been growing in power and influence since the Travails. The Order of Saint Traft also emerged during the Travails, from the cooperation between cathars and benevolent ghosts, called geists.

ODRIC

Once a high-ranking cathar in the Church of Avacyn, Odric's faith was broken during the Travails. Ironically, it was his transformation into a vampire that restored his faith, and now he uses his curse to help humanity.

SIGARDA

The only remaining archangel acknowledged by the Church, Sigarda has always been a steadfast defender of humanity. Her incorruptible nature led her to fight against her sisters after they were transformed by the Eldrazi.

THALIA

The Guardian of Thraben is the stand-out hero of the Travails, having stopped the zombie invasion of Thraben and defeated the Eldrazi angel abomination, Brisela.

THE ORDER OF SAINT TRAFT

Founded by Thalia and the benevolent geist of a long-dead saint named Traft, the Order uses the power of geists in a way the Church once considered anathema. Allowing the benevolent geists to possess living bodies, they were able to withstand the corruption of the Eldrazi titan Emrakul.

THE DAWNHART COVEN

A benevolent coven of nature witches, the Dawnhart were the first to recognize the danger of the encroaching night and the only ones to offer a solution. With their success, the Dawnhart have become a respected force in Innistrad society, even working alongside cathars to complete their rituals.

LIESA

Liesa was an apocryphal archangel who, unlike her sisters, was willing to work with monsters in order to protect the greater good. Centuries ago, Avacyn destroyed her while she was consorting with demons, and her name was forgotten. Liesa has since been reborn after the Travails and has been gathering a small group of former cultists and repentant sinners to forge a new path.

SORIN MARKOV

Sorin Markov is a 7,000-year-old vampire who has seen worlds rise and fall. With that perspective, he set about protecting his home plane and has taken an active role in safeguarding the Multiverse. Despite that, he cares little for individual lives and remains an incredibly dangerous vampire.

VAMPIRE SANGROMANCER
Sorin is an ageless vampire with a mastery of blood magic. He empowers himself by draining the life force of others.

LORD OF INNISTRAD

Sorin Markov is an ancient vampire who does not shy away from his murderous impulses, but he nonetheless views himself as a protector. Six thousand years ago, he mentored a young lithomancer named Nahiri and partnered with the elder dragon Ugin to seal the Eldrazi titans on Zendikar. His vampiric magics helped drain their power to keep them imprisoned. A thousand years ago, he created the Archangel Avacyn to stem the wanton slaughter of humans on Innistrad, fearing they'd be wiped out by his kind's lack of restraint. He used what he had learned from Nahiri to build the Helvault, a moonsilver prison, only to seal Nahiri inside it when she challenged him for not aiding her when the Eldrazi almost broke free.

When the Eldrazi were set loose on Zendikar again, Sorin finally arrived and attempted to reseal their prison, only for his efforts to be stymied by a distrustful Nissa Revane. Surprised that Ugin did not arrive, he sought

> **"I have seen planes leveled and all life rendered to dust. It brought no pleasure, even to a heart as dark as mine."**

out his old ally and discovered the elder dragon hibernating after nearly being killed by his twin, Nicol Bolas. Returning to Innistrad, Sorin found his creation Avacyn turning on the people she was supposed to protect, and he was forced to destroy her. Nahiri had been freed of her imprisonment when the Helvault was destroyed some time prior and had plotted this outcome, summoning Emrakul to the plane, which then lacked a defender. Nahiri attacked Sorin in the ruins she had made of his ancestral manor and imprisoned him in a wall to watch his world end.

But, thanks to the Gatewatch, the world didn't end, and eventually, after much suffering, Sorin clawed his way free of the rock. Enraged with Nahiri, when they crossed paths during Bolas's War of the Spark, they turned on each other until their anger was spent. Sorin has since returned to brood on Innistrad, only to find himself forced to fight his own kind when Olivia Voldaren ensorcelled his grandfather, the vampire progenitor Edgar Markov.

White hair and golden eyes mark Sorin's vampiric nature.

With thousands of years of practice, Sorin is an expert swordsman.

Sorin's blood ruby adorns his millennia-old armor.

VAMPIRIC POWERS

As one of the original vampires of Innistrad, Sorin drinks blood to sustain himself and heal his injuries. His vampirism gives him preternatural strength and speed, and he can levitate for short periods of time.

MARKOV BLOODLINE

Sorin is the grandson of Edgar Markov, the progenitor of vampires on Innistrad, making Sorin vampire nobility, although his creation of Avacyn has led to him being a pariah among the other vampires. Although he is not as powerful as he once was, few vampires would dare challenge a being of his power.

KEY DATA

SPECIES Vampire (formerly Human)

STATUS Planeswalker

SIGNATURE MAGIC Sangromancy

AGE Over 7,000 years old

PLANE OF ORIGIN Innistrad

AFFILIATION None

BASE Innistrad

HAIR White

EYES Black sclera with golden irises

HEIGHT 6 ft 2 in

ALLY Ugin

FOES Bolas, Nahiri

ARLINN KORD

Arlinn Kord is a werewolf with the unique ability to control her transformations. For most of her life, the wolf inside her was a curse that she tried to suppress, but that changed when she traveled the Multiverse and found inner balance. Despite the people of Innistrad hating and fearing her, she protects them with everything she has.

Arlinn bears the scars of her battles as a werewolf.

Arlinn keeps her clothing simple to avoid ripping during transformations.

Arlinn leads a pack of wolves including Boulder, Patience, Redtooth, and Streak.

VOICE OF THE PACK

Arlinn first felt the call of her werewolf nature as a teenager. Summoned into the forest by the Mondronen Howlpack, she quickly became the favorite of the pack's alpha, Tovolar. But after realizing how little the howlpack cared for the people they hurt, she left them and spent years using every bit of magic and charm she could to stave off her transformations. She worked diligently as a mage in the Church of Avacyn, becoming an Archmage of Goldnight, wielding powerful rays of holy light to destroy the undead. Then a devil attack pushed her to her limits, and she lost control for the first time in years. In her wolf form, she attacked her friends as well as the devils. In the aftermath, Arlinn was so horrified she planeswalked away.

On a distant plane, without the silver moon pulling at the wolf spirit within, Arlinn found that she could control her transformations. She returned to her home forest in Kessig and became a protector of humanity, despite the fact that they would have killed her, given the opportunity. During the Travails, Arlinn even made an uneasy peace with her old archmage allies to defeat the corrupted angels and eventually retake Thraben.

When she felt the pull of the planar beacon on Ravnica, Arlinn arrived and answered the call, befriending the Gatewatch and fighting alongside them. Over a year later, when Innistrad was imperiled by the lengthening night, the Gatewatch arrived to help put it right. Arlinn confronted Tovolar and her own past, and reclaimed the key to the Celestus to restore the balance of night and day.

"If you don't speak wolf, allow me to translate: 'One step closer and I'll rip out your throat.'"

Arlinn's werewolf form gives her much greater strength and agility.

WEREWOLF ARCHMAGE

Arlinn has the skill of an archmage in the Church of Avacyn, and she has supernatural speed and strength in her wolf form.

WEREWOLF DUALITY

While on other planes, Arlinn learned to balance the dual natures inside her—that of the human and the wild spirit of the werewolf. It's her greatest hope to teach other werewolves to master this balance, but the task is difficult on Innistrad.

KEY DATA

SPECIES Human werewolf

STATUS Planeswalker

SIGNATURE MAGIC Werewolf and Archmage of Goldnight

AGE Mid-40s

PLANE OF ORIGIN Innistrad

BASE Kessig, Innistrad

HAIR Brown with hints of white

EYES Hazel

HEIGHT 5 ft 7 in

ALLIES The Gatewatch, the Dawnhart Coven

FOE Tovolar

INNISTRAD'S MONSTERS

Innistrad has always been a dangerous place, but with Avacyn gone, the balance could shift out of humanity's favor at any moment. Werewolves grow to unprecedented size and rampage with abandon. Entire villages are slain on a whim to sate a vampire's gluttony. Only by banding together can humanity survive.

WEREWOLVES
Those cursed with lycanthropy live normal lives until the day they hear a howl coming from the forest. From then on, their life is forever torn between a dual nature, that of the person and the wild essence of the wolf. Some try to go back to their normal lives, but even if they manage to stave off the change for a time, it always ends in tragedy when the wolf regains control. Others embrace their new lives and join a howlpack, running with other wolves and preying on human settlements.

TOVOLAR AND THE DIRES
Werewolves of unprecedented size and ferocity have begun emerging since the Travails. The most powerful and influential of these is Tovolar, who has come to lead the largest and most powerful howlpack on Innistrad.

GHOULS AND GEISTS
The greatest fear among the people of Innistrad is being unable to rest even in death. A person's soul can rise again as a geist when they die violently or unfulfilled, which is not uncommon on Innistrad. While some are benevolent, clinging to the bonds that drove them in life, most grow increasingly vengeful over time. Worse yet, opportunistic necromancers use Innistrad's ample graveyards as fodder for their zombie armies or as parts for stitched-together zombies made through alchemy, called Skaabs.

GISA AND GERALF
Ghoulcaller Gisa and stitcher Geralf are necromancers who have horrifically redefined sibling rivalry.

VAMPIRES

Millennia ago, alchemist Edgar Markov used a demonic ritual to become the plane's first vampire. The vampires of Innistrad are not truly undead—instead, upon being turned, the sclera of their eyes becomes black, their skin turns pale and cool to the touch, their canines elongate, and they must drink blood to survive for the rest of their days. In exchange, they gain enhanced strength and agelessness, and can develop a variety of magical powers, such as flight and transfiguring themselves into mist.

OLIVIA VOLDAREN

Olivia Voldaren reigns over the vampires in all but name as her rival houses fell to shambles in the Travails.

DEMONS AND DEVILS

Demons and devils spawn onto Innistrad through gateways from their hellish realms, the largest being the ashmouth. Demons come to the mortal realm in search of souls, bargaining with mortals and even becoming the deity of demonic cults. Devils, by contrast, exist only to torment others with their wicked mischief—usually by burning things down and cackling with glee.

THE SKIRSDAG CULT

The largest and most powerful cult of demon worshippers, the Skirsdag have infiltrated the highest levels of the Church of Avacyn.

TIBALT

A spell gone awry fused Tibalt, a cruel empath, with devilish essence. Now he roams the Multiverse in search of opportunities to inflict exquisite agonies on his unsuspecting victims.

OLD STICKFINGERS

A forgotten nature god became a campfire story until he was summoned to avenge a petty slight.

UMBRIS

An ancient being of shadows that feeds on memories of sorrow, Umbris was once bound to a small town but has since been freed to sample Innistrad's delicacies.

THE GITROG MONSTER

A secret cult on the shore of Lake Zhava worships this hypnotic amphibian that hungers for human flesh.

IXALAN

Ferocious dinosaurs prowl the jungles of Ixalan, their power harnessed by the magic of the Sun Empire. Merfolk shapers move silently through the rainforest, with nature itself bending out of their way. In the seas, pirate marauders and vampiric conquistadors vie for a foothold on the continent, as each civilization searches for ancient treasure.

HISTORY OF IXALAN

Almost 1,300 years ago, the planeswalker Azor attempted to imprison the elder dragon Nicol Bolas on Ixalan using an artifact called the Immortal Sun. The plan failed, and Azor was left trapped and sparkless instead. Azor left the care of the Immortal Sun in the hands of various peoples, but inevitably the power of the artifact brought out their worst impulses, and defenders became conquerors by using its power. On the continent of Torrezon, the vampires of the Dusk Legion have built an empire while searching for the fabled artifact. On the continent of Ixalan, the Sun Empire believes it to be their ancestral right.

The pirates of the Brazen Coalition, descendants of seafaring refugees displaced by the Dusk Legion and rebuffed by the Sun Empire, seek the Immortal Sun simply because it's big, shiny, and gold. The merfolk of the River Heralds have kept it hidden away from all who would covet its power, locking it in an ancient city, the location of which has been lost to time. There, it remained hidden for centuries, until Bolas hired gorgon planeswalker Vraska to locate it and deliver it to him. Vraska's efforts kickstarted a race between the plane's factions for the lost golden city of Orazca and the Immortal Sun hidden within.

AZOR
The ancient sphinx planeswalker is known as the lawbringer, imposing strictures of law and order across the Multiverse. He is most famous for creating the Guildpact of Ravnica. Without a spark, he's been trapped on Ixalan for centuries.

THE IMMORTAL SUN
A trap for Nicol Bolas created with Azor's own spark, the Immortal Sun is a font of power for whoever can lay claim to it … and keep it. It was taken by Bolas for his schemes on Ravnica, where it remains.

THE DUSK LEGION

When Azor took the Immortal Sun from Torrezon, a monk named Elenda set off across the sea in pursuit. She returned years later, having taken on a vampiric curse and ended a civil war that was wreaking havoc on Torrezon. In a sacrament known as the Rite of Redemption, the clergy and nobility took on Elenda's curse in order to extend their lives and start a quest for the Immortal Sun. Afterward, Elenda departed, but without her leadership, the nobility—armed with vampiric powers and burdened with a thirst for blood—began to conquer their neighbors. Torrezon went from a small mountain nation to a continent-spanning empire in a few centuries.

The Dusk Legion turned their eyes to Ixalan once Torrezon was secured. They invaded, searching for the Immortal Sun (and treasure). When they finally reached the golden city, they found Elenda herself, who was infuriated that her vampiric gift had not taught them humility. With the Immortal Sun gone and their Saint causing a schism in the empire, the Dusk Legion was left on shaky ground.

A Dusk Legion cleric offers up a prayer to Saint Elenda.

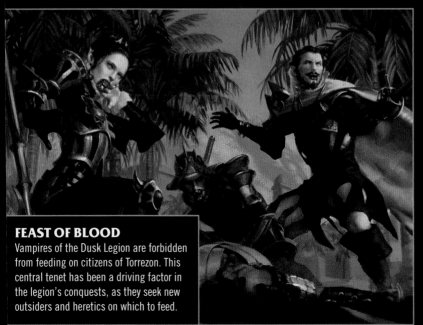

FEAST OF BLOOD
Vampires of the Dusk Legion are forbidden from feeding on citizens of Torrezon. This central tenet has been a driving factor in the legion's conquests, as they seek new outsiders and heretics on which to feed.

ELENDA, THE DUSK ROSE
The curse of vampirism was a holy sacrifice made by Elenda. Her pious nature led her to overcome the worst impulses of the blood thirst, and she believes taking on such a curse to be an act of humility.

KEY DATA

DEMONYM Ixalani

TERRAIN A lush jungle island-continent

KEY LOCATIONS Ixalan (continent), Torrezon

KEY FACTIONS The Dusk Legion, The River Heralds, The Brazen Coalition, The Sun Empire

COMMON SPECIES Dryad, Goblin, Harpy, Human, Imp, Merfolk, Orc, Siren, Vampire

THE SUN EMPIRE

The Sun Empire has spent centuries learning to harness the power of the dinosaurs. Dinosaurs can be seen in many aspects of their society, from war mounts to plowbeasts. The Empire itself reveres a divinity they call the Threefold Sun, and between their dinosaurs and sun clerics, they have a significant edge against the invading vampires of the Dusk Legion. Although they have a rich warrior tradition, the Sun Empire embraces art, with the positon of Warrior-Poet the most coveted in the empire.

THREEFOLD SUN

The people of the Sun Empire worship the three aspects of the sun: Kinjalli, the Wakening Sun, which represents creativity; Ixalli, the Verdant Sun, which represents the sustaining and nourishing aspects of the sun; and Tilonalli, the Burning Sun, which represents its destructive power.

Gishath is the dinosaur avatar of the Threefold Sun, embodying all of its aspects.

DINOSAURS

Ixalan is populated with all manner of feathered dinosaurs, from the long-necked Brontodons and Altisaurs, to the horn-crested Ceratopses, the armored Aegisaurs and Armisaurs, and the flying Aerosaurs. Sharp-toothed raptors command fear and respect in the jungles, but the true tyrants are the massive carnivores known as monstrosaurs, regisaurs, and the towering dreadmaws with teeth the size of a Dusk Legion broadsword.

ADMIRAL BECKETT BRASS

The Brazen Coalition is named for Admiral Beckett Brass, who as a young captain rammed her ship, the Scourge, into her rival's ship. The vessels became impossible to dislodge but, miraculously, neither sank. A parley ended the battle, and the ships became the foundation of the floating city of High and Dry, made up of docked fleets and floating derelicts alike. Today, Admiral Brass commands the Fathom Fleet, the largest armada in the coalition.

THE BRAZEN COALITION

The Brazen Coalition is a loose alliance of pirate crews formed decades ago from refugees fleeing the Dusk Legion. The Brazen Coalition turned to piracy on the outlying islands of Ixalan when they were rebuffed by the indigenous Sun Empire. The pirates of the Brazen Coalition raid the Sun Empire and Legion of Dusk alike, seeking only treasure and a place to live.

GOBLINS

Simian goblins are native to Ixalan, but many choose to join pirate crews in search of shiny treasure and big explosions.

THE BELLIGERENT

The crew of the Belligerent accompanied Vraska on her journey to claim the Immortal Sun. Even after she departed, she remains their beloved captain. The most infamous members of the crew were Malcolm, the siren navigator, and Breeches, the loud goblin cannoneer.

SHAPERS

The Shamans who lead each of the nine tribes are named for the nine tributaries of the continent's great river.

RIVER HERALDS

The merfolk of the River Heralds lived on the continent of Ixalan long before humanity came. The River Heralds coexist with the natural world, their magic manipulating nature and the rivers of the continent. When the Sun Empire inevitably abused the power of the Immortal Sun, Azor entrusted it to the Shapers of the River Heralds to keep it safe and hidden, and they continued that duty for centuries, using their powers to make the interior of the continent impenetrable.

HUATLI

Huatli is a Warrior-Poet with the ability to command dinosaurs. She is always in search of the next great saga to bring to her rapt audience. Her orations draw large crowds in the Sun Empire, although the Empire isn't always happy with the truths she has to tell.

RADIANT CHAMPION

Huatli joined the army of Pachatupa as a young woman, alongside her cousin Inti. She quickly rose through the ranks thanks to her oratory skills and her extraordinary ability to control dinosaurs, well beyond that of other mages of the empire. Huatli was a deft combatant, able to turn back Dusk Legion incursions without a single fatality on either side. This nonlethal prowess was the sign of true skill among the Sun Empire. But despite being the preeminent warrior and orator among her people, she was not awarded the post of Warrior-Poet. A battle with the minotaur planeswalker and pirate Angrath pushed her past her limits and ignited her spark. In that moment, she believed she saw a vision of the lost city of Orazca. Seeing the potential Orazca—and the Immortal Sun—could have for the restoration of the Sun Empire, the Emperor commanded her to find it, with the title of Warrior-Poet being her reward.

> **"The sun banishes darkness every morning. I too will rise with such assuredness."**

Huatli was ultimately too late to secure the Immortal Sun. Instead, she returned atop the elder dinosaur Zacama, the most titanic dinosaur to have walked the surface of Ixalan. She visited the Emperor with a tale of mutual cooperation and nobility among their enemies. When the Emperor gave her a different story to tell, one of the Empire's greatness alone, she told the truth to the people anyway and was ousted. Her cousin stole the Warrior-Poet helm for her, and her family bid her farewell as she sought new stories to tell in the Multiverse, where she discovered wonder and horror alike. During the War of the Spark, she stood alongside the Gatewatch against the elder dragon tyrant Nicol Bolas and his army of Eternals.

Huatli's helm is that of the Warrior-Poet.

Huatli commands dinosaurs, but prefers raptor mounts.

Huatli's razor-sharp fans form a weapon of precision.

FILIGREE DINOSAURS

Once the Immortal Sun left Ixalan, Huatli departed to find the city she'd seen in her vision. On Kaladesh, she discovered the wonders that exist across the Multiverse, and met Saheeli Rai, an inventor and planeswalker. Meeting again by chance a couple of months later, the couple realized their shared interest in one another and began dating.

KEY DATA

SPECIES Human

STATUS Planeswalker

SIGNATURE MAGIC Controls Dinosaurs

AGE Early 20s

PLANE OF ORIGIN Ixalan

AFFILIATION Sun Empire

BASE Pachatupa, Ixalan

HAIR Black

EYES Medium brown

HEIGHT 5 ft 2 in

ALLIES Saheeli Rai, the Gatewatch

FOES Nicol Bolas, Azor, Vraska

TRAPPED BY THE IMMORTAL SUN

Huatli's spark ignited while the Immortal Sun was still active on Ixalan, which trapped her. She saw a vision of Ghirapur on Kaladesh before the Immortal Sun pulled her back from her first planeswalk, and this vision of a golden city drove her pursuit of Orazca.

ZACAMA

The colossal elder dinosaur Zacama is a living embodiment of the Threefold Sun. While Huatli is unable to control a dinosaur of such grandeur, the two share a mutual respect, and she has found she can influence the elder dinosaur as long as their goals are aligned.

KALADESH

Kaladesh is a plane full of filigreed wonder. Decades ago, an inventor discovered the means to refine the plane's abundant aether and kickstarted a revolution in artifice. Inventors and tinkerers now strive with relentless optimism, filling the world with artifacts as beautiful as they are brilliant.

This massive structure is a hub for processing and redistributing aether across the city.

HISTORY OF KALADESH

Centuries ago, Kaladesh was made up of fractious kingdoms, and inventors sought patronage from the nobles of these courts. Over the years, social and political entanglements between these court inventors bound them together in an informal network, until 11 of the kingdoms warred in a massive, bloody conflict that lasted a generation. The court inventors used their influence to negotiate peace, and the city of Ghirapur was founded as neutral ground, with the 11 inventors—each from one of the warring kingdoms—becoming the first consuls of this new city. People flocked to Ghirapur, and the influence of the petty kingdoms waned until they collapsed entirely. Today, the Consulate effectively controls Kaladesh.

The artificers of Kaladesh strive ceaselessly for perfection, progress, and the ultimate expression of elegance.

For many years, inventors tried to harness the power of aether, but it always proved too unstable and unreliable as a fuel source. Then, 60 years ago, something changed. A brilliant inventor discovered a means to refine the aether into a clean, unlimited source of energy. The Consulate, seeing the potential of this discovery, set about creating the infrastructure to collect and distribute it. Because refinement of such a volatile resource was inherently hazardous, only the Consulate itself was allowed to harvest and distribute it.

Decades later, what began as a noble enterprise quickly became tyrannical for those who felt they were being underserved by the Consulate bureaucracy. Those discontented with the situation turned to illicit sources of aether and were labeled renegades. When the nefarious planeswalker Tezzeret launched a coup on the Consulate, the renegades began a revolution that brought him down, and the Consulate has spent the years that followed attempting to regain the public trust.

THE AETHERSPHERE

Aether permeates Kaladesh like no other plane in the Multiverse. The swirling skies known as the Aethersphere contain this magical resource in abundance. The influence of the aether on the plane can be seen everywhere, as life, and the plane itself, follows its patterns. The elves believe there is a spiritual component to the way aether shapes the plane—a phenomenon they call the Great Conduit—and they strive to follow its flow.

GREMLINS

These pests that were once merely a nuisance have become a serious problem. The hardy gremlins of Kaladesh feed on delicious aether, whose supply is now abundant inside the carefully engineered artifacts of Kaladesh, which they seem suited to wrecking ... It is, after all, a crunchy shell around their delicious treats. Keeping gremlin infestations at bay is a major concern in populated areas.

AETHERBORN

A strange by-product of the aether refinement process is the spontaneous creation of Aetherborn, living beings of aether that manifest fully formed and born knowing exactly how long they have to live. Aetherborn are extremely empathetic, able to sense the emotions of others, and their extremely short lifespans propel them into living life to the fullest.

KEY DATA

DEMONYM Kaladeshi

TERRAIN Vibrant fields below an aether-filled sky

KEY LOCATIONS Ghirapur

KEY FACTIONS The Consulate, The Renegades

COMMON SPECIES Aetherborn, Dwarf, Elf, Giant, Gremlin, Human, Vedalken

THE AETHER CYCLE

Kaladeshi philosophy is centered around the aether cycle, the belief that invention and life follow the same cycle as the aether through five stages: Inspiration, the genesis of an idea; Innovation, the refining of the idea; Construction, the creation of the artifact; Liberation, the destruction of the artifact; and Reclamation, the returning of aether to its source to begin the cycle anew.

THE CONSULATE

The Consulate is controlled by 11 consuls, each a lifetime appointment. These consuls are each in charge of a segment of the Consulate's bureaucracy, from the allocation of aether, to taxation, commerce, regulation, and law enforcement. In the view of some, the Consulate is a benevolent regulator that ensures a fair distribution of the aether supply. While aether itself is nearly unlimited, the ability to refine it is not. Refining aether takes time, and it's a dangerous process—as proven by unregulated refining operations often ending in explosive catastrophes. To others, the Consulate is an enormous authoritarian bureaucracy with little oversight. Where the people of Kaladesh fall on their view of the Consulate usually depends on whether or not they benefit from the status quo.

A consulate official patrols with a small mechanical automaton called a Servo.

DOVIN BAAN

Dovin Baan was a planeswalker who thrived in the Consulate's bureaucracy. A skilled engineer with a talent for spotting flaws, he obeyed authority implicitly, even when that trust was placed in usurpers like Tezzeret or tyrants like Nicol Bolas. His own flaws were the only ones he couldn't see, and he was killed after working for Bolas during the War of the Spark.

PIA NALAAR

The Renegade leader turned Consul was once a simple inventor who worked a little outside the Consulate's lines. When her daughter was revealed to be a pyromancer, she was arrested and her husband was executed by a corrupt Consulate captain. Years later, emerging from a secret Consulate prison to a city on the brink of revolution, Pia united the disparate Renegade factions into a true rebellion. When the dust settled, Pia was made a Consul and began working to change the underlying causes of the revolution.

THE RENEGADES

The Consulate refers to those groups and individuals who don't conform to their version of society as Renegades. In truth, the Renegades were disparate groups that never shared a common cause until Tezzeret's coup led to an actual revolt. Most Renegades are merely poor or disaffected inventors, aether smugglers, and street artists.

GHIRAPUR, CITY OF WONDERS

The capital of Kaladesh and beating heart of the enterprising spirit is Ghirapur, the city of wonders. Artificers flock to Ghirapur from across the plane, hoping to earn the attention and resources of the Consulate to continue their work.

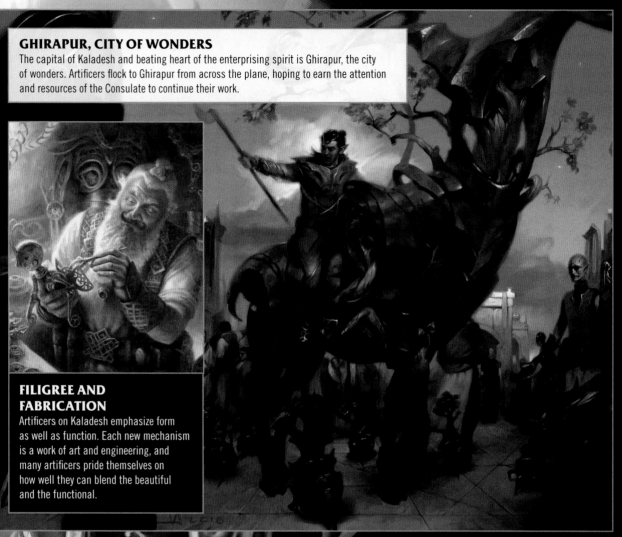

ARTIFICE IMITATES LIFE

Inventors are inspired by the natural world, learning from it to improve their craft.

FILIGREE AND FABRICATION

Artificers on Kaladesh emphasize form as well as function. Each new mechanism is a work of art and engineering, and many artificers pride themselves on how well they can blend the beautiful and the functional.

GLIDERS AND WHEELERS

Motorized vehicles have become commonplace, to the point where the average citizen thinks nothing of riding a floating train across the city or seeing wheeled speedsters dashing down city streets.

LOOK TO THE SKY

Inventions take flight on Kaladesh, from the grandest Skyships in the clouds to the smallest thopters—winged artifacts used as couriers and spies—flying just overhead. Skyships have become the most common method of shipping goods across the plane. However, cruising through the aethersphere carries its own risks, as an unwary skyship may find itself rammed by a massive skywhale or waylaid by pirates.

AUTOMATONS

Most practical inventions on Kaladesh are designed for specific purposes, often using humanoid shapes.

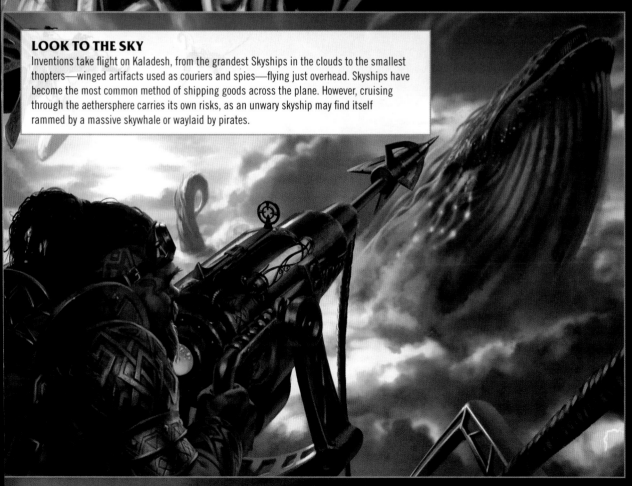

GEARHULKS AND WALKERS

Artificers on Kaladesh don't just dream big, they build big, too. Colossal machines called Gearhulks stomp around the plane, while massive spider-legged walkers transport thopters and other goods across rough terrain.

CHANDRA NALAAR

Chandra Nalaar is a pyromancer with a fiery disposition. Prone to acting first and thinking about consequences later, she found her true calling as a hero with the Gatewatch. Recent years have brought her tragedy and catharsis in equal measure, but her heroic core is unshakeable.

TORCH OF DEFIANCE

Chandra's spark ignited as a teen when she was to be executed by a corrupt Consulate captain. Afterward, she ended up on the volcanic plane of Regatha and was taken in by the monks of Keral Keep. Believing herself responsible for the deaths of her parents, Chandra's self-destructive streak brought her to the attention of the planeswalker Gideon Jura, who tracked her down and helped set her on a better path. The manipulations of Nicol Bolas brought her to the Eye of Ugin on Zendikar, where she was inadvertently involved in releasing the horrific Eldrazi from their prison.

A couple of years later, Gideon returned to ask Chandra for help, alongside former adversary Jace Beleren. Chandra initially refused, but was encouraged by her mentor, an aged planeswalker named Jaya Ballard (in disguise), to follow her heart. Her late arrival saved her friends' lives from the demonic planeswalker Ob Nixilis.

Together with new ally Nissa Revane, they destroyed two of the Eldrazi titans and vowed to protect the Multiverse from similar threats, calling themselves the Gatewatch. Nissa and Chandra developed a deep bond, and Chandra returned home to discover that her mother, Pia, hadn't been killed like she'd always believed. With the Gatewatch's help, she and her mother led a revolution that unseated the scheming planeswalker Tezzeret.

In the aftermath of this, the Gatewatch discovered Tezzeret was merely a pawn in the grand schemes of elder dragon Nicol Bolas. When the Gatewatch tried to take the dragon on directly, they were easily defeated and Chandra and Nissa's relationship suffered for it, with Nissa returning home. They were reunited during Bolas's attack on Ravnica, but the trauma of the day and the death of Gideon, who she loved like a brother, drove them apart. Now the threat of New Phyrexia may reunite them, but with her mentor Jaya slain by her friend Ajani—who himself was turned into a Phyrexian— Chandra is ready to burn New Phyrexia to the ground.

> "Fire is always dancing, leaping, and whirling, seeking more fuel. It never rests, so why should I?"

BOLD PYROMANCER
Chandra is a headstrong pyromancer of unprecedented power.

Chandra's goggles once belonged to her father, Kiran.

Chandra's hair alights when channeling her power.

The regulator on Chandra's arm helped her learn to focus her power.

KEY DATA

SPECIES Human

STATUS Planeswalker

SIGNATURE MAGIC Chandra can conjure and manipulate flame

AGE Mid-20s

PLANE OF ORIGIN Kaladesh

AFFILIATION The Gatewatch

BASE Ghirapur, Kaladesh

HAIR Bright auburn

EYES Amber

HEIGHT 5 ft 6 in

ALLIES The Gatewatch, Saheeli Rai, Arlinn Kord, Wrenn

FOES Nicol Bolas, Tezzeret

PIA AND KIRAN
Practicing pyromancy was illegal on Kaladesh due to the volatile nature of the plane's abundant aether. When Chandra's powers emerged, she destroyed a Consulate foundry by accident and her family was forced to go on the run. They were captured and an overzealous captain executed her father, Kiran. Chandra and her mother, Pia, each believed the other was dead until their joyous reunion.

KERAL KEEP
The monks of Keral Keep were led by the ancient pyromancer and planeswalker, Jaya Ballard—in disguise to avoid the near-mythical reverence Jaya was given at the Keep. Jaya tried to teach Chandra, but the headstrong young woman wasn't receptive until years later, when Jaya revealed her true identity.

SAHEELI RAI

Saheeli Rai has never viewed herself as a hero. As a planeswalker and famous inventor, she had everything she wanted. While she just wants to focus on her work, she finds the Gatewatch inspiring her into heroic acts again and again. She isn't one to be outdone, after all.

SUBLIME ARTIFICER
Saheeli is a famous and skilled inventor on Kaladesh, but her ability to shape quicksilver strands sets her apart.

FILIGREE MASTER

Saheeli Rai was not born into tragedy or conflict. Unlike many of her planeswalker friends, she has no tragic backstory. She doesn't even think of herself as particularly heroic. She's just a person who enjoys inventing, and maybe a little quicksmithing on the side to hone her skills. When her friend Rashmi asked for a favor to complete her Planar Bridge, Saheeli was torn. The Multiverse—of which her friend and the rest of the plane were not yet aware—was a dangerous place. She decided to help, but that choice drew her into a greater conflict as the bridge was stolen by the nefarious planeswalker Tezzeret.

Saheeli quickly found fast friends in the Gatewatch in the fight against Tezzeret. Although she refused to join them formally, she decided to help them out when needed. She had no idea how quickly that would happen—just weeks later, Saheeli, like dozens of other planeswalkers, was lured to Ravnica

"Our creations are more than mere things. They have life in them, little bits of ourselves."

in a trap set by the elder dragon Nicol Bolas, who sought to harvest their sparks. When the opportunity came to cut and run, Saheeli remained and fought alongside the Gatewatch, taking down the elder dragon Nicol Bolas.

A couple of years later, when Teferi came asking for her assistance in building great artifacts the likes of which hadn't been seen in ages, Saheeli jumped at the chance. As she learned of the threat posed by Phyrexia, Saheeli reckoned with her own view of herself and decided that maybe she wasn't a hero—but she was a protector—and she would defend the people and the plane she loved at all costs.

Saheeli's magic allows her to create artifacts faster than human hands.

Saheeli's gold ornamentation doubles as artificer tools.

GIFTED ARTIFICER

Saheeli possess a skill which few— even ancient artificers like Urza— could match. Within just a few short weeks, Saheeli recreated Urza's Sylex in her own style and built a time machine with Teferi. Although Saheeli thinks little of such accomplishments, Teferi has been amazed by her work.

QUICKSMITH

As a rising star in Ghirapur's inventor circles, Saheeli made a name for herself in underground quicksmithing matches where inventors test their skills, building and battling their devices against one another. Saheeli's magic gave her an edge over her competition, building new artifacts faster than human hands would allow.

FILIGREE DINOSAURS

Saheeli discovered a strangely dressed woman one day on the streets of Ghirapur. Quickly realizing this was another planeswalker, she introduced herself to Huatli. Saheeli learned that Huatli came from a plane full of majestic creatures called dinosaurs. Months later, after setting up a date with a mystery woman she had been corresponding with, Saheeli was delighted to realize that this woman was Huatli.

KEY DATA

SPECIES Human

STATUS Planeswalker

SIGNATURE MAGIC Saheeli can create and manipulate strands of liquid metal to create devices

AGE Mid-20s

PLANE OF ORIGIN Kaladesh

BASE Ghirapur, Kaladesh

HAIR Brown

EYES Brown

HEIGHT 5 ft 4 in

ALLIES The Gatewatch, Saheeli Rai, Arlinn Kord, Wrenn

FOES Nicol Bolas, Tezzeret

KALDHEIM

Kaldheim is unique among the planes as it contains the Cosmos, a Multiverse in microcosm connected by the mystical World Tree. Viking clans make a home in the cold light of the World Tree, while narrow passages into other realms provide opportunities for glory and riches. Kaldheim's gods travel the Cosmos, as likely to cause problems as to solve them.

THE WORLD TREE AND THE COSMOS

The realms of Kaldheim are connected by the branches of the World Tree. Dividing the realms is the Cosmos, a dangerous metaphysical space nearly impossible to cross directly without the power of the gods. The Cosmos is home to the Cosmos Monsters, beings worshipped by the elves but feared by humanity and barred from entering the realms of mortals by the power of the gods.

The World Tree appears as branches in the sky of every realm, but the only way for mortals to travel between the realms is through rare gateways called Omenpaths. As the branches of the World Tree rotate through the cosmos, realms sometimes collide in deadly cataclysms called Doomskars, where one or both realms involved risk destruction. There are 11 known realms on Kaldheim, although the exact number varies as realms have been created and destroyed over the millennia.

In the aftermath of the War of the Spark, the devil planeswalker Tibalt was infected by Phyrexians. In exchange for his life, he posed as the trickster god Valki to stir up a war between the realms. While Tibalt was causing chaos, the New Phyrexian praetor, Vorinclex, entered the plane through Tezzeret's planar bridge and stole sap from the World Tree.

Kaya, who was hired to hunt a monster that turned out to be Vorinclex, was caught up in Tibalt's schemes. As she worked to stop the devil planeswalker, she met fellow planeswalkers Tyvar Kell and Niko Aris. Together, the three of them put an end to Tibalt's war of the realms. Afterward, Kaya departed to inform the Gatewatch of what had transpired.

TYRITE
A magical metal made from the sap of the World Tree.

THE GODS
Ruling over Kaldheim are the Skoti, the human gods who usurped the elven gods known as the Einir. The Skoti are imbued with the auroralike energy of the World Tree through the consumption of the Cosmos Elixir, which maintains their divinity. They are led by Alrund, the god of wisdom, who has battled the Cosmos Monsters for the secrets of reality.

KEY DATA

DEMONYM Kaldheimr

TERRAIN Cold realms connected by the mystical World Tree

KEY LOCATIONS Bretagard, Starnheim, Istfell, Axgard, Gnottvold, Immersturm, Karfell, Littjara, Skemfar, Surtland

KEY FACTIONS Einir, Skoti, Beskir, Omenseekers, Skelle, Tuskeri, Kannah

COMMON SPECIES Angel, Demon, Dwarf, Elf, Giant, Human, Troll

GNOTTVOLD

The troll-infested wilds of Gnottvold may have once been home to a mortal civilization, but any evidence of such now lies in ruins.

KARFELL

Karfell was once a land of mortals, not unlike Bretagard, but they were betrayed by the greed of their king and transformed into the undead Draugr.

AXGARD

The realm of the dwarves is full of mountains and rocky flatlands. The dwarves make their homes in underground cities, painstakingly excavated over centuries.

COSMOS MONSTERS

These fearsome creatures inhabit the space between realms.

OMENPATHS

Omenpaths are the only safe passage between realms.

BRETAGARD

The human realm of Bretagard is home to five human clans of Vikings.

IMMERSTURM

Immersturm is a realm of constant warfare ruled by demon warlords.

STARNHEIM

The light of Starnheim shines from atop the World Tree like a sun, providing the light and warmth that nurtures the other realms. The angelic valkyrie who live here judge whether the souls of the dead are worthy to join them.

SKEMFAR

Skemfar is a realm of colossal forests and the elves who make their homes in the branches and roots.

DOOMSKARS

A Doomskar is a cataclysmic collision of realms.

LITTJARA

Littjara is a mysterious and mutable realm of shapeshifters and the lakes and forest they call home.

ISTFELL

Istfell, the realm of the dead, lies at the bottom of the World Tree, farthest from Starnheim's light.

SURTLAND

Surtland is an unstable realm of glaciers and volcanic fissures ruled by rival giant peoples.

TYVAR KELL

Tyvar Kell's great deeds need no introduction, for he will tell you himself! A warrior of incredible strength and agility, Tyvar's skills are matched only by his bravado. On any other being in the Multiverse, Tyvar's grandstanding would be hot air, but Tyvar is every bit the hero he claims to be.

WOOD ELF WARRIOR
Tyvar is a skilled hand-to-hand combatant with the ability to transmute at a touch.

MASTER TRANSMUTER

Tyvar Kell is a wood elf from the realm of Skemfar. The younger brother of the great king, Harald, Tyvar seeks to further his own legend. His boastful personality is paired with real confidence and charisma, as well as martial and magical skill, allowing him to back up any boast he makes. He is quick to make friends and allies, and is as quick to brag about his allies' great deeds as his own. Although his physical prowess is formidable—a fact he shows off with his bare chest, for all to see—his lack of armor isn't merely arrogance. What truly makes him unique are his powers of transmutation. Tyvar can take a material like wood, metal, or even water and change himself and others by touching them. His skin can become the same metal as the blade on his wrist in a moment, making armor redundant.

    Tyvar first learned he was a planeswalker from Kaya while on the trail of the cruel planeswalker Tibalt, who had disguised himself as Valki, the god of lies. Kaya recognized a hedron, a magical stone only found on Zendikar, which Tyvar was wearing as a trophy from what he believed to be just another realm. With his newfound allies in Kaya and Niko, Tyvar learned about what it meant to be a planeswalker. After stopping Tibalt's plan to sow war and chaos throughout the realms of Kaldheim, Tyvar decided to travel the Multiverse, helping those in need … and spreading his own legend in the process.

JASPERA TREES
The great war between the human gods, the Skoti, and the elven gods, the Einir, ended with the human gods imprisoning the seven remaining Einir inside towering Jaspera Trees in Skemfar. The elves continue to revere these trees, with each one capable of a miracle from the imprisoned god inside, from healing wounds to creating indestructible wood.

Tyvar's serpentine tattoos are also in honor of the Cosmos Serpent.

Tyvar's arm blade is a fang design in honor of Koma, the Cosmos Serpent.

Tyvar prefers to be unencumbered ... by weapons, armor, or even a shirt.

"Tyvar Kell. Prince of the elves of Skemfar. Greatest hero in all the realms. Your personal savior."

—TYVAR KELL

KEY DATA

SPECIES Elf

STATUS Planeswalker

SIGNATURE MAGIC Tyvar can transmute himself and others into materials he can touch

AGE Late teens

PLANE OF ORIGIN Kaldheim

BASE Skemfar, Kaldheim

HAIR Red

EYES Purple

HEIGHT 5 ft 8 in

ALLIES The Gatewatch, Niko Aris

FOES Tibalt, New Phyrexia

HARALD, KING OF SKEMFAR

Tyvar's brother is the legendary King Harald, who was granted a vision of a unified Kaldheim after eating the fruit of a Jaspera tree and sleeping beneath its boughs. Over the countless years since, Harald has worked tirelessly to make this dream a reality, forging an alliance between the fractured peoples. Harald believes that it is their right to reclaim the lost power of the Einir, and that it is only possible once the scattered children of the Einir, the shadow and wood elves, are united once more. Harald's alliance is tenuous, and without him holding it together, it's likely that the rift between their peoples will reopen once more.

KAMIGAWA

Kamigawa is a plane inhabited by divine spirits called kami. As the kami realm merges into the mortal realm, the Imperials seek to ease that transition amidst a rapid technological boom. But the Imperials face opposition from groups that resent their rule, and the cultural clash between tradition and modernity rages.

THE KAMI WAR

Over 1,300 years ago, Lord Takeshi Konda committed an unforgiveable crime. On the night of his daughter Michiko's birth, he trespassed into the realm of kami and stole the divinity of the great dragon guardian, O-Kagachi. That divinity manifested as a stone statue in the material realm, and over the years became self-aware. The theft angered the kami so greatly that it ignited 20 years of war between the realms.

The Kami War ended when Michiko learned the truth about her father's crime. Michiko worked tirelessly to end the war with the help of rogue samurai Toshiro Umezawa, freeing her kami sister Kyodai and stopping both O-Kagachi's rampage and Lord Konda's tyranny. Michiko and Kyodai ruled side by side, over mortals and kami alike. In the aftermath of the Kami War, the two once separate realms began to merge. In the aftermath, Toshiro's kami patron, the Myojin of Night's Reach, transported him to Dominaria.

KAMI
Kami are divine spirits that embody aspects of the material realm.

TOWASHI AND THE MODERN AGE

The symbol of modern Kamigawa is Towashi, a cosmopolitan city where all the peoples of Kamigawa live side by side in a way the plane has never seen before. A technological revolution fueled by the merging of the realms coincided with the construction of Towashi, which today is a hub of the technology boom. Towashi once bordered the Jukai Forest, but over the years more and more forest land has been cleared to make way for the city. Construction halted when the kami of the forest revolted at this infringement, and the city began expanding upward into massive skyscrapers. The great tree Boseiju has risen among the skyscrapers, keeping much of the city in its shadow. It is a reminder to the mortals that no matter how high they reach, nature reaches higher.

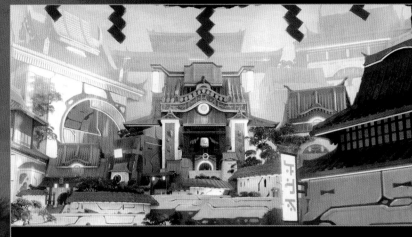

THE IMPERIAL COURT

In the modern day, the merging of kami and material realms occasionally create sites where the kami realm bleeds over. Kyodai founded the Imperials with a mortal emperor in order to mitigate these merges. However, over time their purview has expanded to be the major ruling body over the plane.

MERGE GATES

Merge gates are imperial technology used to manage the unpredictable effects of a merging.

KEY DATA

DEMONYM Kamigawan

TERRAIN High-tech cities coexisting with pastoral landscapes

KEY LOCATIONS Eiganjo, Sokenzanshi, Towashi, Otawara, Sokenzan Range, Takenuma Swamp, Jukai Forest

KEY FACTIONS The Imperials, the Asari Uprisers, the Saiba Futurists, Order of Jukai, Reckoner Gangs

COMMON SPECIES Demon, Goblin, Human, Fox, Moonfolk, Ogre, Rat, Snake

KAITO SHIZUKI

Kaito Shizuki is a skilled warrior who makes great use of his limited telekinetic abilities. A fledgling samurai turned techno-savvy ninja, Kaito cares deeply for his friends. He has spent his life searching the Multiverse for his oldest friend, the Wanderer, and upon finding her, he's stumbled into a greater crisis ...

Kaito's sword can break into smaller origami-like throwing stars.

Himoto never leaves Kaito's side for long.

THE TELEKINETIC FUTURIST

Kaito and his sister, Eiko, were orphaned at a young age and adopted by the Imperials. Trained by the best tutors in diplomacy and combat, they were groomed for Imperial service. When Kaito was paired against the young emperor—the Wanderer—for training, the two became friends. Although Kaito was trained for the life of an Imperial Samurai, he preferred nightly runs along the city's rooftops. One such night, he found Tezzeret implanting technology into Kyodai, causing the emperor to disappear.

When it was clear that the Imperials didn't believe his story, Kaito left them and used his skills with the ruthless Reckoner gangs of Towashi to search for the emperor by himself. When a Reckoner mission introduced him to a technologically-savvy Futurist artificer and Himoto, the Kami of the Spark, he and Himoto bonded and the Multiverse opened up. Since then, he's balanced his time between the Futurists and searching the Multiverse for the emperor. He found her with the help of fellow Kamigawan planeswalker Tamiyo—but stumbled upon a New Phyrexian plot in progress.

HIMOTO, THE KAMI OF THE SPARK
Kaito's planeswalker spark ignited when he bonded with Himoto, a kami offspring of Kyodai. Himoto is protected in a small tanuki-shaped robot which Kaito has nicknamed Pompon, in order to avoid revealing her true identity to those who would take her power.

KEY DATA

SPECIES Human

STATUS Planeswalker

SIGNATURE MAGIC Kaito has limited telekinetic abilities

AGE Early 20s

PLANE OF ORIGIN Kamigawa

BASE Towashi, Kamigawa

HAIR Black

EYES Black

HEIGHT 6 ft

ALLIES The Wanderer, Tamiyo, the Gatewatch

FOES Tezzeret, New Phyrexia

THE WANDERER

The Wanderer typically conceals her identity with her wide-brimmed hat.

The Wanderer's whiplike blade can cleave any foe.

Legends have grown around the mysterious Wanderer, a skilled swordswoman who appears briefly to save the day before disappearing. In truth, the Wanderer is Kamigawa's missing emperor, a planeswalker whose spark is in constant flux, which forces her to live a transient life as she planeswalks with little control.

WHEN WE WERE YOUNG
Kaito and the Wanderer are childhood friends. The Wanderer was always the better fighter, and she doesn't let Kaito forget it.

KEY DATA

SPECIES Human

STATUS Planeswalker

SIGNATURE MAGIC The Wanderer absorbs kinetic energy to reflect back in her sword strikes

AGE Mid-20s

PLANE OF ORIGIN Kamigawa

BASE None

HAIR White

EYES Brown

HEIGHT 5 ft 3 in

ALLIES Kaito Shizuki, Tamiyo, the Gatewatch

FOES Tezzeret, Nicol Bolas, New Phyrexia

REALITY CHIP
The finished Reality Chip allowed the Wanderer to anchor herself to planes once again ... but fell into the hands of New Phyrexia, who used it to compleat Tamiyo.

THE WANDERING EMPEROR

As a young girl, the Wanderer was bonded to the great kami Kyodai and named emperor of Kamigawa. She was trained by the best samurai and given the best student sparring partner available: Kaito Shizuki. Kaito and the Wanderer became best friends. Then the nefarious Tezzeret infiltrated Eiganjo and, using a prototype Reality Chip, he damaged the Wanderer's spark. Forced to planeswalk whenever she loses concentration, the Wanderer earned her nickname as she flitted about the universe, using her skills to help those in need before moving on.

Her skills were vital in stopping the evil elder dragon Nicol Bolas, whose lackey, Tezzeret, had caused her condition. She tracked Tezzeret down, but the conniving planeswalker eluded her again. When Kaito and Tamiyo—on the trail of Tezzeret—recovered the new Reality Chip, she was finally able to return home. However, Tamiyo and the chip were taken by Tezzeret to New Phyrexia, leaving the Wanderer unmoored once more.

The Wanderer walks many paths. Her blade travels only one.

KAMIGAWA'S FACTIONS

The Imperial Court's authority isn't unchallenged on Kamigawa. As technology has developed, factions opposed to Imperial control have emerged from a wide range of ideologies. These factions sometimes bitterly oppose each other as much as they oppose the Imperials.

SAIBA FUTURISTS

The secretive, technocratic Saiba Futurists are at the forefront of scientific research. The Futurists see technology as more reliable than traditional magic, which on Kamigawa often requires a kami patron. Technology allows the Futurists to take control of that power for themselves. To ensure their secrets never fall into the wrong hands, they employ the Veilshapers, a department of professional spies.

RECKONER GANGS

As the city of Towashi expanded, so too did the criminals who made their home there. Imperial edicts have created a market for illicit goods and technology, and Reckoner gangs fill the unsavory margins. Due to magically binding loyalty tattoos, each gang functions effectively as a family, since there is no way to leave once inked. The largest and most powerful of these gangs are the Hyozan Reckoners, who trace their origins all the way back to the kami war and the legendary rogue Toshiro Umezawa. Other gangs include the Mukotai, who specialize in stealth and subterfuge, and the Okiba, a biker gang comprised entirely of nezumi who trace their origins to the ancient nezumi warrior caste.

RECKONER TATTOOS

A tradition carried over from the Kami War, Reckoner loyalty is ensured through binding vows inscribed in magical tattoos. As gang members climb the ranks, they gain additional tattoos that imbue a wide range of abilities.

SATORU UMEZAWA

The ruthless leader of the Hyozan Reckoners claims to be a direct descendant of the legendary Toshiro Umezawa. No one is quite sure if that is true, but no one is brave enough to challenge the assertion, either.

ASARI UPRISERS

The unforgiving Sokenzan Mountains have always bred hardy, independent people. The mountain city of Sokenzanshi is no exception. Bringing together humans, akki, and ogres, the city is a massive foundry where independent tinkerers and artificers thrive. The Asari Uprisers were born from this spirit of independence, rising up against an overzealous Imperial regime. The Uprisers are made up of former Imperial soldiers and Sokenzanshi artisans who seek to cast off Imperial control.

UPRISER TECH

The limited resources of Sokenzanshi have created an environment where tinkerers take pride in repairing and recycling old equipment rather than building something new.

ORDER OF JUKAI

The Order of Jukai is a response to the rapid pace of technological growth that is believed will lead to the destruction of the spirit realm. The monastic order was founded in part by those displaced from the Jukai Forest by kami angry at the deforestation brought about by Towashi. The Order operates as independent cells working to undermine groups like the Futurists attacking technological centers.

TAMIYO

Tamiyo was known as a researcher and explorer who sought to learn about the Multiverse and gather its stories. The last thing she ever wanted was to become part of the stories herself, and she desperately avoided interfering with other planes except as a last resort.

COLLECTOR OF TALES
Tamiyo was a moonfolk who wielded the power of stories into practical magic.

"The pain of exploring is less than the pain of not knowing."

—TAMIYO

THE MOON SAGE

The soratami moonfolk of Otawara were once an insular society that held themselves above the rest of Kamigawa, both literally and metaphorically. Tamiyo, by contrast, found new and different cultures fascinating. A researcher, historian, and storyteller, when the Multiverse opened up to her, she leapt at the chance to explore and learn. She weaved her magic through her story scrolls, each of which imparted an ability based on the metaphor of the story contained within.

During a research trip to Innistrad, she found herself caught during the arrival of the Eldrazi titan Emrakul. Initially reluctant to interfere in the affairs of another plane, she was convinced by the Gatewatch that an extraplanar threat like the Eldrazi required planeswalker intervention. Using one of her restricted iron-banded scrolls, she provided the power to seal Emrakul into Innistrad's silver moon. She would go on to join the Gatewatch again on Ravnica to defeat the elder dragon Nicol Bolas.

When Kaito began asking questions about Tamiyo's adopted son, Nashi, she confronted Kaito, believing him to be an agent of Tezzeret or otherwise a threat to her family. When she learned Kaito was tracking Tezzeret, who was on Kamigawa, they worked together to stop what turned out to be a New Phyrexian plot. While trying to stop Tezzeret and the New Phyrexian praetor Jin-Gitaxias, Tamiyo was abducted by Tezzeret and brought to New Phyrexia.

COMPLEATED SAGE
After Tamiyo was captured by New Phyrexia, the praetor Jin-Gitaxias converted her into becoming the first successful Phyrexian planeswalker. Her first task was to capture other planeswalkers for compleation, the first of which was her longtime friend Ajani. Tamiyo now serves as a living herald for Phyrexia, her love of story transformed into the evangelization of Phyrexia's story, her love of family twisted into the view that all of Phyrexia is her family.

Tamiyo has pledged never to use the stories contained in her iron-bound scrolls.

Tamiyo wields her magic through story-scrolls.

Tamiyo can float through the air with moonfolk magic.

THE STORY-CIRCLE
Tamiyo befriended like-minded planeswalkers Ajani and Narset and formed the story-circle, a small group of planeswalkers who gather to share their stories of the Multiverse.

FOR THE LOVE OF FAMILY
Tamiyo divided her time between her field research and her family. She was happily married to Genku, a moonfolk man, and they had two children together, Hiroku and Rumiyo. They also adopted Nashi, an orphaned nezumi whose village was burned down by agents of Tezzeret. Tamiyo was fiercely protective of her family and would do anything to keep them safe.

KEY DATA

SPECIES Moonfolk

STATUS Planeswalker

SIGNATURE MAGIC Tamiyo weaves story magic in practical magic

AGE Appears mid-30s

PLANE OF ORIGIN Kamigawa

AFFILIATION New Phyrexia (current)

BASE Otawara, Kamigawa (former), New Phyrexia (current)

HAIR White

EYES Purple

HEIGHT 5 ft 10 in

ALLIES The Gatewatch (former), Narset (former), Ajani

FOES The Gatewatch (current)

NEW CAPENNA

The vertical cityscape of New Capenna is controlled by crime families who clash over the dwindling supplies of Halo, the sole remaining essence of Capenna's lost angels. Outside the city lies a world in ruin, left to crumble after a Phyrexian invasion nearly destroyed the plane.

THE HISTORY OF OLD CAPENNA

Centuries ago, Capenna was a hopeful world of castles and sorcery overseen by angel guardians. Then came a threat even the grandeur of the archangels couldn't stop—a force of mechanical horrors from beyond their world: Phyrexians. The archangels built New Capenna as a refuge for the people of Old Capenna, but their power was spent containing the Phyrexian spread. Sensing their rivals' weakness, the archdemons of the plane bound the archangels in a stasis spell and merged with hand-picked successors. These successors became the heads of the five modern crime families.

THE CITY OF NEW CAPENNA
The primary location on this plane is New Capenna, an extreme vertical cityscape that seems as if it is floating in the sky. The city is divided into three boroughs, connected by steep vertical bridges. Each crime family has territory throughout the city, but some are more heavily focused in certain areas. Park Heights comprises the upper tiers of the city, where the upper class live in glitz and glamor. The Mezzio is the city center, the hub of trade and commerce, filled with shops and tradespeople, where most people reside. The Caldaia are the lowest levels of the city, resembling an industrialized dragon's lair, where the working class toil.

HALO
Angelic essence, Halo is a highly sought-after commodity and has many magical uses.

THE MAESTROS

In Old Capenna, the Maestros were aristocratic patrons of the arts. During the great migrations to New Capenna, they were responsible for saving much of the art and culture of the old world. Today, they portray themselves as upstanding citizens with a passion for the arts, but secretly they're also a shadowy cabal of assassins led by vampires. The Maestros are the old money of New Capenna, descended from the wealthy noble class, and the most powerful among them hail from distinguished ancient bloodlines, vampiric or not.

GIADA

Giada is a young girl with an angelic destiny. The first new source of Halo in generations, Giada was sought after by all five families. When Elspeth helped her escape her imprisonment, her latent angelic power awakened.

LORD XANDER

Years ago, Lord Xander was offered a bargain from the archdemons: join them and be blessed with eternal life. They failed to mention that the means for that life would be a vampiric curse. Although Xander was once a notorious assassin, he has now retired from active jobs and spends his days managing the family and curating his museum. Xander was ultimately killed by the Adversary, an interloper named Ob Nixilis. Xander's top lieutenant, the vampire assassin Anhelo, then took over the family.

ANGELS

Once sealed by demonic power, the angels have begun to awaken.

THE MUSEUM OF OLD CAPENNA

Curated by Lord Xander himself, the Museum of Old Capenna is filled with tasteful exhibitions of fine art from across Old Capenna.

KEY DATA

DEMONYM Capennan

TERRAIN A vertical urban cityscape

KEY LOCATIONS Park Heights, The Mezzio, The Caldaia, Old Capenna

KEY FACTIONS The Maestros, the Cabaretti, the Brokers, the Riveteers, the Obscura

COMMON SPECIES Aven, Cephalid, Devil, Elf, Leonin, Ogre, Racoonfolk, Rhox, Vampire, Viashino

THE OBSCURA

Before New Capenna, the Obscura were a society of mages who guided society through their wisdom. Today, after centuries of demonic influence, they've become master manipulators. Using their vast mystical powers, they collect information for blackmail and confidence schemes, turning every situation to their advantage and playing the other families against one another.

RAFFINE

The mastermind behind the Obscura's criminal network is Raffine, a sphinx oracle who runs an unassuming fortune teller shop. In truth, the store front hides a secret entrance to the Obscura base of operations known as the Cloud Spire, from which Raffine perches over the city and sees to her criminal empire. Raffine claims her deal with the archdemons granted her the gift of prophecy, but she never shares the contents of the visions she receives, and many suspect that her prophecies are simply another con.

THE RIVITEERS

The Riviteers were once the artisans and tradespeople who built and maintained the cities of Old Capenna. They became the labor force that constructed New Capenna, and they continue to be indispensable in the upkeep of this vast metropolis. They have complete control of the Caldaia, the lower levels of the city, and work to turn the entire city into a draconic paradise in service to their boss.

ZIATORA

The dragon Ziatora has always been a thrill seeker and collector of trinkets and treasure. Her deal with the archdemons put her in control of the skilled workers of the city, an opportunity to expand her influence and sate her thirst for adventure in the new status quo of the plane. Riveteers have some access to Ziatora's draconic power, manifesting in different ways between the different peoples who belong to her organization.

THE CABARETTI

The Cabaretti formed from the druids of the old world. With the dizzying heights of the metal cityscape separating them from the earth, their druidic festivals slowly became nonstop parties. They're the most open to newcomers of all the families, although fame and influence are preferred in new candidates. Jetmir, the archdruid turned family boss, has final say on all new recruits to the family.

JETMIR

Jetmir still views himself as the paternal high priest he once was before merging with demons. His generosity is boundless, refusing to see anyone in the city go hungry, and he is quick with a laugh and a smile. He encourages the hedonistic pursuits of the family, and he has a merciless streak for anything he views as disloyalty.

THE BROKERS

The Brokers formed from an order of nomadic paladins that could be called upon for aid in exchange for meager tithes to keep the paladins clothed and fed. With the demonic takeover of the city, the Brokers have become more sinister, a law office whose solicitors offer aid to the desperate in exchange for signing shadowy pacts.

FALCO SPARA

Falco developed the Brokers' mystically binding pact magic through years of study, and leapt at the chance to increase his law firm's reach through his demonic bargain. In secret, Falco has ordered the Brokers to hoard as much Halo as they can, in defense against a future doomsday prophecy of which only he is aware.

ELSPETH TIREL

Elspeth Tirel is a knight and combat mage of renown, but she has spent her life searching for a home where she can belong. For years, she was driven to flee from the tragedies of her past, but she has been reborn with a new resolve to vanquish the evils of her past.

NEMESIS OF PHYREXIA

Elspeth was born in horror among the decaying Phyrexian remnants of New Capenna. Growing up in a Phyrexian dungeon, she was forced to watch unspeakable horrors befall the other prisoners. Her planeswalker spark ignited and she was flung across the Multiverse to relative safety. She eventually found a home on Bant, a shard of Alara, where she ascended the ranks until she met the leonin planeswalker Ajani Goldmane. Together, they unraveled Nicol Bolas's schemes for Alara. Elspeth slew Bolas's minion, the demon-dragon Malfegor, but with the undead hordes of Grixis now tainting her home, her idyllic world was shattered. She left, knowing Bant would never be the same.

> ## "Finally, I understand. Home isn't where you rest. It's what you fight for."
>
> —ELSPETH TIREL

On Dominaria, she ran across Koth, who was looking for aid to defeat the New Phyrexian threat on Mirrodin. Elspeth followed him and overcame her trauma to become a valuable member of the Mirran Resistance as the New Phyrexians conquered Mirrodin. After years of fighting, she was forced to planeswalk away and abandon the fight when a last-ditch mission to assassinate the Phyrexian leaders went awry. Still searching for belonging, she traveled to Theros, where she found her sword Godsend years before and where she hoped the gods would have the answers she sought. Instead, Elspeth became embroiled in the machinations of a planeswalker named Xenagos who sought to usurp the gods themselves.

KNIGHT-ERRANT
Elspeth Tirel is a trained knight of Bant and a mage who can empower her allies in combat.

BETRAYED BY HELIOD
The god Heliod made Elspeth his champion, but he was a jealous god and was threatened by her ability to resist his power. When Elspeth slew her lover (and Heliod's oracle) Daxos while under Xenagos's spell, Heliod turned on her. Elspeth defeated Xenagos, but Heliod seized Godsend after her victory and stabbed her in the back, killing her.
 In the Underworld, the nightmare weaver Ashiok tormented Elspeth with visions of Phyrexia. Instead of spiraling into despair like Ashiok intended, it filled Elspeth with a new resolve. She set out to punish Heliod for his betrayal and return to life—and accomplished both. Restored to life, she returned to Ajani, only to find that New Phyrexia was planning to launch a Multiversal invasion, and her home plane of New Capenna could be the key to stopping it.

Elspeth's tiara mimics the two glowing orbs in Godsend ... and her mask from the Underworld.

Elspeth was reborn in a new body, without the scars of the past.

GODSEND
Elspeth acquired Godsend as a youth, unaware of its true power as a god-killer. It was destroyed by Heliod to prevent it from being used against him.

KEY DATA

SPECIES Human

STATUS Planeswalker

SIGNATURE MAGIC Elspeth empowers and fortifies herself and others in combat

AGE Late 20s

PLANE OF ORIGIN New Capenna

AFFILIATION None

BASE Bant, Alara (formerly)

HAIR Brown

EYES Brown

HEIGHT 5 ft 9 in

ALLIES The Gatewatch, Ajani (formerly), Koth, Karn

FOES Heliod, New Phyrexia, Nicol Bolas

LUXIOR
The Halo sword Luxior was a gift from young Giada. It is full of angelic power.

BELOVED BY DAXOS
During her time on Theros, Elspeth fell in love with the charismatic oracle of Heliod, Daxos. To drive a wedge between Heliod and his champion, Xenagos induced a hallucination that resulted in Daxos's death at Elspeth's hands. Although both have now returned to life, the bond between them has been lost.

SHADOWSPEAR
Shadowspear was a mockery of Heliod's own spear, made from Ashiok's nightmares. The nightmare power dissipated once Elspeth left Theros.

NEW PHYREXIA

New Phyrexia is a terrifying plane where a few survivors eke out a life in hiding from the necro-mechanical horrors that have taken over. The plane was created as Argentum, a perfect metal world built by Karn at the height of his powers, and guarded by a golem named Memnarch.

MIRRODIN
Memnarch, the warden of Argentum created by Karn, became bitter that his creator abandoned him for long stretches of time. The warden became obsessed with becoming a planeswalker as well. To that end, he constructed devices to capture living beings from other planes and transformed the surface of Argentum into biomes for them to live in. He renamed the world Mirrodin, and after a generation of adaptation these Mirrans forgot their true origins. Eventually, an elf named Glissa was born with a spark, but she quickly proved to be Memnarch's match, and she and her allies defeated him at the cost of her latent spark.

MYCOSYNTH
Chrome fungal growths whose spores transformed flesh into metal and vice versa. An early stage of Phyrexia's terraforming of the plane, they also became the substrate upon which the spheres of New Phyrexia would be built.

ELESH NORN, MOTHER OF MACHINES
After years of in-fighting between factions among New Phyrexia, the praetor Elesh Norn is ascendant as supreme leader. Taking the title Mother of Machines, Norn put plans into motion to expand to other planes and bring the glory of New Phyrexia to the Multiverse.

NEW PHYREXIA

When Karn had created Argentum, he unwittingly brought with him Phyrexian's final weapon, a mutagenic compound in the form of glistening oil. The oil infected Argentum from its creation, steadily terraforming the plane into something suitable for the rebirth of Phyrexia. New Phyrexia slowly grew in the hidden places of the plane's core, until they were ready to invade the surface, corrupting and transforming the Mirrans until only a handful were left.

THE MACHINE ORTHODOXY
The Machine Orthodoxy is a grim mockery of religion focused around Elesh Norn's writings. The Orthodoxy's tenets can broadly be categorized into two compelling drives: the elimination of flesh and the unity of all things under Phyrexia. The key tenet of the Machine Orthodoxy is that flesh is a sinful barrier which divides individuals and prevents unity. As Norn prepares for Invasion, her faction has become the Machine Legion, the core of the Phyrexian armada.

KEY DATA

DEMONYM New Phyrexian, Mirran (Mirrodin survivors)

TERRAIN A metallic world of nine nested spheres

KEY LOCATIONS Glorious Façade, Mirrex, Furnace Layer, Hunter's Maze, Surgical Bays, Dross Pits, Fair Basilica, Mycosynth Gardens, Seedcore

KEY FACTIONS Mirran Resistance, Machine Orthodoxy, Progress Engine, Steel Thanes, Quiet Furnace, Vicious Swarm

COMMON SPECIES Elf, Goblin, Human, Leonin, Loxodon, Phyrexian, Vampire, Vedalken

New Phyrexia has five suns, each charged with a color of magic.

THE NINE SPHERES
Years after their conquest of the surface, New Phyrexia has finished its transformation of the plane. What was once merely a surface world and a core is now nine nested spheres after the original Phyrexia.

GLORIOUS FAÇADE
This sphere was constructed above the former surface, populated with horrifying and incomprehensible monuments to mark New Phyrexia's total victory over Mirrodin.

MIRREX
The former surface of Mirrodin has become a barren wasteland. The resources of this sphere have been harvested to construct the rest of New Phyrexia.

FURNACE LAYER
Rivers of molten metal traverse this sphere, destined for titanic forges and for repurposing into new construction.

HUNTER'S MAZE
A tangled copper wilderness constructed from the transplanted artificial forests of Mirrodin's surface.

SURGICAL BAYS
Harsh, sterile laboratories rise from islands in a sea of quicksilver and glistening oil.

THE DROSS PITS
A fetid sphere of acidic pools and toxic vents spewing necrotic gasses.

THE FAIR BASILICA
A sphere modeled after Elesh Norn herself, where the horrific beauty of every cathedral and statue testify to her greatness.

MYCOSYNTH GARDENS
A slice of the former core of Mirrodin, where the mycosynth grows unchecked.

SEEDCORE
An incubation chamber for New Phyrexian's Invasion Tree, Realmbreaker.

NEW PHYREXIA

The New Phyrexians spent centuries gestating in Mirrodin's core. Subjected to Mirrodin's five suns, each of which radiated with a different color of mana, the Phyrexians, too, became split into five ideological factions. Although Elesh Norn's Machine Orthodoxy currently reigns over them all, each has their own agenda.

THE PROGRESS ENGINE

The Progress Engine is the New Phyrexian faction most obsessed with science and experimentation. Seeking what they deem "The Great Synthesis," they believe that iterative experimentation is key to creating the perfect Phyrexian. The Progress Engine is divided into groups called sectives, each of which is responsible for a different area of research, from improving the methods used to convert individuals into Phyrexians, to determining what forms those Phyrexians should take.

A Phyrexian experiments on a captured elf.

JIN-GITAXIAS

The praetor of the Progress Engine believes his vision for New Phyrexia is the most accurate, although he's content to follow Elesh Norn's lead so long as it doesn't interfere with his experiments. Recently, Jin-Gitaxias has achieved something that has eluded Phyrexia for millennia: creating a Phyrexian planeswalker.

SHEOLDRED

Sheoldred was Elesh Norn's main rival for control of New Phyrexia. To eliminate her as a threat, Elesh Norn lured her into invading Dominaria, the Phyrexian's ancestral home, which Sheoldred was all too happy to do. But Sheoldred's failure on Dominaria has removed the last major threat to Elesh Norn's power.

THE STEEL THANES

The seven Steel Thanes are a loose feudal faction led by Sheoldred, a master manipulator who uses her vast networks of spies, saboteurs, and assassins to maintain control. Sheoldred has had visions of Yawgmoth's Phyrexian Scriptures, and as the black-mana aligned faction, the Steel Thanes are the closest to old Phyrexia in nature. Each Thane bides their time until they can seize power from the others.

THE QUIET FURNACE

The Quiet Furnace dwells in the Furnace Layer, with no goals other than to continue their Great Work, the reforging of the old into the new. As the red-aligned faction, the Quiet Furnace is most opposed to ideas of hierarchy, and they've begun to show glimmers of something akin to empathy, or at least apathy, toward the Mirran Resistance, even allowing the Mirran survivors to hide among them.

URABRASK

Urabrask has declared the Mirran Resistance be left alone, so long as they don't interfere with the Great Work. Urabrask does not engage with the other factions unless forced, but Elesh Norn's ambitions represent a grave threat to the Great Work, and he believes they must be opposed. As such, he has begun cooperating with the Mirran Resistance and several Steel Thanes in planning a revolt against Elesh Norn's control.

THE VICIOUS SWARM

The Vicious Swarm believes in a survival of the fittest philosophy. It takes the idea of Phyrexian's Grand Evolution from scriptures literally and creates an environment where the strongest predators emerge from their version of nature.

VORINCLEX

The praetor of the Vicious Swarm is an apex predator who kills and feeds on any challengers to his supremacy. Although he is intelligent, he rarely speaks and prefers to follow his bestial instincts.

GLISSA

Once considered a great hero of the plane, Glissa is now a high-ranking Phyrexian. While Vorinclex is the nominal head of the Vicious Swarm, he prefers to delegate most of his responsibilities to Glissa. As such, Glissa controls much of the fighting force of the Swarm and often speaks as Vorinclex's voice.

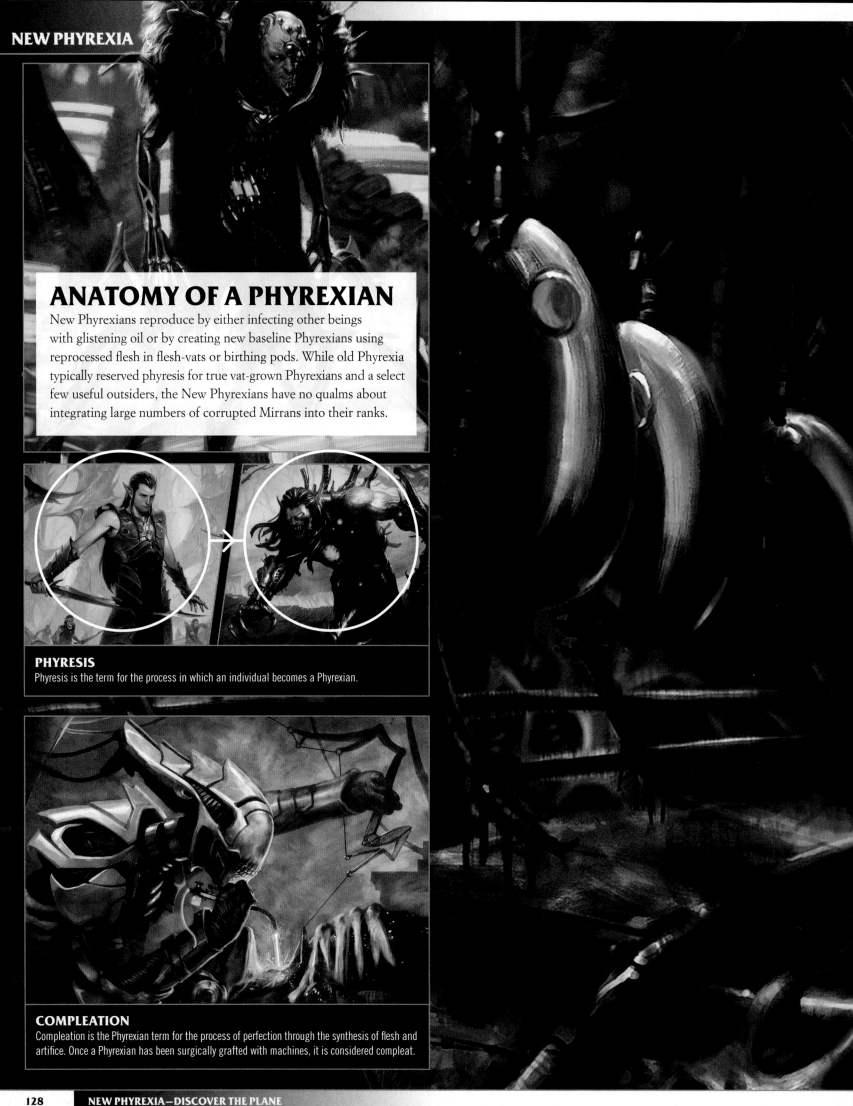

ANATOMY OF A PHYREXIAN

New Phyrexians reproduce by either infecting other beings with glistening oil or by creating new baseline Phyrexians using reprocessed flesh in flesh-vats or birthing pods. While old Phyrexia typically reserved phyresis for true vat-grown Phyrexians and a select few useful outsiders, the New Phyrexians have no qualms about integrating large numbers of corrupted Mirrans into their ranks.

PHYRESIS
Phyresis is the term for the process in which an individual becomes a Phyrexian.

COMPLEATION
Compleation is the Phyrexian term for the process of perfection through the synthesis of flesh and artifice. Once a Phyrexian has been surgically grafted with machines, it is considered compleat.

FLESH STOCK

New Phyrexians are created through two separate processes: the conversion of outside hosts and the creation of new baseline Phyrexians. New Phyrexia relies heavily on the conversion of new hosts—however, these compleated beings are rarely afforded the same respect as a Phyrexian created in the core. A baseline vat-grown Phyrexian is called a newt and is similar in appearance to a human, although heavily genetically modified. Only a compleated newt is considered a true, core-born Phyrexian.

GLISTENING OIL

Phyrexian oil, also known as glistening oil, is the primary mechanism for phyresis. The oil acts as a mutagen that twists the minds of those infected (often involving memory loss and personality changes) and modifies their bodies for compleation. The oil has become more virulent over time, although its efficacy will depend on both the host and the environment. Early stages of phyresis are characterized by oil leaking from an infected host's eyes. Eventually, the oil replaces the vital liquids in the host's body.

COMPLEATION

Once a host has been corrupted, vat-priests or splicers oversee the surgical modification of the host to fulfill a specific purpose. This process may also involve necromancy, as such procedures are usually fatal. When the host's body is fully integrated with machinery, they are considered Phyrexianized or compleat. The degree to which a body is altered can vary drastically in this process, as can the level of intelligence they retain after compleation. The higher a Phyrexian ranks, the more intelligence they are usually granted.

PHYREXIAN ARTIFACTS

Phyrexians also use a wide array of artifact creatures and undead, but where an artifact begins and the Phyrexian ends is usually questionable. Phyrexians can corrupt artifacts in much the same way as they corrupt organic beings, and generally make little distinction between living tissue, dead tissue, and inanimate objects, as they have no understanding of the nature of the soul.

PHYREXIAN PLANESWALKERS

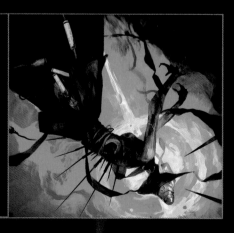

Because Phyrexians lack the concept of a soul, they could not comprehend the nature of the planeswalker spark. Compleation destroyed the spark as surely as death. Through experimentation on Kamigawa, the praetor Jin-Gitaxias learned to harness the intangible spirit. This breakthrough allowed for the successful compleation of Tamiyo, the first Phyrexian planeswalker.

RESISTING AND CURING PHYRESIS

There have only been a handful of instances of phyresis being resisted or cured, but it is possible. Dominaria and New Capenna both resisted Phyrexian incursions and phyresis through technological and magical means. On New Phyrexia, the Mirran human known as Melira was born with a natural immunity to phyresis. After an encounter with the mysterious blinkmoths of Mirrodin, she was magically enhanced with the ability to confer this immunity on others. Melira's immunity can reverse severe infections up until the host is completely corrupted, but the effects of her powers are growing weaker as the glistening oil has grown more virulent. Some of the Mirran Resistance, as well as the planeswalkers Elspeth, Koth, and Karn, have all benefited from the immunity she has granted. Tezzeret also received an inoculation against phyresis—of unknown origin—by another agent of Bolas.

KOTH

Koth is the leader of the Mirran Resistance, the survivors of the New Phyrexian invasion of Mirrodin. Koth searched the Multiverse for allies to stop them, but was too late to prevent the New Phyrexian takeover of the plane. Although the situation seems hopeless, Koth will never stop fighting for his people.

AVENGER OF MIRRODIN

When the Vulshok tribes went to war for the first time in generations over corrupted ore, Koth was able to negotiate a peace by purifying the ore. As the corruption grew worse, Koth investigated the source and discovered the impending New Phyrexian conquest of the surface. As a planeswalker, he traveled the Multiverse looking for other planeswalkers who could help and met Elspeth and Venser, both of whom had experience dealing with Phyrexians or their technology.

With Elspeth and Venser at his side, the three planeswalkers descended into Mirrodin's core, only to find the situation far worse than they had imagined. The New Phyrexians had created an army to conquer the surface, and the conquest was already underway. Freeing Karn, the creator of Mirrodin kept prisoner by the New Phyrexians, was their only hope. During their journey, they made a tentative alliance with Tezzeret, a ruthless planeswalker who infiltrated Phyrexia on behalf of the elder dragon Nicol Bolas. Tezzeret gave them Melira, a curious Mirran who was immune to both metallic growths endemic to Mirrans and to the glistening oil. Taking Melira to a Mirran encampment, they discovered that she had developed the ability to pass her immunity along to others.

VULSHOK GEOMANCER
Koth has command over tectonic forces. He is able to control earth, ore, and metal and heat them into magma.

Freshly immunized, Koth and his allies descended to the core in search of Karn, fighting the forces of Phyrexian elf Glissa along the way. When they reached Karn's throne room, it was clear he was corrupted beyond healing. Venser, who was dying of a terminal illness, teleported his immunized spark into Karn. With his mind clear, Karn helped them fight their way out of the core, but it was apparent that even Karn could not defeat New Phyrexia by himself, and he went in search of the mysterious sylex that his mentor had detonated millennia before. Koth and Elspeth continued the fight in the meantime, but even they were overwhelmed. Koth forced Elspeth to planeswalk away during an ill-fated assassination attempt on the praetors, but remained behind to continue the fight. He continues to lead the surviving Mirrans in a guerrilla campaign against New Phyrexia.

"If there can be no victory, then I will fight forever."

—KOTH OF THE HAMMER

MIRRAN RESISTANCE
The Mirran Resistance is made up of the survivors of Mirrodin. Peoples who were once bitter enemies now fight side by side for their survival and the glimmer of hope of a Mirrodin restored. They've survived, thanks in part to the sanctuary they found in the Furnace Layer, where Urabrask ordered his minions to leave the Mirrans alone if they don't interfere with the Great Work. From their encampments in the Furnace Layer and the remains of Mirran, they launch guerrilla strikes against the New Phyrexians.

Mirrans all possess metallic growths to survive the harsh metal environment of their home plane.

KEY DATA

SPECIES Human (Mirran)

STATUS Planeswalker

SIGNATURE MAGIC Koth is a geomancer with a command over earth and ore

AGE Late 30s

PLANE OF ORIGIN Mirrodin

AFFILIATION Mirran Resitance

BASE Mirrex, New Phyrexia

HAIR None (obsidian stone)

EYES Black

HEIGHT 6 ft

ALLIES Elspeth, Karn

FOES New Phyrexia

Koth's forearms are full of orelike growths that turn molten with his magic.

HAMMER TRIBE SHAMAN

Koth is a Vulshok, a human tribe from Mirrodin who adapted to the metallic world with orelike growths coming from their bodies. The Vulshok were divided into tribes around their specializations, and Koth's tribe was that of the Hammer. They were renowned blacksmiths, and Koth himself is incredibly adept at fashioning weapons out of molten ore.

RAVNICA

The world-city of Ravnica is one of the most populous—and prosperous—planes in the Multiverse. The world is controlled by 10 rival guilds whose ambitions are kept in check by the mystical Guildpact. Guild rule has resulted in the expansive growth of the city over the millennia, and today the cityscape covers the entire world.

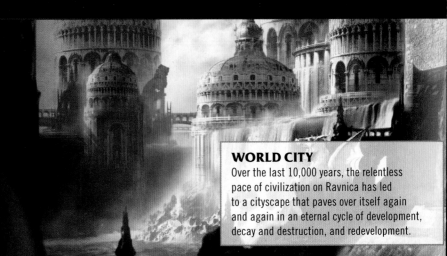

WORLD CITY
Over the last 10,000 years, the relentless pace of civilization on Ravnica has led to a cityscape that paves over itself again and again in an eternal cycle of development, decay and destruction, and redevelopment.

CITY OF GUILDS

Ten thousand years ago, the sphinx planeswalker Azor ended the ongoing war between the forces of order and chaos on Ravnica by binding them all to the Guildpact. Each of the 10 factions was given their own sphere of influence in which to do what they did best and to keep them out of each other's way. For 10,000 years, the system worked. Then Szadek, the guildmaster of House Dimir, finally succeeded in creating a paradox that destroyed the Guildpact. In the following decades, chaos reigned as each of the guilds attempted to seize power in their own way. Weakened by this struggle, the guilds began to decline as their members abandoned them in droves.

Azor had hidden a failsafe in case the Guildpact were to ever fall. Planeswalkers Jace Beleren and

As the city grew, so too did the forgotten spaces. Beneath the surface lies an expansive domain of tunnels, caverns, and ruins collectively known as the Undercity.

Ral Zarek discovered the failsafe and raced to decipher the meaning of the maze Azor had left behind. When Jace discovered that the failsafe would destroy the Tenth District unless the guilds could come to a new accord, he used his telepathic abilities to unite them again. In the process, the failsafe granted him the power of the Living Guildpact— to be the personified arbiter of law on the plane.

Jace was at best an inattentive leader, frequently leaving the plane for long periods of time with the Gatewatch. When he discovered that Nicol Bolas planned to lead an interplanar invasion of Ravnica, he returned just in time for Bolas to destroy the Hall of the Guildpact, severing Jace from the Guildpact's power. To defeat Bolas, former Izzet guildmaster Niv Mizzet was resurrected as the new Living Guildpact.

Some structures are enchanted to float above the ground.

Tall, wide buildings accommodate most species.

Deep crevasses serve as entry points to the Undercity.

> ## "Ravnica is not its buildings or markets, or even its guilds. Ravnica is its people. As long as we're here, we can rebuild the rest."
>
> —TEYSA KARLOV

ARCHITECTURE

Each of the guilds has its own preferred style of architecture (up to and including "rubble"), but the city itself is composed of white stone with a skyline dominated by domed rooftops, vaulted archways, and towering spires.

THE TEN GUILDS

Ravnica is a vast metropolis controlled by a tenuous alliance between 10 rival guilds. A delicate balance of power between these guilds is maintained by the Guildpact, a magically binding charter guiding the powers, roles, and responsibilities of each of the guilds.

KEY DATA

DEMONYM Ravnican

TERRAIN Urban

KEY LOCATIONS The Tenth District, The Rubblebelt, The Undercity

KEY FACTIONS The Azorious Senate, the Boros Legion, House Dimir, the Cult of Rakdos, the Golgari Swarm, the Gruul Clans, the Izzet League, the Orzhov Syndicate, the Selesyna Conclave, the Simic Combine

RULER The Guildpact

COMMON SPECIES Angel, Centaur, Cyclops, Demon, Devil, Djinn, Dryad, Elf, Faerie, Giant, Goblin, Gorgon, Harpy, Homunculi, Human, Imp, Kraul, Loxodon, Merfolk, Minotaur, Ogre, Sphinx, Troll, Vampire, Vedalken, Viashino

TENTH DISTRICT PLAZA

The expansive plaza is a popular destination for interguild meetings, recreation, shopping, and dining. It is seen as one of the few places on the plane that is truly neutral territory for both the guilds and the guildless.

HALL OF THE GUILDPACT

Serving as both the office of the Living Guildpact and the council chambers for guild representatives on Guildpact business, the Hall of the Guildpact is the crown jewel of the Tenth District. The mystical leylines of Ravnica converge on this point, fueling the enchantment that binds the guilds together.

THE GUILDS OF RAVNICA

Ten guilds share power on Ravnica, each with a different domain and role to play. Despite 10,000 years of relative peace, skirmishes between the guilds aren't uncommon, and given the opportunity, many of them would attempt to take control of the plane. It is up to the Living Guildpact to keep the balance of power and the peace.

PARHELION II

The pride of the Boros is *Parhelion II*, a flying citadel capable of deploying scores of angels and skyknights anywhere on Ravnica within minutes. The original Parhelion was destroyed decades ago when it crashed into Prahv, the former Azorius guildhall.

Tajic is a Boros commander and influential advisor to Aurelia.

AURELIA

The angel Guildmaster of the Boros Legion is a passionate advocate of justice.

BOROS LEGION

The Boros Legion is a militant guild of shining paladins and resplendent angels. Responsible for maintaining order on the plane, the Legion is the counter to the military overreach of other guilds. Usually, that means putting down Rakdos riots. In the aftermath of Nicol Bolas's invasion of the plane, the Boros are also the first line of defense for the plane itself.

AZORIUS SENATE

As the guild responsible for making and enforcing the laws of Ravnica, the Azorius Senate is both the legislative and bureaucratic wing of Ravnican governance. Founded by the planeswalker Azor, the creator of the Guildpact, the guild is similarly disposed to imposing its will on what it sees as chaos, much to the chagrin of the other guilds.

LAVINIA

Lavinia was an Azorius arrester who, through a series of cruel ironies, is now the acting guildmaster of the Azorius Senate. Thanks to the complexity of Azorius debates, it may take the rest of her natural life for them to name a permanent guildmaster.

NEW PRAHV

The Azorius guildhall is New Prahv, built after the old Prahv was destroyed in the conflicts that followed the fall of the original guildpact. Each of the three towers is home to one of the three Columns of the Azorius: the Sova, or the judiciary; the Jelenn, or the legislature; and the Lyev, or the constabulary.

TROSTANI

The guildmaster of the Selesnya Conclave is Trostani, the fusion of three dryad sisters who act in harmony.

SELESNYA CONCLAVE

The Selesnya Conclave is a nature-oriented faith surrounding worship of Ravnica's worldsoul (or ultimate elemental embodiment), Mat'Selesnya. The Conclave believes itself to be the voice of Mat'Selesnya's will on Ravnica, and on the face of it seeks peace and harmony for the plane—but in doing so often neglects the individual.

VITU-GHAZI

The Selesnya guildhall is Vitu-Ghazi, known as the city-tree. It is said that the soul of the world herself, Mat'Selesnya, slumbers inside Vitu-Ghazi. The tree was uprooted during the War of the Spark, animated into an elemental titan in the war, before being nearly destroyed by the god-eternals. Weakened, Vitu-Ghazi has one more taken root in Ravnica's soil to recover.

SIMIC COMBINE

The Simic Combine reinvented itself in the last few decades with the influence of the previously forgotten merfolk of Ravnica's long paved-over oceans. Its mission is to preserve and adapt the natural world through biological mutation and augmentation. The guild is divided, however, on whether that should be a slow, deliberative process of acclimation or a sudden explosive adaptation.

ZONOTS

Zonots are massive sinkholes that opened up across the city decades ago, exposing the surface to the long-forgotten oceans of the plane, and the merfolk who inhabit them.

VANNIFAR

The current guildmaster of the Simic is Vannifar, leader of the Adaptationist faction. Vannifar was the driving influence behind the Guardian Project, an effort to create bioengineered soldiers for the Simic. Her chief rival is Zegana, leader of the Utopian faction, who believes Vannifar is too reckless and aggressive.

HOUSE DIMIR

House Dimir is a secretive guild of spies and assassins. Its visible branches include newspapers and libraries, but these are a front for the covert activities of the guild. The Dimir agents themselves are decentralized, operating in individual cells unaware of one another.

Historically, the Dimir leadership has worked against the Guildpact, but in light of the recent extraplanar attacks, it has been a key ally in defeating the elder dragon Nicol Bolas.

LAZAV

The true goals of the shape-shifting Guildmaster of House Dimir are known only to himself.

ETRATA

Etrata is a younger generation of Dimir who believes the old guard has caused the guild to become stretched thin and that Lazav should never have allowed the existence of the Dimir to become public knowledge.

CULT OF RAKDOS

No one is quite sure why the demon-worshipping Cult of Rakdos was founded as a guild, but leading theories suggest it was to help contain the destructive power of their lord, Rakdos. Rakdos is kept pacified by the entertainment provided by his guild, who are among the most skilled—and dangerous—entertainers, musicians, comedians, and performers on Ravnica.

JUDITH

Judith is the voice of a growing number of cultists who are dissatisfied with Rakdos's "leadership." She's tired of the demon getting all the credit for her acts and plots with like-minded guild members against the demon.

LORD RAKDOS

The guildmaster of the Cult of Rakdos slumbers in his volcanic lair, his awakening a portent of destruction.

Nikya is a centaur druid who leads the Zhur-Taa clan. The Zhur-Taa are practitioners of the Old Ways, the ancient Gruul faith.

DOMRI RADE

A young beastmaster and planeswalker, Domri Rade was manipulated and tragically murdered by the elder dragon Nicol Bolas.

GRUUL CLANS

Millennia ago, the Gruul Clans were responsible for protecting Ravnica's wild space. The overwhelming pace of civilization destroyed that mission, and today the Gruul are known as the anarchists of the plane, fighting back against urbanization and the overreach of other guilds. The colossal cyclops Borborygmos is chief of the strongest Gruul tribe, the Burning-Tree Clan, and is nominal guildmaster of the Gruul Clans.

THE UTMUNGR

The Gruul faith, called the Old Ways, believes in a pantheon of gods called the Utmungr, nature gods that will return to raze Ravnica to the ground. When Nicol Bolas launched his invasion of Ravnica, Ilharg, the boar god, appeared to destroy civilization.

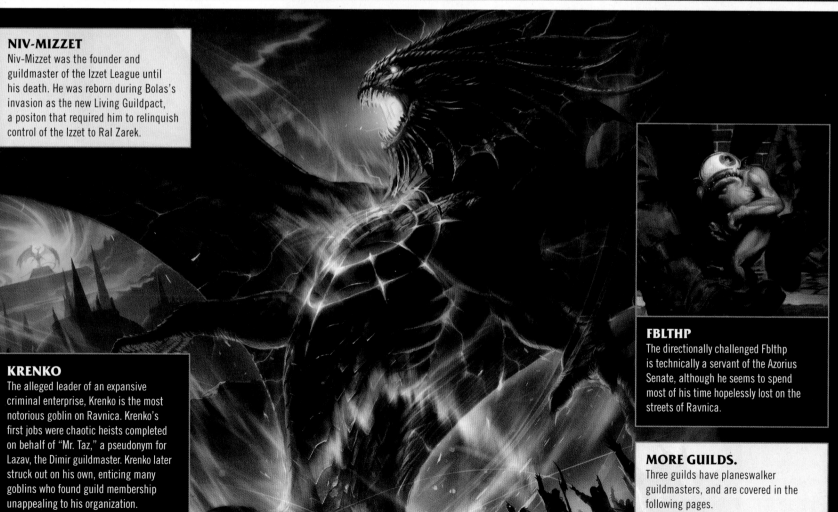

NIV-MIZZET

Niv-Mizzet was the founder and guildmaster of the Izzet League until his death. He was reborn during Bolas's invasion as the new Living Guildpact, a position that required him to relinquish control of the Izzet to Ral Zarek.

FBLTHP

The directionally challenged Fblthp is technically a servant of the Azorius Senate, although he seems to spend most of his time hopelessly lost on the streets of Ravnica.

KRENKO

The alleged leader of an expansive criminal enterprise, Krenko is the most notorious goblin on Ravnica. Krenko's first jobs were chaotic heists completed on behalf of "Mr. Taz," a pseudonym for Lazav, the Dimir guildmaster. Krenko later struck out on his own, enticing many goblins who found guild membership unappealing to his organization.

MORE GUILDS.

Three guilds have planeswalker guildmasters, and are covered in the following pages.

KAYA

Kaya has spent years of her life traveling from plane to plane using her skills to exorcise the undead. Although she has taken on questionable jobs in the past, her strong sense of justice has driven her to join the Gatewatch and use her skills for the greater good.

GHOST ASSASSIN
Gifted with the ability to shift into a ghost form, Kaya makes a living as a ghost hunter. Her ability to turn herself intangible is handy for getting out of scrapes, and spirits quickly learn they're not as untouchable as they thought around her.

BANE OF THE DEAD

Kaya makes her living as a ghost assassin for hire across the Multiverse, sending lingering spirits to their final rest. Although she's not one to shy away from less reputable jobs, she has firm moral boundaries she's unwilling to cross for any price. After taking a job on Fiora to assassinate the spectral tyrant Brago, she was hired by the elder dragon Nicol Bolas for a job on Ravnica, in exchange for help fixing her home plane, Tolvada.

On Ravnica, Kaya found more than she bargained for. Upon eliminating the Obzedat, the ghost council that led the Orzhov Syndicate, Kaya found herself bound by the chains of soul-debt that linked the ghost council to their guild. Kaya had become the new Orzhov guildmaster by default, much to the chagrin of Orzhov scion Teysa Karlov. With the help of a young law mage named Tomik Vrona, Kaya quickly realized that she had been used as a pawn by Bolas and worked to stop his machinations to destroy Ravnica.

> ## "So much wealth. So much splendor. So much temptation to believe the gilded lie."
>
> —KAYA

Kaya fought alongside the Gatewatch during Bolas's invasion of Ravnica and joined them as the dust settled, giving Tomik control of the Orzhov while she was off-plane. A new job on Kaldheim, secretly orchestrated by Tezzeret, saw her tracking down the Phyrexian praetor Vorinclex, who had escaped New Phyrexia by unknown means. Reporting back on this strange event to the Gatewatch, Kaya became central to the group's plans to destroy New Phyrexia once and for all.

THE ORZHOV SYNDICATE
Known as the church of deals, the Orzhov Syndicate is responsible for much of Ravnica's commerce. While the Orzhov claim that it's the source of prosperity on Ravnica, in truth a handful of oligarchs control the entirety of the guild's wealth, while everyone else finds themselves increasingly in debt with loans they will have to continue to work off after their deaths. Kaya found this practice so abhorrent she began releasing souls still indebted to the guild.

TEYSA KARLOV
Teysa has long believed that the corrupt oligarchs of the ghost council had to go and that she should run the guild in their place ... while making a tidy profit doing so. Kaya's assassination of the ghost council almost delivered on that dream, but when Kaya herself became guildmaster instead, Teysa began working on solutions to remove her new obstacle.

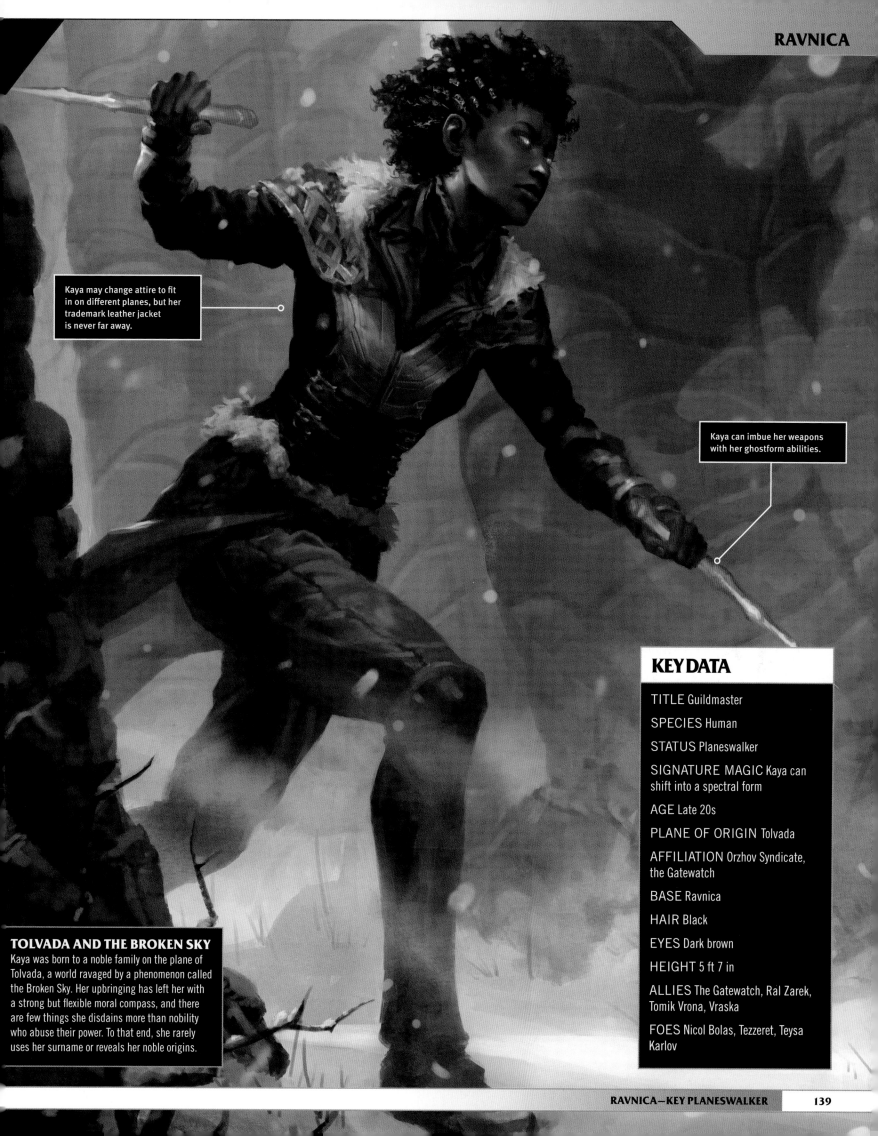

Kaya may change attire to fit in on different planes, but her trademark leather jacket is never far away.

Kaya can imbue her weapons with her ghostform abilities.

KEY DATA

TITLE Guildmaster

SPECIES Human

STATUS Planeswalker

SIGNATURE MAGIC Kaya can shift into a spectral form

AGE Late 20s

PLANE OF ORIGIN Tolvada

AFFILIATION Orzhov Syndicate, the Gatewatch

BASE Ravnica

HAIR Black

EYES Dark brown

HEIGHT 5 ft 7 in

ALLIES The Gatewatch, Ral Zarek, Tomik Vrona, Vraska

FOES Nicol Bolas, Tezzeret, Teysa Karlov

TOLVADA AND THE BROKEN SKY

Kaya was born to a noble family on the plane of Tolvada, a world ravaged by a phenomenon called the Broken Sky. Her upbringing has left her with a strong but flexible moral compass, and there are few things she disdains more than nobility who abuse their power. To that end, she rarely uses her surname or reveals her noble origins.

RAL ZAREK

The storm mage Ral Zarek once spent his life ruthlessly demanding the respect he believed he'd earned, unable to fully trust other people and resorting to using them instead. When powerful forces conspired against his home, Ral was forced to finally rely on other people and found himself all the stronger for it.

STORM CONDUIT
Ral Zarek can summon storms and harness wind and lightning into destructive spell casting. To help channel his abilities, he has built an electrostatic accumulator to store electricity and release it through his gauntlet.

THE IZZET LEAGUE
The Izzet League is a guild of mage-scientists founded by a brilliant but eccentric dragon named Niv-Mizzet. The League is responsible for Ravnica's infrastructure, and its inventors created most of the technological advances of the plane. The Izzet believe there's no such thing as a failed experiment, even if the explosive result wasn't the one it had intended—it's still useful knowledge for later. As such, the League is known for pushing boundaries and taking risks, often with destructive results.

IZZET VICEROY

Ral Zarek was born into poverty in an outlying district of Ravnica and struck out on his own at an early age. He made a living as a "rain mage," until he met the elder dragon Nicol Bolas, disguised as a human. Bolas played the part of a local crime lord, sending Ral on tasks that increasingly pushed the boundaries of his morality, all the while influencing Ral's lover, Elias, at the time into betraying him. Ral's spark ignited in that moment of betrayal, and he built a new life for himself on another plane as he apprenticed as an artificer. Bolas's plans to turn Ral into the perfect lackey backfired when Ral also became determined to leave Bolas behind.

Returning to Ravnica years later—and joining the Izzet League—Ral quickly and ruthlessly made his way up through the ranks. Ral discovered Azor's failsafe and did everything he could to seize the power of the Guildpact for himself. Ultimately, he failed and bitterly resented Jace Beleren, an outsider who Ral viewed as an interloper. But when an Izzet project threatened to expose Ral as a planeswalker to Ravnica—a carefully guarded secret of his—Ral begrudgingly worked with Jace to sabotage the machine: a device to detect planeswalkers. As Jace was pulled away from Ravnica for longer and longer intervals with the Gatewatch, Ral learned of Bolas's plans to invade the plane. His guildmaster, Niv-Mizzet, left him in charge to prepare a defense while he worked on other projects.

Forced to work cooperatively with other guilds for the first time, Ral began to feel a grudging respect and fellowship with Kaya and Vraska, both of whom had been entrapped by Bolas into their positions. Alongside his husband, Tomik, the planeswalkers worked to thwart Bolas's invasion … and failed. Ral became the Izzet guildmaster when Niv-Mizzet was killed by Bolas and leveraged the Izzet in defense of the plane, eventually aiding the Gatewatch in defeating the elder dragon.

> ## "Good ideas don't take time. They take a lot of bad ideas first."
> —RAL ZAREK

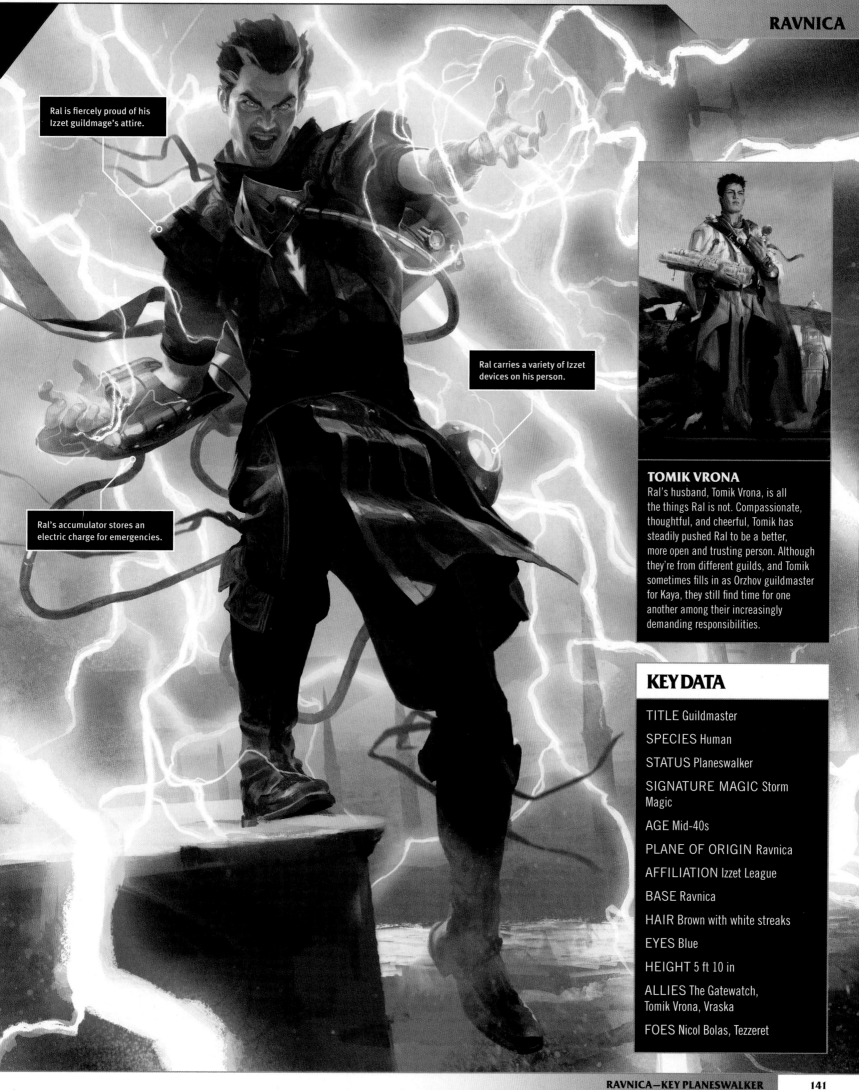

Ral is fiercely proud of his Izzet guildmage's attire.

Ral carries a variety of Izzet devices on his person.

Ral's accumulator stores an electric charge for emergencies.

TOMIK VRONA

Ral's husband, Tomik Vrona, is all the things Ral is not. Compassionate, thoughtful, and cheerful, Tomik has steadily pushed Ral to be a better, more open and trusting person. Although they're from different guilds, and Tomik sometimes fills in as Orzhov guildmaster for Kaya, they still find time for one another among their increasingly demanding responsibilities.

KEY DATA

TITLE Guildmaster

SPECIES Human

STATUS Planeswalker

SIGNATURE MAGIC Storm Magic

AGE Mid-40s

PLANE OF ORIGIN Ravnica

AFFILIATION Izzet League

BASE Ravnica

HAIR Brown with white streaks

EYES Blue

HEIGHT 5 ft 10 in

ALLIES The Gatewatch, Tomik Vrona, Vraska

FOES Nicol Bolas, Tezzeret

VRASKA

The gorgon planeswalker Vraska has lived a tough life in Ravnica's Undercity. Her harsh upbringing has given her a profound sense of empathy for the downtrodden and a ruthless sense of poetic justice for oppressors. She now reigns as Queen over the Golgari Swarm, the guild most reviled by the rest of surface-dwelling Ravnica.

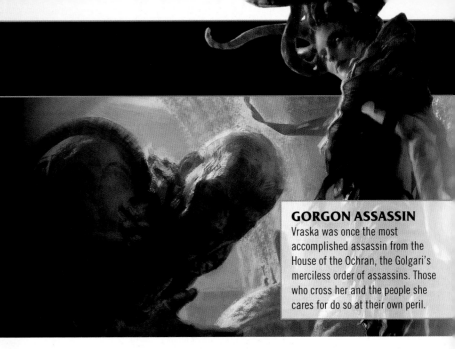

GORGON ASSASSIN
Vraska was once the most accomplished assassin from the House of the Ochran, the Golgari's merciless order of assassins. Those who cross her and the people she cares for do so at their own peril.

> "The continual rise of the downtrodden is as inevitable as vines usurping a forest."
>
> —VRASKA

VRASKA'S THRONE ROOM
At first glance, Vraska's Throne Room is a statuary of exquisitely carved stone, until one remembers the gorgon who reigns there. Her throne is carefully crafted from the petrified bodies of her enemies, a message to would-be usurpers.

EMPEROR OF THE UNDERREALM

Vraska was born into a life of poverty in the Undercity, subjected to raids from the surface guilds and abuse from those who feared her gorgon abilities—or wished to use them as a weapon. When she was arrested in an Azorius sweep of the Undercity, she was blindfolded and beaten by guards and her fellow prisoners alike. Her spark ignited during a prison riot where she was forced to use her powers against her cruel guards. Years later, she joined the Golgari's Ochran assassins to use her abilities against the enemies of the Undercity.

Her outlook changed when she was recruited by Nicol Bolas to find the Immortal Sun on Ixalan. Spending months as the captain of her own pirate ship gave her confidence in her abilities as a leader. When she discovered an amnesiac Jace Beleren—the Living Guildpact of Ravnica and a hated enemy—washed up on a deserted island, she took pity on the wretched castaway and brought him into her crew. The two bonded over their weeks together and fell in love, even after Jace recovered his memories. They plotted to sabotage Bolas's plans and parted ways, with Vraska completing her mission but planning to undermine the elder dragon in secret.

Upon returning to Ravnica, Vraska staged a coup against the devkarin lich Jarad, who had grown cruel after many decades undead. With the fate of her guild under threat from Bolas, Vraska couldn't pass up the chance to assassinate Isperia, the sphinx guildmaster of the Azorius who ordered the raid that captured her years ago. Eventually, Vraska was able to root out the Bolas sympathizers in her midst and turn the tables on the elder dragon, leading the Golgari against the dragon's invasion.

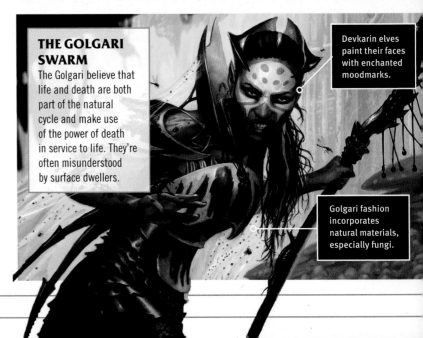

THE GOLGARI SWARM
The Golgari believe that life and death are both part of the natural cycle and make use of the power of death in service to life. They're often misunderstood by surface dwellers.

Devkarin elves paint their faces with enchanted moodmarks.

Golgari fashion incorporates natural materials, especially fungi.

Eyes alight with
golden power
to petrify foes.

Prehensile hair
appears to be
snakelike tails.

Hands can
become claws in
an emergency.

LIFE AND DEATH
IN THE UNDERCITY

The Golgari recycle the waste of the city,
using it to fertilize rot farms that provide
nutritious (if not very appetizing) free
food for the city proper. The rot farms
are usually staffed by various undead,
so it's best not to think too hard about
the food you're eating ...

Elegant Golgari
fashion denotes
high status.

KEY DATA

TITLE Guildmaster

SPECIES Gorgon

STATUS Planeswalker

SIGNATURE MAGIC Able to turn
living beings to stone, poison touch

AGE Early 40s

PLANE OF ORIGIN Ravnica

AFFILIATION Golgari Swarm

BASE Korozda, Ravnica Undercity

HAIR Prehensile tendrils

EYES Yellow

HEIGHT 5 ft 10 in

ALLIES Jace Beleren (love interest),
The Gatewatch

FOES Nicol Bolas, Tezzeret

JACE BELEREN

Jace Beleren has been many things: a con man, a researcher, a pirate, and a reluctant leader. At his core, Jace struggles to reconcile the good that people can do with their selfish inner thoughts. Jace struggles with his desire to be a hero with the great harm his powers can bring—and what that makes him.

THE MIND SCULPTOR

Waking up on Ravnica, Jace had no memory of his past. He used his powers to make easy money as a con artist, until he was approached by Tezzeret to join the Infinite Consortium. Tezzeret pushed Jace's abilities to their limits, and then pushed beyond them, again and again. But Jace couldn't stomach the ruthless nature of the criminal organization's work, and after Tezzeret revealed his true, abusive nature by torturing him for a failed mission, Jace fled. He met Liliana Vess, who manipulated him into taking Tezzeret down. Jace learned of her betrayal and left her behind after defeating Tezzeret.

Jace's travels took him to Zendikar, where he ran into the pyromancer Chandra Nalaar and the dragon mage Sarkhan Vol while tracking down a lead. During a fracas between the three, they unwittingly unlocked the Elrdrazi prison, and Jace fled. Sometime later, Jace stumbled across a mystery on Ravnica that led him to the sphinx planeswalker Azor's failsafe, which inadvertently resulted in him becoming the Living Guildpact, the arbiter of the guilds of Ravnica. Jace's unwanted duties strained him, until the arrival of Gideon Jura, who was looking for planeswalkers to help stop the Eldrazi threat on Zendikar. Acknowledging his guilt—and his responsibility—Jace joined Gideon, and together with Nissa

MIND MAGE
Jace Beleren is a mind mage and illusionist, able to telepathically communicate, invade the minds of others, and conjure illusions using light and mental trickery to deceive.

Revane and Chandra Nalaar formed the Gatewatch and stopped the Eldrazi titans.

With the Gatewatch, Jace discovered that Tezzeret still lived and that his elder dragon master, Nicol Bolas, had plans to invade Ravnica. The Gatewatch rallied their allies, but they were too late to stop the invasion. Worse, the power Jace commanded on Ravnica as the Living Guildpact was the first thing Bolas destroyed. After a desperate struggle, the elder dragon lost his spark to his own spell, and Gideon sacrificed himself to save Liliana Vess, who had saved the day—but only after siding with Bolas for most of the conflict. Despite their history, Jace decided to let Liliana go, and at the behest of Bolas's twin, Ugin, kept secret the fact that the elder dragon still lived. Now, Jace finds himself as the leader of the Gatewatch and works tirelessly to prepare a defense against whatever schemes the malignant New Phyrexia has in store for the Multiverse.

> ## "For all our lofty talk of keeping watch, we had no idea what we were getting into."
> —JACE BELEREN

VRASKA AND THE BELLIGERENT
Jace's love is Vraska, a gorgon assassin turned pirate captain who once tried to assassinate him. After an ill-fated confrontation with Nicol Bolas on Amonkhet, Jace washed ashore on Ixalan bereft of his memories. Vraska, always one to take pity on the downtrodden, brought him aboard. The amnesiac Jace's purity of spirit and curiosity endeared him to her, and the two fell in love. Vraska feared it would end when Jace regained his memories, but the man she fell in love with—the only man to look her in the eyes without fear—was still there. Even when they're arguing, there is nothing in the Multiverse that would keep these two apart.

A Gruul shaman gave Jace his tattoos.

Jace isn't from Ravnica, but he considers it his home.

Jace's cloak is patterned on the half-remembered Mage-Rings of Vryn.

JACE'S FORGOTTEN ORIGIN

Jace Beleren was born on one of Vryn's ancient Mage Rings. His natural gift for telepathy earned the attention of the sphinx arbiter of Vryn, Alhammarret. After years spent studying with the sphinx, Jace discovered Alhammarret had been manipulating him, editing his memories so that he would forget the sphinx's corruption … and his own planeswalker spark. Furious, Jace poured everything he had into a mental assault on Alhammarret, wiping the sphinx's mind, as well as his own memories.

KEY DATA

TITLE None

SPECIES Human

STATUS Planeswalker

SIGNATURE MAGIC Telepathy, Illusions

AGE Late 20s

PLANE OF ORIGIN Vryn

AFFILIATION The Gatewatch

BASE Ravnica

HAIR Dark brown

EYES Light blue

HEIGHT 5 ft 10 in

ALLIES The Gatewatch, Vraska (lover), Ral Zarek

FOES Nicol Bolas, Tezzeret

WAR OF THE SPARK

The elder dragon planeswalker Nicol Bolas foresaw that mending the time rifts on Dominaria would have sweeping consequences. Where planeswalkers were once godlike beings, they would be reduced to mortals once more. This, Bolas could not allow for himself. Even as he felt his power begin to drain away, he set a plan into motion to regain what he had lost.

NICOL BOLAS'S SCHEMES

To regain the divinity he had lost during the Great Mending—the Multiversal event that saw planeswalkers lose their near-omnipotent powers—Nicol Bolas sowed the seeds of a plan across the Multiverse, culminating in an invasion of Ravnica. While the seemingly disparate elements of Bolas's cunning main plan finally came together, Bolas had seeded many other plots across the Multiverse in an effort to restore his power.

THE GATEWATCH

A group of do-gooding heroes was exactly what Bolas needed to rally as many planeswalkers as possible to Ravnica for his endgame. He set about loosing the Eldrazi from their prison on Zendikar and luring planeswalkers together to fight them, around whom a group of heroes could form. Similarly, he cultivated grudges with planeswalkers across the Multiverse who would wish to come and find him when given the chance.

INTERPLANAR BEACON

On Ravnica, Bolas planted agents among the guilds to further his goals. He allowed the Izzet, led by Niv-Mizzet and Ral Zarek, to build the Interplanar Beacon to summon planeswalkers across the Multiverse for aid. When the planeswalkers arrived, drawn by the pull of the beacon, the Immortal Sun was activated, trapping them as Bolas's Eternal Army marched through the Planar Bridge.

THE IMMORTAL SUN

On Ixalan, the very trap once set for Bolas would be one for the planeswalkers he planned to lure to Ravnica. He dispatched the expendable assassin Vraska to find the Immortal Sun, a device that combined the magic of his twin, Ugin, and the sphinx lawbringer Azor, to prevent planeswalking away from a plane.

THE PLANAR BRIDGE

On Kaladesh, Bolas's minion, Tezzeret, finally discovered a means to once again travel between the planes. Bolas had known it was still possible and had investigated planes from across the Multiverse where such technology might be uncovered. With the Planar Bridge under his control, Bolas could transport his army to Ravnica.

THE DREADHORDE

On Amonkhet, Bolas subverted the gods and made them believe he had been their god-pharaoh all along. Bidding them to test their people in murderous trials, the gods produced an army of zombie warriors that retained the skills Bolas desired, all encased in the magical substance Lazotep.

THE ELDERSPELL

After the initial incursion, Bolas revealed his true plan: the Elderspell. An ancient magic that harvests the spark—and soul—from unwilling planeswalkers, it was channeled through the Dreadhorde, whose very touch could rip away a planeswalker's soul for Bolas's consumption. With enough sparks gathered, Bolas would return to his former divinity.

LILIANA'S BETRAYAL

Bolas's plan depended on the necromancer Liliana Vess, whose soul he owned after brokering four demonic contracts on her behalf. Liliana was an unwilling servant, however, and at the crucial moment turned on the elder dragon, using the God-Eternals to harvest his spark and defeat him.

> "We were gods, once, Beleren.
> Did you know that?"
>
> – NICOL BOLAS

THE PRISON REALM

To the planeswalkers in attendance, Bolas appeared to be killed. In truth, Ugin ferried his brother to the former Meditation Realm, now dubbed the Prison Realm, as Bolas's spark faded. Jace Beleren agreed to hide this fact from the others using illusions, convinced to keep this knowledge a secret because death had never been permanent for either of the elder dragon planeswalkers. Bolas had already died once and returned, as had Ugin, so the elder dragon persuaded Jace that imprisonment was the better solution.

TEYO VERADA

A shieldmage acolyte from the plane of Gobakhan, Teyo's planeswalker spark ignited when the Planar Beacon was activated, drawing him into the conflict. Despite his heroic nature, he decided not to join the Gatewatch in the aftermath of the war, instead opting to build his skills before journeying out to the rest of the Multiverse.

TARKIR

Tarkir is a plane ruled by broods of dragons led by mighty dragonlords. But it was not always this way: once, khans ruled the land, evenly matched with the dragons who ruled the skies. When that balance was disrupted, the khans and their clans were overrun by dragons, and the records of their history were erased.

DRAGONSTORMS

Five dragon clans, each led by a fierce elder dragon called a dragonlord, hold dominion over all the people of Tarkir. The dragons of the plane are spawned from the elemental dragonstorms that wrack Tarkir, metaphysically connected to the elder dragon planeswalker Ugin.

KHANFALL

There are rumors that Tarkir was once a very different place, not ruled by dragons but by human khans. The hidden lore of these clans is buried in ancient mountain archives or passed down in whispers between tribal leaders. Those who find it can learn that the dragonlords usurped the clans from great khans of the past. The truth is that 1,200 years ago, Ugin was attacked by his twin, the evil Nicol Bolas, and he was encased in stone hedrons for the intervening years to recover. During his convalescence, the dragonstorms spawned out of control. Eventually, the dragons outnumbered the clans so greatly that the delicate balance between dragons and khans was disrupted, and the khans were toppled one by one.

ABZAN HOUSES
The Abzan were a tight-knit clan who built stone cities amid a harsh desert. They were merchants, artisans, and soldiers who valued family above all else. Each family planted and nurtured a kin-tree, where the family's dead were laid to rest, and the tree became a conduit to the family's ancestors. The Abzan definition of family extends beyond blood relations to adoptees (especially war orphans, called krumar) and those who share close bonds of friendship.

AINOK
The ainok are dogfolk, humanoid canids who can be found most commonly among the Abzan.

Shu Yun was the last Jeskai khan, but he hid the ancient lore of the Jeskai in a secret vault.

JESKAI WAY

The Jeskai were a clan who valued martial arts as a means of reaching spiritual enlightenment. They were monks, artisans, and scholars on a constant journey of discovery. The lived in isolated mountain strongholds and river valleys, supported by local farming villages. The Jeskai revered age and wisdom, and their leader was usually among the oldest and most accomplished warrior-scholars in their ranks.

SULTAI BROOD

The Sultai were a clan ruled by a decadent noble caste supported by a workforce of the undead. Corrupt, treacherous, and cruel, their leaders made demonic pacts to secure their status among the clan's elite.

NAGA

The snakelike Naga were among the Sultai elite, feared and respected for their necromantic abilities.

MARDU HORDE

The Mardu were a clan of fierce warrior raiders known for their lightning-fast raids on the other clans' territory. Mardu encampments would appear and disappear with great speed as the clan feasted between raids. To come of age, a Mardu warrior had to prove themselves in battle and earn their war name, or their name as an adult.

KEY DATA

DEMONYM Tarkiri

TERRAIN Evergreen rainforests, windswept deserts, arid mesas, and frigid mountain peaks

KEY LOCATIONS Ayagor the Dragon's Bowl, Arashin and the Great Aerie, Screamreach, Cori Mountain Sanctuary, Marang River Fortress

KEY FACTIONS The Atarka clan, the Dromoka clan, the Kolaghan clan, the Ojutai clan, the Silumgar clan

RULER The five Dragonlords

COMMON SPECIES Ainok, Aven, Demon, Djinn, Dragon, Efreet, Goblin, Human, Loxodon, Naga, Ogre, Orc

TEMUR FRONTIER

The Temur were a hardy clan of nomads made up of shamans, hunters, and foragers who eked out a living among the frozen mountains. They lived off the bounty of the land and respected the natural order of the wilderness. Their shamans, called whisperers, communicated mystically to keep each individual band in touch with the others and warn of dangers. The Temur were led by the Dragonclaw, a title passed to warriors who could complete a sacred ritual to prove themselves worthy.

RAKSHASA

The rakshasa were powerful demons with the appearance of a humanoid tiger, who live among mortals in order to secure their power through demonic pacts.

SARKHAN VOL

Born on a version of Tarkir where the dragons had all died out, Sarkhan Vol has spent his life seeking dragons worthy of his respect. Instead, he found the elder dragon Nicol Bolas, under whose thrall he committed terrible crimes. Now free of Bolas's clutches, Sarkhan wishes only to enjoy his freedom and enjoy the dragons of Tarkir in peace.

DRAGON SHAMAN
Sarkhan is an accomplished warrior and military leader, as well as a shaman who can influence lesser dragons. He can shapeshift into a dragon form.

UNBROKEN DRAGONSOUL
Sarkhan feels an intrinsic connection to dragonkind. He has spent his life seeking dragons throughout the Multiverse, and especially searching for beings like the elder dragons who could help give his life meaning. After indebting himself to the wrong elder dragon, however, Sarkhan is determined to never serve another master, although he is willing to work with—not for—the spirit dragon Ugin.

THE DRAGONSPEAKER

Sarkhan Vol was born among the Mardu Horde on a timeline of Tarkir that no longer exists. In Sarkhan's timeline, the elder dragon Nicol Bolas killed his brother Ugin in the ancient past, causing the dragons of the plane to go extinct and the khans to reign supreme. Sarkhan grew up with a fascination for these long-dead creatures and spent time among the Temur shamans learning of them. When Sarkhan heard whispers from an ancient dragon's spirit during a battle, he unleashed a massive spell that destroyed friend and foe alike. His spark ignited in the process.

During his travels, Sarkhan pledged himself to Nicol Bolas, who he believed to be the pinnacle of dragonkind. However, he discovered that the elder dragon was not just wise and ferocious, but also cruel. He suffered greatly under Bolas and committed terrible acts in his name. Sent to linger at the Eye of Ugin on Zendikar for months, Sarkhan began to hear the voice of the ancient dragon spirit again—Ugin himself. After completing his task, he returned home to Tarkir with a chunk of a stone monolith from Zendikar called a hedron. There, with the help of Narset, the Khan of the Jeskai, Sarkhan journeyed to the final resting place of Ugin … and was transported back in time.

Sarkhan arrived in the past just moments before Ugin and Bolas's climactic battle. As Ugin fell, the hedron Sarkhan had brought resonated with unknown magic, encasing the spirit dragon in stone and saving his life. Sarkhan returned to the future, arriving on a timeline of Tarkir where he had never been born. Even the ancient and wise Ugin did not know how such a feat was accomplished. For Sarkhan, erasing his own history was a small price to pay to create the paradise of a Tarkir where majestic dragons reign.

> ## "The dragon is a perfect marriage of power and the will to use it."
>
> —SARKHAN VOL

Sarkhan has thrown off the shackles of shirts to ease his draconic transformations.

Sarkhan wields a spear as a memento of his days as a Mardu general.

Sarkhan's hands can be transformed into dragon heads that breathe dragonfire.

WAR OF THE SPARK

Sarkhan would never truly be free until Nicol Bolas was defeated. Alongside Ugin, he worked behind the scenes during the War of the Spark to defeat Bolas. He transported Niv-Mizzet's spirit to safety after the Ravnican dragon was killed in battle with Nicol Bolas, and helped raise the Hekma again on Amonkhet.

SON OF A LOST TARKIR

Sarkhan erased himself from existence when he changed the timeline and saved Ugin's life. No alternate version of him exists on Tarkir. To the Multiverse at large, he simply appeared one day, remembering a different version of Tarkir. For all intents and purposes, Sarkhan was spawned by Tarkir itself like the dragons were— from nothing.

KEY DATA

TITLE None

SPECIES Human

STATUS Planeswalker

SIGNATURE MAGIC Sarkhan can communicate with dragons and transform into one

AGE Appears early 40s (objectively over 1,200 or under 10)

PLANE OF ORIGIN Tarkir (Khans timeline)

AFFILIATION None

BASE Tarkir (Dragons timeline)

HAIR Black with a streak of white

EYES Brown

HEIGHT 5 ft 11 in

ALLIES Ugin, Narset, Ajani

FOES Nicol Bolas, Tezzeret

THE DRACONIC CLANS

After the fall of the khans, the dragonlords erased much of the history of the clans. While each dragonlord felt a kinship of sorts with the clans they conquered, they suppressed elements of those clans that they disdained or felt may become subversive. Now, over a millennia later, the dragonlords are elder dragons in their own right, metaphysically connected as the oldest of their respective broods.

DRAGONLORD SILUMGAR

The ruthless dragonlord Silumgar rules his clan with a gilded claw. After killing the last khan of the Sultai a millennia ago, he languishes in his den of accumulated wealth, displaying the reanimated corpse of the last khan from chains around his neck. Silumgar is an acidic dragon, whose magics lean toward decay and necromancy.

THE SILUMGAR CLAN

Under Silumgar, the opulence of the clan has become unrivaled decadence, with a small handful of dragon elites controlling great hordes of undead. Any semblance of caring about the natural order has been erased. The dragons of the clan care little about the people they view as beneath them and are as likely to kill their underlings for showing too much ambition as reward them. The demonic Rakshasas have fallen out of favor with the clan, as Silumgar secretly fears their powers.

THE KOLAGHAN CLAN

The Kolaghan clan little resembles the organized Mardu Horde. The clan fights among itself for position under Kolaghan, who herself is hostile, violent, and cruel toward the clan. Kolaghan commands the clan's fear and awe, and they respect her unbridled freedom.

DRAGONLORD KOLAGHAN

The ferocious dragonlord Kolaghan does not rule her clan so much as guide the storm of her horde. She is the only dragonlord who does not speak, and simply expresses herself in destructive lighting attacks.

THE ATARKA CLAN

The fiercely independent survivalists of the Temur have become subsistence hunters under Atarka, spending their days hunting game for their draconic overlords. The clan has adapted to this new reality, and what meager meals they can hunt go to pay tribute to the dragonlords, leaving little for their own bellies. The clan continues to do what it has always done—survive.

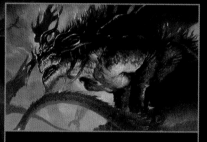

DRAGONLORD ATARKA

Atarka is the consummate hunter. She is less concerned with ruling a clan than sating her ravenous hunger. She cares nothing for diplomacy and only acknowledges the lower beings of her clan when they provide her next meal … or become it.

THE DROMOKA CLAN

The Dromoka clan is the only clan where the dragons work closely with their human counterparts in a truly interdependent way. The desert fortresses have become desert aeries. Community has replaced family as the intrinsic bond of the clan, with family units—usually led by lesser dragons— being defined by bonds of loyalty rather than blood. Children are raised communally in an aerie away from their biological parents and taught to value the clan above all else. Even the practice of calling on ancestor spirits has been outlawed as a form of necromancy.

DRAGONLORD DROMOKA

The imperious dragonlord Dromoka wields the light of the sun itself as her weapon. Unlike many of the other dragonlords, she is involved in the day-to-day workings of her clan and values the community she has built.

KHAN REBELLION

Despite their best efforts, the dragonlords have not been successful at stamping out all memory of the khans, nor at suppressing dissent. The Silumgar and Kolaghan clans care little for history, but would overthrow their dragonlord at any sign of weakness. Among the Atarka, shamans have continued to practice forbidden magic in secret, keeping alive the traditions of the ancient Temur. Dromoka was not successful in wiping out all of the Abzan's kin-trees, and rebels learn from their ancestors in secret. Before submitting to Ojutai, the khan of the Jeskai hid away their scrolls and lore in secret mountain vaults, waiting for the day their descendants could claim their wisdom.

NARSET

Narset was exceptional from a young age, gaining the attention of Dragonlord Ojutai himself and quickly rising through the ranks of the Ojutai clan to the rank of master. Although she now walks a new path, her insatiable hunger for knowledge is her defining trait, and she walks the Multiverse to learn and discover.

ENLIGHTENED MASTER
Narset is a master martial artist, using her skills to channel magical abilities into her strikes, as well as weave elemental spells. She excels at using her opponent's own strength against them, redirecting or reflecting their spells.

THE ANCIENT WAY
Narset started learning the ancient lore of the Jeskai after she stumbled across their hidden archive. Using their ancient scrolls, she began mastering the ways of Jeskai magic, learning from their core mystical disciplines called fires.

PARTER OF VEILS

As a young girl, Narset earned the attention of Dragonlord Ojutai. Narset had always processed information differently than other people, but in training and study she found a place she belonged—and where she excelled. For years, she studied, impressing all of her teachers, until the day she reached mastery. Faced with the horrifying prospect that she had nothing left to learn, she ran from the clan. On her journey, she found a hidden Jeskai archive that revealed the true history of the plane, of the khans that had been defeated and supplanted by dragonlords. Upon the revelation of the truth, her spark ignited, but she held on to Tarkir. She had to talk to her mentor first. After consulting with Ojutai, he encouraged her to seek enlightenment … even if that path would take her away from Tarkir.

On her journeys, she met like-minded planeswalkers, and her formidable skills have kept her safe from any threat. After all, when one learns martial arts from a dragon, what threat are Ikoria's monsters? After meeting Sarkhan Vol, who told her of another version of Tarkir that was ruled by khans instead of dragons, Narset began to study the ancient ways of the Jeskai in earnest. Her efforts and nature earned her the attention of an even greater dragon, the spirit dragon Ugin. With her help, Ugin was able to stop his brother's ambitions during his invasion of Ravnica.

JESKAI KHAN
In Sarkhan's timeline, a version of Tarkir where the dragons had gone extinct, Narset had ascended to the rank of khan among the Jeskai. While helping Sarkhan reach Ugin's final resting place, she was killed before her planeswalker spark could ignite. This version of Narset now only exists in Sarkhan's memories, but he has made friends with the new timeline's version of Narset as well.

> ### "Still the mind and quiet the heart. Only then will you hear the Multiverse's great truths."
>
> —NARSET

Narset can channel the wind into her attacks, giving the appearance of flying kicks.

Narset still wears the robes of an Ojutai master.

THE STORY-CIRCLE
During her travels, Narset has met and befriended Ajani Goldmane and Tamiyo, planeswalkers who share her passion for learning, exploration, and discovery. Together, they meet informally as "the story-circle" to share tales of the Multiverse.

KEY DATA

TITLE Master

SPECIES Human

STATUS Planeswalker

SIGNATURE MAGIC Narset channels elemental forces through martial arts

AGE Mid-50s

PLANE OF ORIGIN Tarkir

AFFILIATION Story-circle

BASE Tarkir

HAIR Black

EYES Brown

HEIGHT 5 ft 8 in

ALLIES Ugin, Sarkhan, Ajani, Tamiyo

FOES Nicol Bolas, Tezzeret

DRAGONLORD OJUTAI
While most dragonlords rule through might and fear, Ojutai rules through respect. The Ojutai Clan reveres age and wisdom, and as the oldest living dragon of his brood, Ojutai is known as the Great Teacher. Ojutai is an ice dragon and has an intrinsic affinity for ice magic.

OJUTAI CLAN
The monastic lifestyle of the Jeskai continues much the same under the Ojutai clan. The fact that Ojutai himself has not always been the leader of the clan is hidden from them, and he has suppressed certain disciplines that the ancient Jeskai used to fight and kill dragons, such as the secret of Ugin's ghostfire. The Ojutai strive to reach enlightenment, and revere the dragons as honored beings due to their age and wisdom.

THEROS

Theros is a land of gods, heroes, and monsters. History and myth are indistinguishable on Theros, a plane where the gods light up the night sky in brilliant constellations. Wonder abounds on Theros, with its idyllic tropical islands near the edge of the world and looming, volcanic mountains that hide paths into the Underworld itself.

NYX, THE GOD-REALM

The god-realm of Nyx lights up the night sky on Theros, appearing as moving constellations of myths, stories, and the gods. This realm is connected to the collective unconscious of Theros, and mortal belief shapes the gods who reside here. Neither the gods nor the mortals who shape them are aware of this intrinsic connection, nor does any mortal left alive remember a time before the gods. Creatures and artifacts born of Nyx bear a telltale shadow marked by a constellation of stars.

HELIOD
The self-proclaimed lord of the gods wields the power of the sun.

THE SUN'S CHAMPION

Years ago, the planeswalker Xenagos learned of the truth behind the gods—that they were not all-knowing but mere manifestations of mortal belief. Enraged, Xenagos sought to show everyone the falseness of the gods and set a plan into motion to secure his own ascension into godhood. When the New Capennan planeswalker Elspeth Tirel arrived on Theros, armed with a long-lost godslaying blade called Godsend, Heliod reluctantly made this stranger his champion. Xenagos saw Elspeth as a threat and enchanted her to believe Phyrexians were attacking her, leading her to kill her love—and Heliod's oracle—Daxos. Xenagos ascended to godhood that very night in a grand revel.

Determined to prove her innocence and return Daxos to the living, Elspeth ascended to Nyx itself with the help of her old friend, the leonin Ajani Goldmane. Elspeth challenged Xenagos, slaying him and fulfilling her duty to Heliod, but her reward was betrayal. Heliod ran her through with her own blade, shattering Godsend. Elspeth languished in Ilysia, the eternal resting place of heroes in the Underworld, but a chance visit from the nightmare weaver Ashiok set her into motion once more. Ashiok's nightmares reminded Elspeth that her work was not finished, and she set about luring Heliod into the Underworld. Her plan succeeded and, as a boon, the god of the Underworld, Erebos, returned her to the living, healthy and whole.

Elspeth delivers the killing blow to Xenagos, ending the nascent god's life.

EREBOS
Melancholy god of the Underworld, who wishes only for mortals to accept their fates.

RETURNED
Intrepid mortals who wish to return to life have to give up their identity, donning a gold funerary mask. When they emerge on the surface, they retain their skills from life but not their memories, and their soul—or eidolon—is split from them to wander the plane as a ghost.

KEY DATA

DEMONYM Theran

TERRAIN A sun-dappled peninsula rising into arid mountains

KEY LOCATIONS Meletis, Akros, Setessa, Skophos, Oreskos, Nyx, the Underworld

KEY FACTIONS Arkoans, Melitians, Stessans

RULERS Heliod (self-proclaimed king of the gods), Taranika (Akros), The Twelve (Meletis), Anthousa (Setessa), Brimaz (Oreskos)

COMMON SPECIES Centaur, Cyclops, Dryad, Giant, Gorgon, Hag, Harpy, Human, Leonin, Merfolk, Minotaur, Satyr, Sphinx

DAXOS
After Daxos's death, Elspeth made a deal with Erebos to return him from the dead. What emerged from the Underworld, however, was a Returned, a grim shadow of the man Daxos used to be. Years later, Heliod had a need for Daxos again and merged his eidolon, or his spirit, with his Returned body. Infused with the power of Nyx, Daxos became a demigod.

THE UNDERWORLD
Upon a mortal's death on Theros, their soul is transported to the Underworld, a realm of the dead from which little returns.

THE MORTAL REALM
Theros itself is a flat plane where if one were to journey too far into the unknown, they might risk falling off the grand waterfalls at the edge of the world. Most of its peoples live in a polis, a city-state, usually dedicated to one or more of the gods.

EPHARA, GOD OF THE POLIS
Ephara is god of the city and of civilization.

MELETIS
The coastal polis of Meletis is home to democracy and a rich philosophical tradition. In the ancient past, Ephara, god of civilization, helped the Meletians overthrow a mystical tyrant. Unwilling to suffer more despots, Meletis turned to democracy, and is now overseen by a council of philosophers called the Twelve. The city's location along the sea makes it a hub for trade and travel, and besides humans you'll often find centaurs and merfolk in the city's bustling marketplaces.

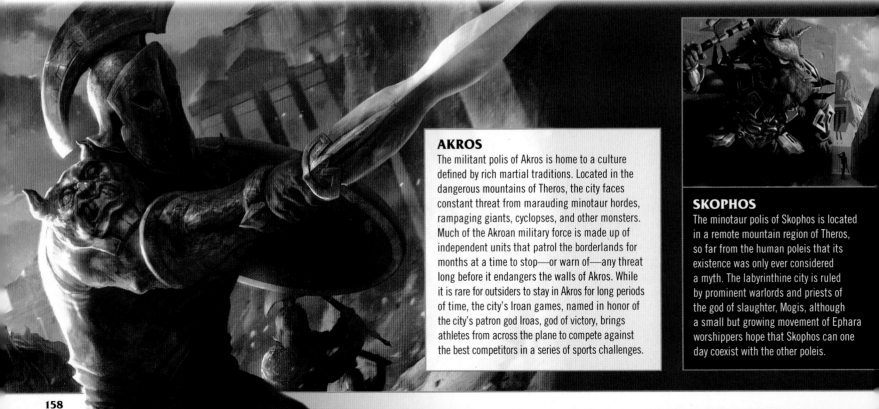

AKROS
The militant polis of Akros is home to a culture defined by rich martial traditions. Located in the dangerous mountains of Theros, the city faces constant threat from marauding minotaur hordes, rampaging giants, cyclopses, and other monsters. Much of the Akroan military force is made up of independent units that patrol the borderlands for months at a time to stop—or warn of—any threat long before it endangers the walls of Akros. While it is rare for outsiders to stay in Akros for long periods of time, the city's Iroan games, named in honor of the city's patron god Iroas, god of victory, brings athletes from across the plane to compete against the best competitors in a series of sports challenges.

SKOPHOS
The minotaur polis of Skophos is located in a remote mountain region of Theros, so far from the human poleis that its existence was only ever considered a myth. The labyrinthine city is ruled by prominent warlords and priests of the god of slaughter, Mogis, although a small but growing movement of Ephara worshippers hope that Skophos can one day coexist with the other poleis.

TRITONS

Theros's amphibious merfolk are called tritons. Many tritons live among human settlements for short periods of time before returning to the sea.

THASSA

Thassa is the god of the sea and the patron god of the Tritons, whose form she usually takes.

SETESSA

The verdant polis of Setessa is home to a culture of rugged woodland hunters who live close to nature. A matriarchal society, the men of Setessa are sent on a peregrination upon reaching adulthood to find their place out in the world, while the women train to defend the polis and reap the harvest. Orphans are always welcome in Setessa, and much of the population was adopted into Setessa rather than being born there. Families live in a designated quarter of the city, although once they reach adulthood, men are not welcome outside of that quarter.

KARAMETRA

Karametra is the god of the harvest and the patron god of Setessa.

IROAS AND MOGIS

Iroas is the god of war, honor, and victory, distinct from his brother Mogis, who is the god of slaughter.

ORESKOS

The valley of Oreskos is home to the nomadic leonin tribes of Theros. Living on the fringes of known Theros, the leonin were driven out of their ancestral home in Meletis for serving the overthrown tyrant. This singular event has created a lot of mistrust and animosity between the leonin and humans of Theros, a gap that King Brimaz, their current chief, hopes to bridge.

GIDEON JURA

Born Kytheon Iora of Akros, Gideon Jura was one of the greatest heroes the Multiverse ever knew. Gideon sacrificed himself during the War of the Spark on Ravnica, but his legacy lives on in the Gatewatch, the team of heroes he brought together.

OATHSWORN PALADIN

In his youthful arrogance, Gideon made a tragic mistake that killed his friends and caused his planeswalker spark to ignite. The guilt from that event drove him to a life of heroism. He sought out organizations where he could do good: first with the knights of Bant and later with the Order of Heliud. The similarity between the historical Heliud and the god Heliod of Theros intrigued him. Through the Order, Gideon was tasked with hunting down a rogue pyromancer from Regatha—Chandra Nalaar—and to bring her in for justice. Gideon tracked Chandra across several planes, and ultimately the two ended up becoming friends. Gideon fulfilled his duty to bring Chandra in to face the Order of Heliud, but did not help the overzealous Order when Chandra brought their headquarters down around their heads.

When Gideon attempted to find Chandra afterward, he tracked her to the plane of Zendikar, where the Eldrazi had been freed. Torn between saving people from the Eldrazi on Zendikar and his sense of duty to other planes, such as Ravnica, where he helped the Boros keep order, Gideon finally realized he needed help. He began enlisting fellow planeswalkers Jace Beleren, Chandra, and Nissa Revane into the fight. Together, they were able to stop the Eldrazi Titans. Each of the planeswalkers took an oath to protect the Multiverse and dubbed themselves the Gatewatch. Gideon led them in battles across many planes, eventually discovering Nicol Bolas's plan for an invasion of Ravnica. They traveled to Amonkhet to confront the elder dragon.

The Gatewatch had grown overconfident from their victories and were unprepared for the battle with Bolas on Amonkhet. Gideon watched helplessly as the dragon defeated them one by one, neutralizing Gideon by slamming him against a wall repeatedly. Gideon was unharmed … but unable to help, either. Demoralized, they gathered on Dominaria, where Gideon bonded with Liliana Vess, a less scrupulous member of the Gatewatch. Gideon saw the potential for good in Liliana when no one else did. During the War of the Spark, when Liliana had seemingly betrayed them all, Gideon still believed in her. He was proven correct when Liliana sacrificed herself to kill Nicol Bolas. As Bolas's curse began to kill her, Gideon took the curse upon himself, which saved Liliana's life.

KYTHEON'S IRREGULARS

Kytheon Iora was born on Theros in the polis of Akros. Orphaned at a young age, Kytheon led a gang of streetwise urchins called Kytheon's Irregulars. He was eventually caught and arrested, but in prison the warden, a warrior-mage named Hixus, took an interest in Kytheon, training the youth to realize his full potential. When Akros was threatened by monsters, Kytheon was set free to help defend the city. His defense, alongside his friends, the Irregulars, became the stuff of legends.

Afterward, Heliod himself appeared to Kytheon and gifted him a blessed spear to strike down the titan behind the monster attacks. But in Kytheon's hubris, he attempted to use the spear against the god of the dead, Erebos, who had sent the titan to the surface. Erebos easily deflected the weapon back at Kytheon and his friends. While Kytheon's indestructible aura protected him, his friends perished. Kytheon's spark ignited in his horror, and on Bant he took on the name Gideon Jura.

> "No one hero will save this day. Today, we must all be heroes."
>
> —GIDEON JURA

Gideon could channel his magic into the blades of the whiplike sural for extra control.

Gideon's armor came from Bant, where he trained as a knight.

GIDEON'S SACRIFICE

Gideon is remembered as a hero across the Multiverse, who gave his all and sacrificed himself to save someone he believed in, even if no one else did.

Gideon's small shield was mostly for show, but it helped him focus his power.

Gideon's sural was a gift from his mentor, Hixus. Wielding it required extreme skill.

KEY DATA

TITLE None

SPECIES Human

STATUS Deceased

SIGNATURE MAGIC Gideon has an aura of invincibility

AGE Late 20s (upon death)

PLANE OF ORIGIN Theros

AFFILIATION The Gatewatch

BASE Ravnica

HAIR Black

EYES Amber

HEIGHT 6 ft 4 in

ALLIES The Gatewatch, The Boros Legion

FOES Nicol Bolas, Tezzeret, Ob Nixilis

CHAMPION OF JUSTICE

Gideon manifested a golden aura that made him impervious to harm, although that protection could slip if he was tired or distracted. He could extend this protection to others with great effort and channel its power into his attacks.

CALIX

Calix is an agent of Klothys, created to enforce the will of the god of destiny. When his target, Elspeth Tirel, escaped the plane—and Klothy's reach—Calix's planeswalker spark ignited. But in the Multiverse at large, Calix is no longer so sure in his convictions.

Calix wields a spear empowered with the hair of the god Klothys.

Calix is a Nyxborn, a being created by the gods through the power of Nyx.

DESTINY'S HAND

Calix was created to return Elspeth Tirel to her eternal rest in Ilysia, the section of the Underworld reserved for heroes. But as Calix hunted her through the Underworld, Elspeth always proved to be one step ahead, her skill a match for Calix at every turn. When Elspeth returned to the living, she planeswalked away, leaving Calix behind. Calix had failed in his destined mission—his reason for existing. In that moment, Calix felt the pull of not just the threads of destiny on Theros, but of the Multiverse at large. His planeswalker spark ignited, and he began tracking Elspeth once more. Although Elspeth has continued to be elusive, Calix may soon find himself tracking another who defied destiny …

"Calix was patient, steadily following Elspeth until their destined confrontation."

KLOTHYS, GOD OF DESTINY

Klothys is the god of destiny on Theros, hidden from view in the Underworld, where she kept the Titans imprisoned. After Xenagos attempted to usurp her place among the gods, Klothys took an active hand among the mortal realm again, sending her agents to reweave all those who have defied destiny back into their appointed places.

KEY DATA

SPECIES Nyxborn Human

STATUS Planeswalker

SIGNATURE MAGIC Calix wields strands of destiny to reweave those who leave their assigned place

AGE Appears mid-30s (actually only a few years old)

PLANE OF ORIGIN Theros

BASE Theros

HAIR Brown

EYES Brown

HEIGHT 5 ft 10 in

ALLIES None

FOES Elspeth Tirel, Niko Aris

NIKO ARIS

Niko Aris was a javelin prodigy who felt stifled by their destiny. Seeking to use their skills to help others, Niko defied destiny and became a hero instead. As a planeswalker, they're excited for new experiences and the opportunity to use their skills to help others, away from the expectations of home.

Niko wields their mirror-shards with the precision of an expert javelineer.

> "Countless worlds unfolded before Niko, every one in need of heroes."

KEY DATA

SPECIES Human

STATUS Planeswalker

SIGNATURE MAGIC Niko manifests mirror-shards that can temporarily imprison beings

AGE Late teens

PLANE OF ORIGIN Theros

BASE Theros

HAIR Black with a lilac streak

EYES Blue-gray

HEIGHT 5 ft 10 in

ALLIES Kaya, Tyvar

FOES Tibalt

MIRROR MAGIC
Niko is able to manifest mirror-shards, which, on contact, have the ability to trap other beings for a limited time. Niko can throw these shards with pinpoint precision to manipulate events on the battlefield.

DESTINY DEFIED

Niko Aris is a javelin champion on Theros. As a child, they were the subject of a prophecy that said they would become one of Theros' greatest athletes, a javelin prodigy who would never miss. Niko trained their whole life to fulfill this prophecy, and when the time came, they won competition after competition. But while Niko's fans adored them, Niko dreamed of becoming a hero and using their skills to make the world a better place. During the finals of the Akroan Games, the biggest athletic competition on Theros that drew crowds from across the plane, Niko seized their chance. Niko intentionally missed their target, defying their destiny.

Klothys, god of destiny, sent one of her agents after Niko to reweave them back into their destiny, but Niko was able to trap them in one of their mirror-shards. Panicked, and not wanting to return to their already mapped-out life, Niko's planeswalker spark ignited and they planeswalked away. Arriving on one of the realms of Kaldheim, Niko met and befriended planeswalkers Kaya and Tyvar Kell while working to stop the machinations of the cruel planeswalker Tibalt.

ZENDIKAR

A vibrant plane teeming with life and wracked by violent elemental turmoil, few places in the Multiverse are as alive as Zendikar. Home to a diverse array of cultures but few permanent settlements, Zendikar is a land of exploration, where expeditionary houses compete to discover the ancient secrets of the plane buried by centuries of tectonic upheaval.

THE HISTORY OF ZENDIKAR

Most of Zendikar's past is lost to history or hidden in forboding ruins. Six thousand years ago, the kor lithomancer Nahiri allied herself with fellow planeswalkers Ugin and Sorin Markov to seal away the Eldrazi titans, with Nahiri herself acting as their warden. Over the centuries spent guarding their prison, Nahiri grew distant from the kor people and eventually went into a hibernation, to awake if the Eldrazi were ever set free. The great Kor Empire of the time, already in decline, fell completely.

A millennia ago, Nahiri awoke to find the walls of the Eldrazi prison beginning to crack. Investigating the cause, she found Eldrazi-worshipping cultists attempting to free the titans. She put a stop to them and left to find her old companions. She did not return, but just a few years ago, Sorin arrived to find the Eldrazi threatening to break free once more. Allying himself with planeswalker Nissa Revane, they journeyed to the Eye of Ugin, the central hub for the hedron network. Nissa betrayed Sorin and destroyed the eye, believing the Eldrazi would simply leave the plane. Instead, the freed titans began to consume Zendikar.

When Gideon Jura discovered Zendikar's peril, he recruited fellow planeswalkers Jace Beleren, Chandra Nalaar, and Nissa Revane—each of whom was partially responsible for the Eldrazi release—to help solve the crisis. They formed the Gatewatch, named after the fallen city of Sea Gate, and together they slew two of the Eldrazi titans. In the wake of their victory, Zendikar began to flourish once more. The great city of Sea Gate was rebuilt over the years, and a new age of explorations and discovery began.

THE ROIL

Zendikar is a land where nature is both wild and unchecked, and those who live there have adapted to the wild surges of elemental magic that regularly batter the unwary. A symptom of Zendikar's unchecked elemental forces is the Roil, the locals' name for the wide array of cataclysms that regularly stymie any attempt to create more permanent settlements on the plane. The Roil is as destructive as it is unpredictable. It can take any form, from a sudden upswell that launches massive boulders into the sky, only for them to come crashing back down moments later, to sudden cyclones or tidal waves that swallow unlucky vessels at sea. The denizens of Zendikar have adapted to its hostile climate, building a few permanent settlements where the Roil is weakest, but also by simply being ready to move at a moment's notice.

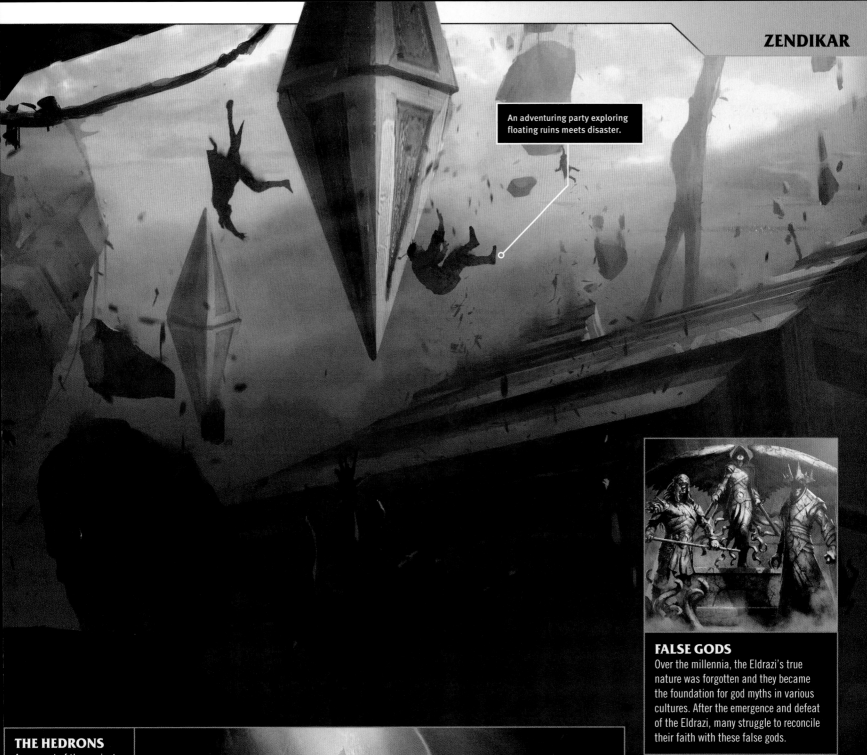

An adventuring party exploring floating ruins meets disaster.

FALSE GODS

Over the millennia, the Eldrazi's true nature was forgotten and they became the foundation for god myths in various cultures. After the emergence and defeat of the Eldrazi, many struggle to reconcile their faith with these false gods.

KEY DATA

DEMONYM Zendikari

TERRAIN A constantly shifting landscape of skyscraping forests and treacherous mountains

KEY LOCATIONS Akoum, Bala Ged, Guul Draz, Ondu, Tazeem, Murasa, Sejiri

KEY FACTIONS None

RULER None

COMMON SPECIES Angel, Demon, Dragon, Elf, Giant, Goblin, Human, Imp, Kor, Merfolk, Minotaur, Ogre, Surrakar, Troll, Vampire

THE HEDRONS

A remnant of the ancient prison built for the Eldrazi titans, the hedrons comprise a network of stone megaliths found across the plane. The hedrons have become an everyday fact of life for the locals, with many taking advantage of their power. Goblins fashion weapons from the powerful artifacts or even regularly consume pieces of them. Small settlements are built in the shadow of massive fallen hedrons, and networks of hooklines can be found linking the hedrons as an aerial path across deadly terrain.

Zendikar's goblins have grown hardened carapaces from eating hedrons.

AKOUM

The volcanic mountains of Akoum are virtually uninhabitable due to tectonic instability. The largest semipermanent settlement in Akoum is the Goma Fada caravan, a wagon train the size of a small city, home to people from every culture on the plane.

DRANA, THE LAST BLOODCHIEF

When the Eldrazi emerged from their prison, many vampires became enthralled to the titan Ulamog, whose influence had corrupted them ages before. The free vampires, led by the bloodchief Drana, were successful in escaping the Ulamog's thralls, but at the cost of the rest of the remaining bloodchiefs. Today, Drana searches for the secret to creating more bloodchiefs.

BALA GED

The marshy rainforests of Bala Ged were home to insular tribes of elves, such as the militant Joraga and the secretive Mul Daya. Bala Ged was hit hard by the Eldrazi, and the elves who survived have begun the long process of rebuilding.

GUUL DRAAZ

To the south of Bala Ged lies Guul Draaz, a fetid swampland continent notable only because the vampire city of Malakir was located there. Malakir was the oldest and most well-developed city on the plane, but lays in ruins after the Eldrazi caused a vampire civil war.

NULLS

Only vampire bloodchiefs can create new vampires. If a lower vampire attempts to turn another being, the victim instead becomes a slavering zombie called a Null.

MURASA AND SEJIRI

The remote Murasa is the most dangerous and inaccessible of continents, full of towering cliffs, deep forests, and priceless artifacts hidden in ruins. To the north, some merfolk have settled in Sejiri, in the permafrost steppes of the most inhospitable continent on Zendikar, living in glacial lakes deep beneath the ice.

TAZEEM

Across a narrow sea lies Tazeem, a lush continent of twisting forests and deep inland seas. Tazeem is home to Sea Gate, the most cosmopolitan city on the plane, built against a massive seawall at the continent's tip. Farther inland lies the mysterious sky ruin Emeria, a floating rock archipelago that was once a massive citadel, as well as Coralhelm, a merfolk enclave along the continent's enormous river gorge.

The lighthouse at Sea Gate is a beacon of hope for the plane. The planeswalkers known as the Gatewatch took their name from this city.

SKYCLAVES

Thousands of years ago, as the ancient Kor Empire fell, so too did their seven imposing aerial fortresses, the skyclaves. Each skyclave once stood as a symbol of their power on every continent, but they were destroyed one after another as the peoples of the plane revolted against their rule. In the wake of the Eldrazi's defeat, explorers slipped into the skyclave known as Emeria, the sky ruin, and accidentally reactivated it. Across the plane, each of the skyclaves returned to the sky, despite many being shattered and in disrepair.

The Skyclaves have become highly sought after ruins by expeditionary parties. Ancient kor weapons and secrets have become a prized commodity, with each skyclave holding a wealth of relics for any who are brave—or foolhardy—enough to plumb their depths. Beyond their material wealth, the skyclaves hold something even more precious: knowledge. The ancient kor's preserved history is the first time the plane's scholars have truly been able to discover the history of their world.

EXPEDITIONARY HOUSES

Expeditionary Houses are companies that organize voyages through the treacherous landscape of Zendikar to explore ruins. These houses have always been a fact of life on Zendikar, but in the aftermath of the Eldrazi's destruction, the focus turned to the newly emerged Skyclaves. Nahiri has become a silent partner in the Sea Gate Expeditionary House, but her true purpose is to recover the means to restore Zendikar to what it once was.

ONDU

The continent of Ondu is the primary home of the nomadic kor tribes, where settlements of rope, piston, and canvas hang nestled in the relative shelter of the deep trenches that criss-cross the continent. The temperate forest known as Turntimber is home to the Tajuru elves, the largest tribe of elves on the plane and the most welcoming and diplomatic.

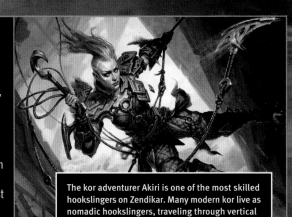

The kor adventurer Akiri is one of the most skilled hookslingers on Zendikar. Many modern kor live as nomadic hookslingers, traveling through vertical canyons with an ease most others can't match.

KIORA

Kiora is an independent trickster at heart, unwilling to allow her actions to be dictated by uninspiring leaders. Although she has spent much of her time working alone, she always believes herself to be acting for the common good, even if her methods sometimes run counter to the establishment.

MASTER OF THE DEPTHS
Kiora is a merfolk trickster and summoner, able to call bonded sea creatures to her over long distances. Her power is enhanced by Dekella, the bident of a sea god from Theros, which gives her mastery over the waves.

MERFOLK OF ZENDIKAR
The surface world of Zendikar is known for its wild dangers, but the oceans and seas are no less hazardous. The hardy merfolk have fared better in maintaining civilization than their terrestrial counterparts over the millennia. Merfolk scholars founded the Lighthouse at Sea Gate, the greatest repository of knowledge on the plane, and it's a poor expedition party that departs without a merfolk guide. Jori En, a close friend of Kiora, is one such scholar and guide.

> **"When your enemy flees, send the sea to pursue them."**
>
> —KIORA

THE CRASHING WAVE

Kiora was once a follower of Cosi, the merfolk trickster god. Cosi's tricksters worked outside the strictures of merfolk society in the name of the greater good, sometimes humbling overzealous leaders and sometimes working behind the scenes to protect the tribe. Kiora brought this philosophy with her across the Multiverse and she explored its deep waters, returning often to tell her sister, Turi, of her adventures.

Then came the Eldrazi, three titan abominations who were once believed to be the gods of the merfolk. Cosi was not a benevolent trickster, but a titanic warper of reality named Kozilek. Upon this realization, Kiora lost her faith. She traveled the Multiverse in search of the mightiest krakens, leviathans, serpents, and giant octopi that could battle the Eldrazi. On Theros, she came close to claiming the greatest kraken she had ever seen, a living island of colossal stature, but she was stymied by Thassa,

the sea god, and left with a different prize: Thassa's divine weapon, the bident Dekella.

With Dekella, Thassa finally had a weapon capable of challenging the gods. She aligned herself with the defenders of the last refuge on Zendikar, the city of Sea Gate. When the titans Ulamog and Kozilek arrived, Kiora wielded the power of the bident against them, but it was not enough. Just as all seemed hopeless, the Gatewatch saved the day in an awe-inspiring display of magic. Kiora, embarrassed and humbled, did not stay for the afterparty.

When the planar beacon summoned planeswalkers from across the Multiverse to Ravnica, Kiora arrived to aid in the fight. She had enough of false gods, and the elder dragon Nicol Bolas was everything she despised. She defended the Simic enclaves and stayed to fight even when she had the chance to escape. She even swallowed her pride to fight alongside the Gatewatch, for whom she harbored some resentment for outshining her on Zendikar.

Kiora wields the bident of the sea god Thassa.

Kiora commands the creatures of the deep.

DEKELLA, BIDENT OF THASSA

Kiora traveled to many planes searching for creatures of the deep who could aid her in the battle against the Eldrazi. On Theros, she discovered the massive kraken Arixmethes. But in trying to wrest control of Arixmethes, she ran afoul of the Theros god of the sea, Thassa … who she may have also been impersonating at the time. Kiora and Thassa battled, and as Thassa threw her bident to pin Kiora to the sea floor, Kiora grabbed the bident and planeswalked away.

KEY DATA

SPECIES Merfolk

STATUS Planeswalker

SIGNATURE MAGIC Kiora summons sea creatures and can control the sea itself

AGE Early 20s

PLANE OF ORIGIN Zendikar

BASE Zendikar

HAIR None

EYES Black

HEIGHT 5 ft 7 in

ALLIES Jori En, Turi

FOES Thassa, god of the sea

NAHIRI

Nahiri, the ancient guardian of Zendikar, has lost everything in her long life. Betrayed by her mentor, imprisoned for a thousand years, and freed only to find her home devastated by the Eldrazi, Nahiri committed horrific acts in the name of revenge. Now she seeks a way forward, for herself and her plane.

KOR LITHOMANCER
Nahiri is a kor with a mastery over lithomancy, the power to shape stone to her will. With her abilities, she can levitate stone and hurl it at her enemies or forge weapons from stone at will.

ZENDIKAR RESURGENT
Returning from her revenge on Sorin and finding Zendikar in recovery, Nahiri dedicated herself to rebuilding her plane. She backed a new expeditionary house based out of Sea Gate to explore the newly reemerged Skyclaves. However, in truth, Nahiri was searching for the lithoform core, the means of stopping the Roil and reforging Zendikar to what it once was. She was stopped by Nissa Revane, a child of modern Zendikar, and the two have held a grudge against one another ever since.

HEIR OF THE ANCIENTS

Millennia ago, as a fresh planeswalker, Nahiri encountered the vampiric planeswalker Sorin Markov. Sorin quickly realized that Nahiri did not yet have a grasp on her planeswalking abilities, and rather than run her off Innistrad, he mentored her. During their travels, they encountered a plane overrun by eldritch creatures. As they watched these titanic beings consume the plane, unable to stop them, the spirit dragon Ugin appeared to them and explained all about these creatures, called the Eldrazi. Together, they devised a plan to imprison the Eldrazi by combining their abilities and creating a network of stone hedrons on Zendikar to lure and imprison the Eldrazi there.

Once their work was complete and the Eldrazi were secure, Nahiri remained their eternal jailor while Ugin and Sorin departed. Over the years, the sorrow at those she loved dying while she remained ageless weighed heavily on her, so she separated from her people and encased herself in stone, to wake only if the Eldrazi prison was threatened. When this happened, neither of her former allies arrived to aid her as they had pledged. Nahiri went to Innistrad, where she found Sorin constructing the Helvault as a means of protecting his plane, unable to hear her summoning him to Zendikar. Enraged, Nahiri leapt into attack, but Sorin's pet archangel Avacyn intervened and sealed her in the Helvault.

A thousand years later, she was freed when the Helvault was destroyed, only to find Zendikar devastated by the Eldrazi. Left with nothing but a fierce desire for vengeance, Nahiri plotted to destroy Innistrad, just like Zendikar had been. She lured the Eldrazi titan Emrakul to Innistrad, forcing Sorin to destroy Avacyn, his creation, as Emrakul's influence over her drove her mad. After defeating Sorin and sealing him in a temporary prison of stone so he could helplessly watch his plane die, Nahiri departed.

WAR OF THE SPARK
Nahiri encountered Sorin again during the War of the Spark, where the former companions ignored the threat of Nicol Bolas and spent much of the war trying to kill one another. Weakened by the Mending, Sorin and Nahiri were evenly matched, and it wasn't until the interference of Ugin, through his agent Narset, that they cooperated again for the greater good.

> "Zendikar has suffered enough. It is time, at last, for my home to know peace."
>
> —NAHIRI

Nahiri can create stoneforged blades from rock, their edges still aglow with inner heat.

Nahiri is the inspiration for modern-day kor lithomancers, who have imitated her garb.

KEY DATA

SPECIES Kor

STATUS Planeswalker

SIGNATURE MAGIC Nahiri is a lithomancer with the ability to shape stone

AGE Over 6,000 years old

PLANE OF ORIGIN Zendikar

AFFILIATION None

BASE Zendikar

HAIR White

EYES Pale gray

HEIGHT 5 ft 9 in

ALLIES Ugin

FOES Nissa Revane, Sorin Markov

NISSA REVANE

Nissa Revane was born among the insular Joraga, but her worldview has evolved as she learns from past mistakes and travels with her friends in the Gatewatch. Through her friends' eyes, she has come to see how every plane is full of natural wonder and beauty, if you only know how to look.

WORLDWAKER
Nissa is an animist, able to call upon the elemental forces of the world to rise and fight alongside her. On Zendikar, her powers are unmatched, as the plane itself has chosen her to be its voice.

MY FRIEND, MY ENEMY
Nissa formed a cautious friendship with Nahiri, a fellow planeswalker who also cared deeply for Zendikar. But when she realized Nahiri wished to stop the Roil—the wild soul of the plane she loved—their burgeoning friendship turned to enmity, and they came to blows.

VOICE OF ZENDIKAR

Nissa was once an outcast among the insular tribes of the Joraga. Her animist powers were forbidden, and so she hid them from her people. To learn more about the world, she spent time among the Tajuru Nation on Ondu, which is where she discovered Eldrazi drones laying waste to everything in their path. Joined by the vampire planeswalker Sorin Markov, Nissa journeyed to the Eye of Ugin, the magical control center of the Hedron Network. Nissa's distrust of vampires ran deep, and she betrayed Sorin by destroying the central hedron—rather than helping him repair it—in the hope that Sorin was lying and the Eldrazi would leave once they were freed.

The truth was far worse. Nissa unleashed the Eldrazi titans themselves, unfathomable beings of cosmic hunger that immediately set about devouring the mana and life essence of the plane. Nissa spent years attempting to stem the tide, but her success only came when she embraced her elemental powers and allied herself with planeswalkers Jace Beleren, Gideon Jura, and Chandra Nalaar to form the Gatewatch. Together, they destroyed the Eldrazi titans on Zendikar and tracked down the final titan, Emrakul, on Innistrad.

During the Gatewatch's time together, Nissa grew close to Chandra Nalaar as they explored her home plane of Kaladesh. When the Gatewatch discovered Nicol Bolas was planning an invasion of Ravnica, they tried to stop him on the plane of Amonkhet. Bolas defeated them brutally, and Nissa decided to go back to Zendikar to ensure it healed, rather than watch more worlds burn under Bolas. Jace eventually convinced her to return to the fray, and during the invasion of Ravnica, she rejoined the Gatewatch to vanquish the elder dragon.

> ## "My heart and Zendikar's beat as one. Together, we will endure."
> —NISSA REVANE

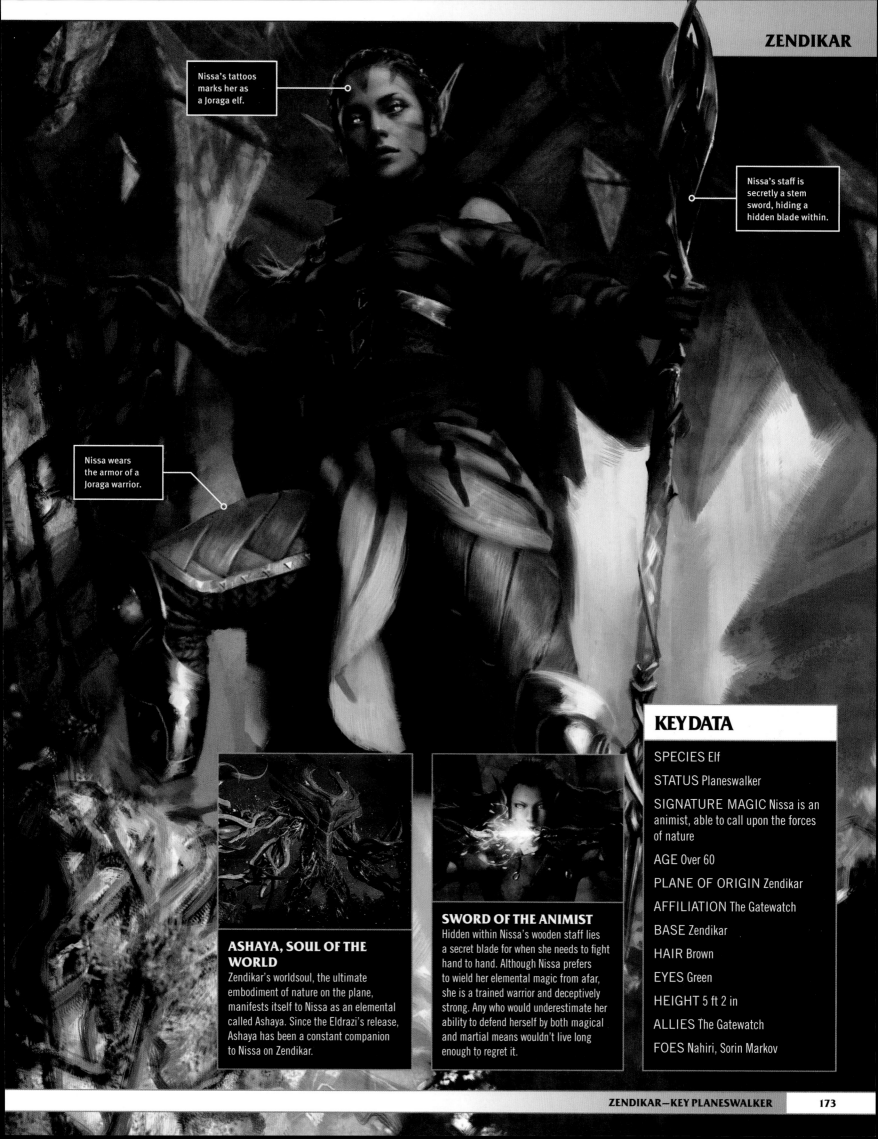

Nissa's tattoos marks her as a Joraga elf.

Nissa's staff is secretly a stem sword, hiding a hidden blade within.

Nissa wears the armor of a Joraga warrior.

KEY DATA

SPECIES Elf

STATUS Planeswalker

SIGNATURE MAGIC Nissa is an animist, able to call upon the forces of nature

AGE Over 60

PLANE OF ORIGIN Zendikar

AFFILIATION The Gatewatch

BASE Zendikar

HAIR Brown

EYES Green

HEIGHT 5 ft 2 in

ALLIES The Gatewatch

FOES Nahiri, Sorin Markov

ASHAYA, SOUL OF THE WORLD

Zendikar's worldsoul, the ultimate embodiment of nature on the plane, manifests itself to Nissa as an elemental called Ashaya. Since the Eldrazi's release, Ashaya has been a constant companion to Nissa on Zendikar.

SWORD OF THE ANIMIST

Hidden within Nissa's wooden staff lies a secret blade for when she needs to fight hand to hand. Although Nissa prefers to wield her elemental magic from afar, she is a trained warrior and deceptively strong. Any who would underestimate her ability to defend herself by both magical and martial means wouldn't live long enough to regret it.

KYLEM

Kylem is a peaceful plane that embraces its rich history and diverse cultures. The people of Kylem have all rallied around a shared love of competition, camaraderie, and the excitement of sports. And no sport is more beloved than that of martial magic, where duos compete in explosive magical brawls at Valor's Reach arena.

CLOUDSPIRE CITY
Cloudspire draws crowds from across the plane for its magnificent views. Located literally above the clouds, the awe-inspiring locale is the perfect setting for the biggest sport on the plane.

VALOR'S REACH
Valor's Reach is the massive arena at the pinnacle of Cloudspire City. Founded generations ago by the wealthy elves of the city, it's a marvel of magical technology. The battlefield at the center of the enormous arena can transform into any type of terrain, providing new challenges for the competitors at any time.

HOMUNCULI
The homunculi of Kylem are employed as referees and caretakers, overseeing pivotal competitions on a variety of levels. Homunculi referees arbitrate matches while safeguarding the crowds from errant magic. Lacking mouths, the homunculi of Kylem also use a form of sign language to communicate, which is taught to all students on Kylem.

AZRA
Azra are beings with distant demonic ancestry, which is reflected in their purple skin tones and facial horns.

THE RULES OF MARTIAL MAGIC
Martial magic is played by teams of partners called duos. Each duo begins with a certain number of points, and getting hit by spells, holds, or other attacks incur penalties determined by the homunculi referees. Matches are nonlethal, with enchantments in place to blunt the worst attacks and healers on standby for every competition. Duos compete not just for skill, but for style, with some formats of the game encouraging "style points," where winners are determined by fans.

KEY DATA

KEY LOCATIONS Cloudspire City

COMMON SPECIES Angel, Aven, Azra, Cyclops, Demon, Dragon, Dryad, Dwarf, Giant, Goblin, Homunculus, Human, Orc

VRYN

Vryn is a plane locked in perpetual warfare over control of the Mage Rings, ancient devices that channel mana throughout the plane. The feuding sides of the conflict are ever changing, but life for those caught in the middle is the same toil and drudgery it has always been.

MAGE RING NETWORK

No one living knows how old the Mage Rings are, or who built them. To the rival factions that are in a constant state of war over control of them, those factors matter very little. The Mage Rings channel the magical essence of mana throughout the plane, and whoever controls them, controls the flow of magical power. An enormous amount of maintenance is required to keep the Mage Rings functioning, and a working class of ring-mages are caught between the opposing factions.

RINGERS

Those who reside on the enormous Mage Rings are called Ringers. Ringers usually become mage-technicians who maintain the Mage Rings, both ensuring an optimal flow of mana through the rings and keeping them from falling apart due to age. Jace Beleren was born a "ringer"— his father was a ring-mage—but he now considers Ravnica his home.

TROVIAN SEPARATISTS

The Trovian Separatists are made up of rebel factions from outlying states on Vryn. While their stated purpose is independence from the Ampryn League, they simply want control of the Mage Rings for themselves.

ALHAMMARRET THE HIGH ARBITER

Arbitrating the disputes between the Ampryn League and Trovian Separatists was Alhammarret, a sphinx mind mage who had recruited a teenage Jace Beleren as his apprentice. After a few years, Jace learned that Alhammarret was using him to prolong the conflict and enrich himself, keeping Jace a prisoner by erasing his memories of any wrongdoing. When Jace discovered this, their duel left Alhammarret brain dead and Jace an amnesiac.

THE AMPRYN LEAGUE

The dominant power on Kylem is the Ampryn League, a coalition of "Core States" situated at the nexus of the mage-ring network.

KEY DATA

KEY LOCATIONS Silmot's Crossing, The Core States

COMMON SPECIES Human, Sphinx

LORWYN

Lorwyn is a plane caught in a perpetual summer, where the sun never sets and fae creatures live simple lives among its picturesque landscape. At the heart of this seemingly idyllic world is a sinister secret—every few centuries, their world is twisted into a dark parody of itself.

GREATER ELEMENTALS
Greater elementals sprout from the fabric of reality on Lorwyn, born of the abstract feelings of the creatures of the plane. Elementals are hopes, fears, dreams, and nightmares given form.

FLAMEKIN
Flamekin are living, intelligent elementals who burn with a cold fire and seek to live in harmony with the other creatures of Lorwyn. They look upon their greater elemental cousins with a spiritual awe.

KITHKIN
Kithkin are about half the height of a human and live in tight-knit villages on Lorwyn's rolling plains. Kithkin are united by the thoughtweft, an intrinsic connection to the collective consciousness of the minds of other kithkin.

ELVES
The cruel elves of Lorwyn have created a society where beauty is the only standard of importance, and any creature who doesn't meet their vision of perfection—called an eyeblight—is ruthlessly hunted.

CHANGELINGS
Changelings are semi-intelligent shapeshifters who reflexively mimic other creatures.

MERROW
Merfolk with fish tails that control the rivers and act as couriers and merchants.

BOGGARTS
The goblins of Lorwyn are pesky pranksters organized into warrens led by a matriarch (and sometimes patriarch) called an Auntie. Lorwyn boggarts have a wide range of morphology and are primarily driven to seek out new sensations and share it with their warrens.

KEY DATA

KEY LOCATIONS Gilt-Leaf Wood, Glen Elendra, Goldmeadow, The Merrow Lanes

COMMON SPECIES Elemental, Elf, Faerie, Giant, Goblin, Kithkin, Merfolk, Shapeshifter, Treefolk

SHADOWMOOR

Transformed by the Great Aurora into a perpetual night every three centuries, Lorwyn became Shadowmoor, a wicked reflection of itself. The last cycle was broken when Oona, the queen of the fae, was defeated and replaced by her own avatar, Maralen, who restored the normal cycle of day and night.

THE GREAT AURORA

The perpetual day of Lorwyn became the everlasting night of Shadowmoor every three centuries with the coming of the Great Aurora. The Mending disrupted this cycle, and Oona created Maralen to ensure that her mind survived the transition. However, Maralen grew independent and chose to break Oona's cycle instead and destroy the fae queen.

CINDERS

Cinders are the extinguished and bitter remnants of the Flamekin. They want nothing more than for the world to suffer as they do.

KITHKIN

Kithkin are about half the height of a human and live in armed fortresses on Shadowmoor's gloomy plains. Kithkin are linked by the mindweft, a collective xenophobia and shared paranoia of the unknown.

ELVES

The benevolent elves of Shadowmoor are charged with protecting beauty—for where there is beauty, there is also hope. They fight back against the darkness any way they can.

BOGGARTS

The boggarts of Shadowmoor are mercurial marauders, organized into bestial gangs, primarily driven by their hunger to roam and consume anything to sate their empty stomachs.

FAERIES

The fae were unaffected by the Great Aurora and continued their work as Oona's agents.

MERROW

Merfolk with fish tails that dominate the rivers as cutthroats and thieves.

KEY DATA

KEY LOCATIONS Wilt-Leaf Wood, Glen Elendra, Mistmeadow, The Dark Meanders

COMMON SPECIES Elemental, Elf, Faerie, Giant, Goblin, Kithkin, Merfolk, Shapeshifter, Treefolk

SHANDALAR

Shandalar does not have a fixed location in the Multiverse, forever drifting through the Blind Eternities. Abnormally mana-rich, Shandalar is a place where magic flows freely, from the wilds of Kalonia and the bright kingdom of Thune, to the shadows of Xathrid, the volcanic peaks of Valkas, and the azure shores of the Eastern Sea.

LIM-DÛL'S WAR

Nearly 1,600 years ago, at the end of the Ice Age on Dominaria, the necromancer Lim-Dûl was transported to Shandalar by his planeswalker patron. Using the plane's abundant mana, Lim-Dûl played his master, the villainous Leshrac, against the demonic Tevesh Szat, and after a duel, they both fled the plane. Freed, Lim-Dûl set about waging wars of conquest on Shandalar, even moving beyond his own body to possess others. The archmages of the plane united to stop him, and he was imprisoned in an artifact that was used to power a Great Barrier to protect the plane from further invasions.

THE AMPHIN

The Amphin are an amphibious people who dwell in the shallows and seas of Shandalar. They have spent years masking their presence from the other peoples of Shandalar as they prepare for an invasion.

THE ONAKKE

Deep in the Kalonian Wilds lie the ruins of an ancient civilization of ogre artificers known as the Onakke. Where once they controlled an empire, now only their ghosts remain, haunting their catacombs as they await a vessel to make use of the Chain Veil. With the Veil destroyed, it's unknown what is left of the Onakke.

SLIVERS AND THE SKEP

Beyond the Kalonian Wilds, on the shores of the Eastern Sea, lies the Skep. A buzzing hive-mind of shapeshifting drones called Slivers have made their home along the cliffs there, beyond the notice of the kingdoms that could threaten them. The slivers are adaptive shapeshifters, taking on the advantageous characteristics of other species and spreading those adaptations to nearby members of the hive. Fossils indicate that an ancient calamity brought the slivers to Shandalar's shores, although the few researchers who believe in their existence can only speculate as to their true origin.

REGATHA

Regatha is a mountainous landscape of volcanic and tectonic instability.

KERAL KEEP

The monastery of Keral Keep was founded in honor of the ancient planeswalker pyromancer Jaya Ballard. She considered the gesture both endearing and annoying, mainly because its monks took her sarcastic comments as profound wisdom. Their monastic approach to pyromancy makes them a unique sect, and their more serene approach was a poor fit for planeswalker Chandra Nalaar, who spent a lot of time there as a youth learning to harness her abilities.

THE PURIFYING FIRE

The Order of Heliud would send mage-criminals to be judged in the living flame known as the Purifying Fire, which would burn away their abilities if it found them guilty. When they sentenced Chandra to the flame, a personal epiphany helped her overcome it, and she brought the Order's headquarters down around their heads.

THE ORDER OF HELIUD

The capital city of Zinara is run by a league of hieromancers called the Order of Heliud. The Order was founded in honor of a religious figure known as Heliud, and the Order is said to have expanded to several planes.

PLANE OF MOUNTAINS AND SEAS

The Plane of Mountains and Seas is a bountiful land of wondrous treasures and strange animals.

MU YANLING

Yanling is a planeswalker elementalist who commands the seas and the winds. Orphaned by a tidal wave as a child, her adoptive father Li Shan disappeared, and she searches for the truth of whether he is alive or dead.

JIANG YANGGU

An amnesiac who cannot remember his past or his real name, Yanggu is a kind soul who can empower beasts, including his loyal companion Mowu.

MOWU

Mowu is Yanggu's loyal hound, a dog made of stone and magic who can grow from his small stature into a titanic hound when threatened.

THE ELDRAZI

The Eldrazi are eldritch creatures from the Blind Eternities, the space between realities. What is known of the Eldrazi is only speculation, drawn from their physical manifestations within the planes. They're attracted to strong or unusual manifestations of mana, a fact used to lure them to Zendikar, and later to Innistrad. When they manifest on a plane, they feed on the mana until the plane can no longer sustain itself and it collapses into nothingness.

ULAMOG

Ulamog was the smallest and weakest of the Eldrazi titans, a being of eternal hunger whose appetite outstripped that of his larger cousins. With disturbing humanoid features, Ulamog was a terror to behold. As he consumed, he also created spawns of his lineage and spewed deadly plagues and parasitic entities. His passing transformed the landscape, draining any vestiges of life and leaving behind a wasteland of chalky white husks.

THE ELDRAZI TITANS

Three Eldrazi titans have been documented, each of which has distinct characteristics. These titans are believed to be the "true" Eldrazi, the physical manifestations of beings that ordinarily exist outside of planes. Each of the titans has a Brood Lineage, although scholars can only speculate as to their true nature and if they're merely extensions of the titans themselves. Two of the titans, Ulamog and Kozilek, were destroyed by the Gatewatch in an event that nearly destroyed Zendikar. The third and most powerful titan, Emrakul, is currently imprisoned in Innistrad's silver moon.

ULAMOG'S BROOD

Ulamog's brood look and act much like their titan, with tentacles, horrifying bifurcated arms, and eyeless bony face-plates eerily similar to a human face. The lowest drones merely consume, while the larger of the lineage act as spawnsires for more of their kind. Smaller drones attach to the faces of Zendikar's vampires, controlling them as if they were extensions of his brood.

KOZILEK

Kozilek was the most feared of the titans on Zendikar. A reality shaper, Kozilek's presence would subvert the laws of physics in his vicinity and warp the minds of those who came near him. Kozilek fed on the landscape as Ulamog did, but in strange and inscrutable ways. His passing through a region left behind iridescent geometric patterns.

KOZILEK'S BROOD

Kozilek's drones are more varied than Ulamog's, best signified by floating geometric shapes hovering around their heads.

EMRAKUL

The final titan, Emrakul, is also the mightiest, dominating the horizon like a monstrous alien jellyfish. Latticelike structures build to a central dome that has continued to grow as she recovers from her long imprisonment, and sickening tendrils trail freely beneath her as she passes by. Gravity itself warps around her, as she does not so much fly as defy physics to remain aloft. Her presence is desolation itself, driving those who gaze upon her to despair and eventually succumb to madness, as they lose their identities and become part of her.

BRISELA

The fusion of the Eldrazi-corrupted archangels Bruna and Gisela was destroyed during the Travails, just before Emrakul was sealed away.

HANWEIR

The township of Hanweir fused together under Emrakul's influence and slithered away. It hasn't been seen since the Travails.

EMRAKUL'S BROOD

Emrakul's brood are not created but transformed. Her influence warps the mind and the flesh of sapient beings, and those affected by her presence may find strange latticelike fleshy growths on their body as they're slowly transformed into extensions of her will. As they're transformed, they begin to lose all sense of self until there is only Emrakul.

"This is all wrong. I am incomplete, unfulfilled, inchoate. There should be blossoms, not barren resentment. The soil was not receptive. It is not my time. Not yet."

—EMRAKUL

ELDRITCH MOON

While in psychic contact with Jace Beleren, the Gatewatch's mind mage, a mental construct of Emrakul indicated that her manifestation on Innistrad felt incomplete. Influencing the mind of the moonfolk planeswalker Tamiyo, Emrakul sealed herself into Innistrad's silver moon with a massive infusion of mana, leaving the Gatewatch befuddled as to her true purpose.

MORE PLANESWALKERS

ANGRATH

Angrath is a minotaur blacksmith with a thirst for exploration and a deep love of his family. He also has an unyielding rage for anything that would curtail his freedom. When his wanderlust took him away from his family for over a decade, he vowed to spend more time with his now adult daughters—that is, until he gets the itch to travel again ...

Angrath glows internally like a forge when wielding his magic.

Angrath fights with a near-molten chain and blacksmith tools.

CAPTAIN OF CHAOS

Angrath is a blacksmith and a family minotaur, from a minotaur people who value their freedom more than anything else. His planeswalker nature has instilled in him a desire to see the Multiverse, but unfortunately his travels brought him to Ixalan, where he was trapped by an artifact called the Immortal Sun. Unable to return home to his daughters, he instead vented his rage as a pirate on the high seas of Ixalan, hoping to find a means to escape.

"Gold without freedom might as well be lead."

He aided the planeswalker Huatli (whether she wanted him to or not) in the race to Orazca on Ixalan, and was finally free of the plane when the Immortal Sun was taken off-plane as part of elder dragon Nicol Bolas's schemes. Angrath returned home to a joyful reunion with his daughters, but soon the Planar Beacon summoned him to Ravnica, where he was trapped again. He helped the Gatewatch defeat Nicol Bolas, where they learned the furious-seeming Angrath also possessed a great well of wisdom when it comes to grief, having dealt with the loss of his wife.

DESPERATE FATHER
Angrath's daughters are named Rumi and Jamira, and he loves them more than anything in the Multiverse. During their father's long absence, they became blacksmiths themselves and now run the family forge, a fact he couldn't be more proud of. In the wake of being trapped off-world—twice—Angrath has vowed to settle down with his daughters. Woe betide any being that tries to keep him from returning to his family a third time, for Angrath has a merciless rage for anyone who would stand between him and his family.

KEY DATA

SPECIES Minotaur

STATUS Planeswalker

SIGNATURE MAGIC Angrath creates scorching heat that he imbues into his metal tools

AGE Late 40s

PLANE OF ORIGIN Unknown

BASE Unknown

HAIR Auburn

EYES Amber

HEIGHT 7 ft

ALLIES The Gatewatch, Huatli

FOES Azor, Nicol Bolas

ASHIOK

Ashiok thinks of themself as a Multiversal artist, using nightmares as the medium with which to create exquisite masterpieces. To Ashiok, people are merely blank canvases upon which they will create their latest work of art, and Ashiok will go to any lengths for their art.

Ashiok is missing the upper half of their face, almost like an unfinished dream.

Ashiok always floats just above the ground, never deigning to touch it.

NIGHTMARE WEAVER
Ashiok can telepathically invade the minds of others and then manifest their fears physically as shadowy nightmares. They can also use their powers to disguise themselves with illusions.

SCULPTOR OF FEARS

The true origins of the Ashiok are unknown. In recent years, they've taken a liking to Theros for its unique metaphysics tied to the collective unconscious and dreams. To hide from the notice of the gods, they made a bargain with Phenax, god of deception. In exchange for a new polis for Phenax's undead Returned, Ashiok would be hidden from the gods' sight. Ashiok tricked the leonin and humans of the small polis of Iretis into destroying each other by playing on their fears of one another.

Later, Ashiok experimented with the creation of a god, incepting a proto-god named Cacophony out of the nightmares of the city. The would-be god was absorbed by Ephara, who was already a god of the city, but she was unable to locate Ashiok. Finished with the Theran god-realm of Nyx, Ashiok went into the Underworld to further experiment with dreams on the plane. Their actions brought them to the attention of planeswalking thief Dack Fayden, who followed them into the Underworld. Due to Dack's interference, Ashiok relented their assault on the living and turned instead to tormenting the dead.

Ashiok sensed the nightmares of Elspeth Tirel and Phyrexia, and decided to find this horrific plane. On New Phyrexia, they sculpted their true masterpiece: causing the dreamless Phyrexian leader Elesh Norn to have a nightmare about Elspeth, thus ensuring a collision course between the revived Elspeth and Norn.

> **"Every nightmare is a caged bird that yearns to be set free."**

KEY DATA

SPECIES Unknown

STATUS Planeswalker

SIGNATURE MAGIC Ashiok manifests nightmares

AGE Unknown

PLANE OF ORIGIN Unknown

BASE Unknown

HAIR None

EYES None

HEIGHT 6 ft 10 in

ALLIES None

FOES Elspeth Tirel

DAVRIEL

Davriel wants nothing more than to be left alone. Once, he wielded a power that would make planes tremble ... but it turned out that dominating a plane was a lot of work. Instead, he'd rather spend his time doing things he enjoyed, only spurred to action when absolutely required.

LANGUID DIABOLIST

Davriel has the ability to pluck spells from the minds of others and use them as his own, although they fade over time and with use. He's also an expert diabolist, creating demonic contracts that leave him with the better of the deal every time. Secretly, he harbors an ancient force of terrible power within his mind, one he is loath to use.

THE ENTITY
Years ago, Davriel came across a dying man. Reaching into his mind with his powers, he absorbed a being of immense power that now resides in his mind. The Entity is a worldsoul, the ultimate elemental force of a dead plane. It heals Davriel and urges him to draw upon its power, but Davriel fears what he would become should he ever draw upon it again.

SOUL BROKER

Davriel was once a young accountant on his home plane, and it's his attention to detail that has served him well as a diabolist who makes pacts with demons. After absorbing the power of a mysterious Entity that now resides inside his mind, he spent years traveling the Multiverse. As he learned how to wield his abilities, manipulate demons, and exact vengeance when someone wronged him, he grew to believe he was special. He decided that he should finally use the power of the Entity and conquer a plane for himself.

The result was horrifying and disastrous, however. Davriel succeeded, but the price was too high, even for him. Worse, the cost of keeping a throne meant constant vigilance and constant toil with little time for any of the activities he enjoyed. Even worse, the act of using the Entity alerted the allies of the dying man—from whom he had taken the Entity—to his location. So Davriel took the only sensible action: he hid.

> ## "It's a bit much, I know, but it reminds my visitors who really holds the power here."

Today, Davriel lives in relative obscurity. Taking on a variety of pseudonyms, the name Cane being the latest, Davriel now rules as an extremely minor lord of an incredibly remote region in the hinterlands of Kessig on Innistrad. His quiet existence was disrupted by the revelation that his Entity had influenced this particular hiding spot, intending for Davriel to absorb the power of another Entity hidden in the remote village. Instead, he allowed a local girl, Tacenda Verlasen, to absorb this new entity, much to the annoyance of the being inside his mind. Despite the disruption to his simple existence— and a side trip to Ravnica at the summons of the Planar Bridge to fight Nicol Bolas—Davriel has gotten used to Innistrad and continues to live there. For now.

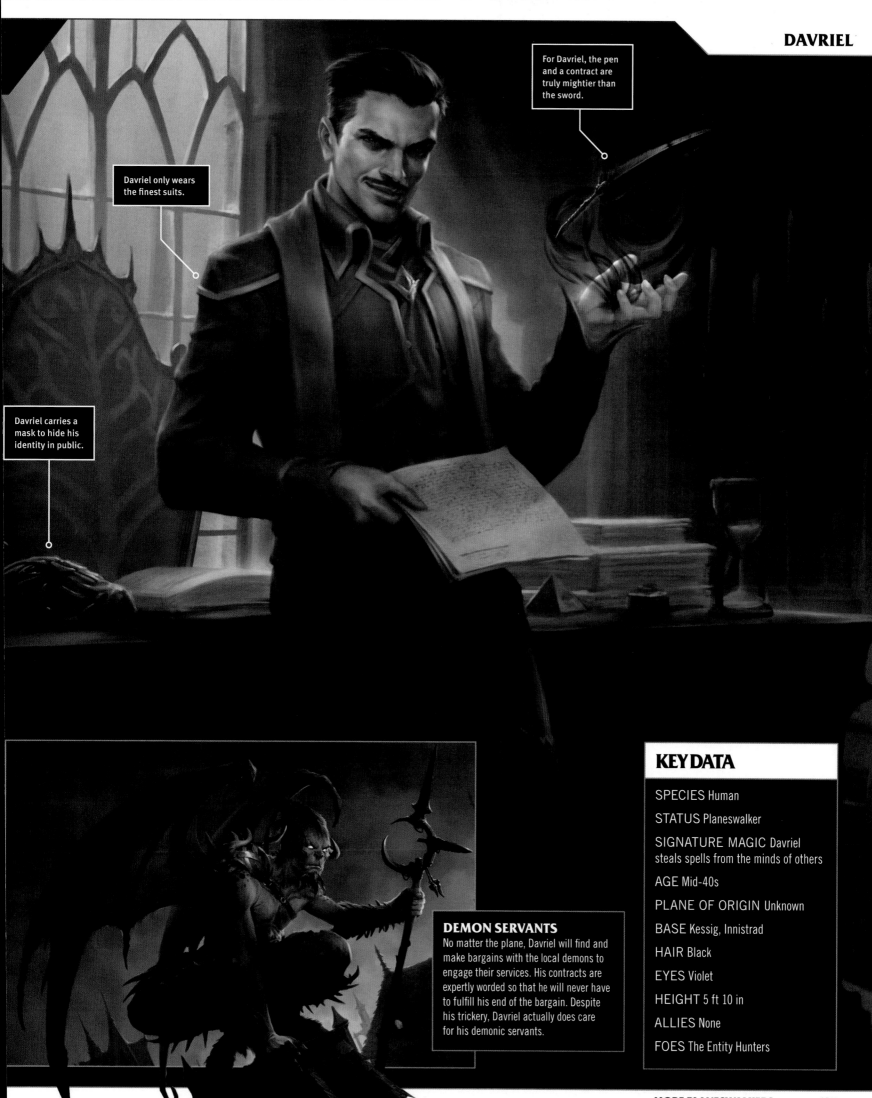

For Davriel, the pen and a contract are truly mightier than the sword.

Davriel only wears the finest suits.

Davriel carries a mask to hide his identity in public.

DEMON SERVANTS

No matter the plane, Davriel will find and make bargains with the local demons to engage their services. His contracts are expertly worded so that he will never have to fulfill his end of the bargain. Despite his trickery, Davriel actually does care for his demonic servants.

KEY DATA

SPECIES Human

STATUS Planeswalker

SIGNATURE MAGIC Davriel steals spells from the minds of others

AGE Mid-40s

PLANE OF ORIGIN Unknown

BASE Kessig, Innistrad

HAIR Black

EYES Violet

HEIGHT 5 ft 10 in

ALLIES None

FOES The Entity Hunters

GARRUK WILDSPEAKER

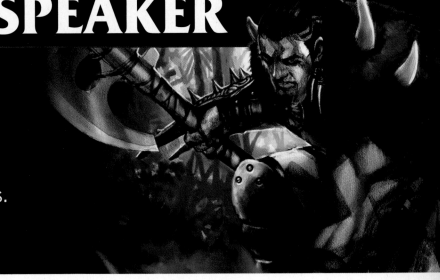

Garruk was orphaned as a young boy and grew up in the wilds alone. He shuns civilization and lives by the laws of nature, although in a battle with Liliana Vess, he was cursed by the Chain Veil and became a murderous hunter of planeswalkers. Now cured, Garruk is reexamining his place in the Multiverse.

THE WILDSPEAKER
Garruk is a massive physical specimen, towering over most other beings and wielding an imposing ax. He is a master hunter, tracker, and beastcaller, able to summon nearby creatures to his aid.

CURSED BY THE CHAIN VEIL
Although he is now free of its influence, Garruk was cursed by the Chain Veil, slowly being turned into a demonic form. There were many times he came close to a cure—an angelic blessing on Innistrad and a hedron to bind his power—but it wasn't until he stumbled upon the Cauldron of Eternity that he was cured for good.

CALLER OF BEASTS

When Garruk was a boy of 10, his father, Raklan, was arrested by the local sheriff for refusing to allow Garruk to be conscripted into the army. Garruk grew up in the local woods, surviving by using his nature magic to live alongside beasts that would have otherwise eaten him. When he had become a man, he ventured back into town to find that the sheriff had murdered his father not long after his arrest. In a fury, Garruk summoned the beasts and wurms of the forest and leveled the town.

Since then, Garruk has spent most of his life aimless, staying away from civilization and seeking only to live in the moment and live off the land. That was disrupted when Liliana Vess cursed him with the Chain Veil after a clash on Shandalar. Garruk began a slow demonic transformation, becoming a hunter of planeswalkers instead of beasts. His worsening curse brought him to the attention of Jace Beleren, who hired planeswalkers to try and stop him. They began falling to Garruk's ax, until finally one succeeded in binding the curse with a hedron taken from the demonic planeswalker Ob Nixilis.

The hedron slowed the curse, but did not stop it. As Garruk hunted down a fae planeswalker named Oko, the trickster cast a glamor that enslaved

> ## "The predator knows the true way of the world. Life is conflict. Only the strong survive."
> —GARRUK WILDSPEAKER

the huntsman's will. Responding only to "dog," Garruk helped Oko carry out his nefarious plans for Eldraine, including keeping watch over the meddling young Kenrith Twins. Will Kenrith showed genuine empathy for Garruk, and his friends removed the hedron implanted in Garruk, thinking they were helping. Garruk's curse raged out of control, but he was free of Oko's thrall. Aiding the Kenriths even while cursed, Garruk fell into a river, where the Cauldron of Eternity emerged and drained his curse, saving his life. After running Oko off Eldraine, Garruk found a strange affection for the twins and vowed to the King and Queen to watch over their children—as much as any civilization-avoiding planeswalker could, that is.

Garruk's helm was taken from the sheriff who murdered his father.

Garruk prefers to wear only the furs of creatures he has hunted himself.

KEY DATA

SPECIES Human

STATUS Planeswalker

SIGNATURE MAGIC Garruk summons beasts and can enhance their strength and size

AGE Late 30s

PLANE OF ORIGIN Unknown

BASE None

HAIR Brown

EYES Brown

HEIGHT 7 ft 7 in (varies by around 1 ft depending on his mood)

ALLIES Will and Rowan Kenrith

FOES Liliana Vess

KASMINA

Little is known about the enigmatic Kasmina, who has acted as a wise mentor to many nascent planeswalkers. Kasmina is the leader of a secret organization and is dedicated to stopping an unrevealed future crisis. Of late, she has shown a great deal of interest in Rowan Kenrith and Liliana Vess.

Kasmina uses artificial owls to surveil her targets.

Kasmina never goes anywhere without her archwizard's staff.

ENIGMA SAGE
Kasmina's specialty is the ability to scry across planes and locate embers—planeswalkers whose sparks have not yet ignited. She is also a wizard with a wide array of spells at her disposal, including transfiguration and hypnotism.

ENIGMATIC MENTOR

The mysterious Kasmina is the leader of a secret order of planeswalkers which seeks out embers. Her motives remain unclear, although there are indications that she has foreseen some great catastrophe for which she patiently prepares by helping embers reach their true potential. She has been known to employ ruthless means to ensure their sparks ignite.

Kasmina first revealed herself to the greater planeswalker community during the War of the Spark, where she took an active role in fighting the elder dragon Nicol Bolas's Dreadhorde. She has since influenced the Kenrith twins into attending Strixhaven University and seems to have taken an active interest in Rowan. She had high hopes for Lukka with her organization, but his actions on Strixhaven proved him a threat rather than an ally. She has also befriended Liliana Vess, formerly of the Gatewatch, although it is not known whether Liliana has joined her secret organization or is merely an ally.

"Every Planeswalker remembers the first time their mind touched the staggering vastness of the Multiverse."

KEY DATA

SPECIES Human

STATUS Planeswalker

SIGNATURE MAGIC Kasmina can scry between planes

AGE Appears to be early 40s

PLANE OF ORIGIN Unknown

BASE Unknown

HAIR Auburn

EYES Blue

HEIGHT 5 ft 10 in

ALLIES Kasmina's Secret Organization, Will and Rowan Kenrith, Liliana Vess

FOES Lukka

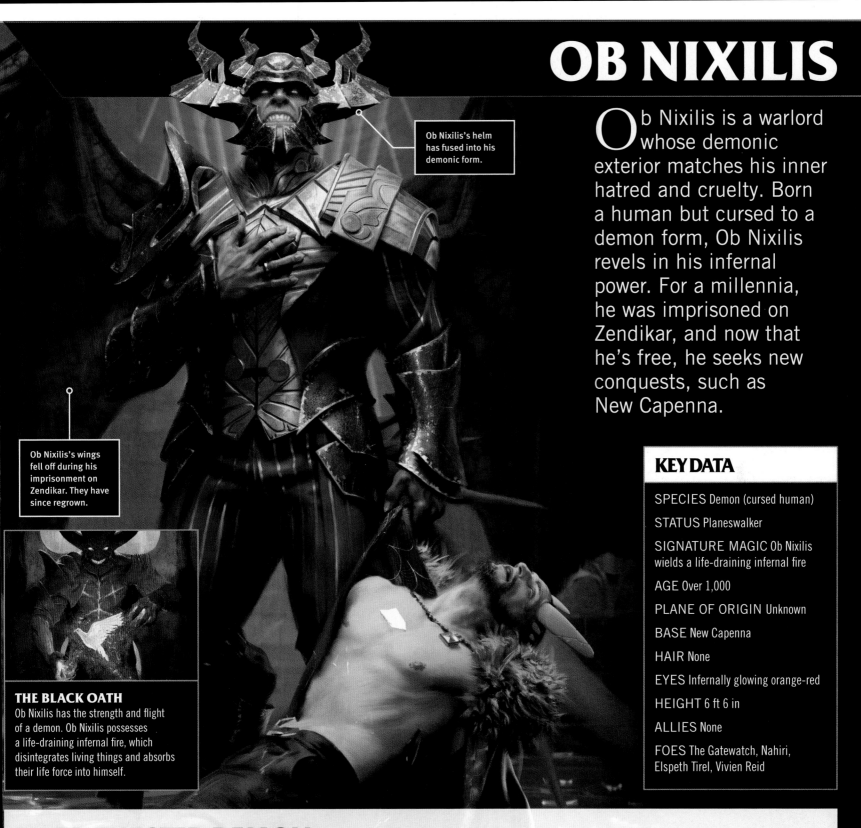

OB NIXILIS

Ob Nixilis is a warlord whose demonic exterior matches his inner hatred and cruelty. Born a human but cursed to a demon form, Ob Nixilis revels in his infernal power. For a millennia, he was imprisoned on Zendikar, and now that he's free, he seeks new conquests, such as New Capenna.

Ob Nixilis's helm has fused into his demonic form.

Ob Nixilis's wings fell off during his imprisonment on Zendikar. They have since regrown.

THE BLACK OATH
Ob Nixilis has the strength and flight of a demon. Ob Nixilis possesses a life-draining infernal fire, which disintegrates living things and absorbs their life force into himself.

KEY DATA

SPECIES Demon (cursed human)

STATUS Planeswalker

SIGNATURE MAGIC Ob Nixilis wields a life-draining infernal fire

AGE Over 1,000

PLANE OF ORIGIN Unknown

BASE New Capenna

HAIR None

EYES Infernally glowing orange-red

HEIGHT 6 ft 6 in

ALLIES None

FOES The Gatewatch, Nahiri, Elspeth Tirel, Vivien Reid

HATE-TWISTED DEMON

Ob Nixilis was a human warlord who conquered his world and made a demonic pact that wiped out life on his plane. His spark ignited and he traveled the Multiverse, conquering plane after plane and then leaving it behind, enjoying the thrill of the conquest but with little desire to rule. He sought out the Chain Veil on Shandalar, but the Veil's curse transformed him into a demon, which he views as a gift.

When he came to Zendikar, the planeswalker guardian Nahiri saw the danger he posed and implanted a binding hedron in his body, which trapped him without his spark for a millennia. When he finally tricked an unsuspecting planeswalker into removing the hedron, Nixilis's full demonic abilities returned. He sabotaged Zendikar's efforts to reimprison the Eldrazi and took the power unleashed to reignite his spark. He nearly killed the Gatewatch, until they combined their abilities and forced him to retreat.

After being lured to Ravnica for the War of the Spark and leaving the others to die as soon as possible, Ob Nixilis set his sights on the plane of New Capenna. A world run by demon mob bosses appealed to him, and he began to recruit from each of the families, until he was powerful enough to challenge them all directly, even killing Xander, the leader of the Maestros.

> **"Morality is just shorthand for the constraints of being powerless."**

OKO

Oko is a charming but unpredictable fae shapeshifter who travels the Multiverse sowing chaos. He uses his abilities to subvert authority, believing himself to be a liberator, but in truth he is simply a capricious trickster in search of any excuse to cause a little mayhem.

Oko's true form is unknown, although he prefers a human-sized form.

Oko's pale skin and blue face markings mark his heritage while in a humanoid form.

FAE CHANGELING

Oko is a faerie shapeshifter, capable of transforming himself and others into different forms. He also possesses fae glamors that make others believe him to be a friend.

THIEF OF CROWNS

No one is quite sure where Oko comes from, but to hear him tell it, he was born on a plane ruled by a rigid faerie society, where the natural mischievousness of the fae had to be suppressed. What the ruling class believed to be a perfect society was anathema to Oko, and so he attempted to hold a mirror up to the hypocrisy of the plane. As a dissident, the authorities tried to suppress his powers, but his planeswalker spark ignited instead. He has spent his indeterminately long life employing his powers to take down the established order. When the cursed Garruk Wildspeaker began to track him through the Multiverse, he enchanted the huntsman to become his servant.

No matter the cruelty of Oko's jokes, he's always guaranteed the sycophant's laughter.

Then came Eldraine, where Oko decided that the Realm was overbearing and would be better off without a pesky high king. He befriended the young Kenrith twins, and then impersonated the High King's closest advisor and transformed the king into a stag. He wanted to reignite a war between the elves of the Wilds and the knights of the Realm, and so he gifted the stag to the elves for their annual wild hunt. Thanks to the Kenrith twins, his plans were foiled, and the meddling teens also freed Garruk from his glamor. Unable to fight the huntsman directly, Oko fled, to find somewhere a bit easier to sow his mischief.

KEY DATA

SPECIES Faerie

STATUS Planeswalker

SIGNATURE MAGIC Oko is a shapeshifter who employs glamors

AGE Appears mid-20s

PLANE OF ORIGIN Unknown

BASE Unknown

HAIR Black with a blue sheen

EYES Light greenish-blue (variable)

HEIGHT 5 ft 5 in (variable)

ALLIES None

FOES Garruk Wildspeaker, Will and Rowan Kenrith

VIVIEN REID

Vivien Reid is a ranger searching for meaning. Her plane, Skalla, was destroyed by the malicious planeswalker Nicol Bolas, but with the elder dragon defeated at the end of the War of the Spark, she has nothing left to avenge. Now she travels the Multiverse, searching for balance in the constant war between nature and civilization.

Vivien typically wears the clothes of a Smaragdi Ranger from Skalla.

Vivien never lets the Arkbow, the last remnant of Skalla, out of her sight.

KEY DATA

SPECIES Human

STATUS Planeswalker

SIGNATURE MAGIC Vivien wields the Arkbow to summon spirits

AGE Late 20s

PLANE OF ORIGIN Skalla

BASE None

HAIR Black with white undercut

EYES Green

HEIGHT 5 ft 10 in

ALLIES The Gatewatch, Elspeth Tirel

FOES Nicol Bolas, Lukka

THE ARKBOW

Vivien is a ranger by training who wields the Arkbow, the last artifact of her lost plane Skalla, which has the ability to store animal spirits and summon them by firing arrows. Vivien has used it to preserve the lost creatures of Skalla and has also added creatures from across the Multiverse.

NATURE'S AVENGER

Vivien Reid is a druidic ranger from the dead plane of Skalla. Years ago, Nicol Bolas destroyed her world, leaving her and the Arkbow she carries as all that remains of that lost world. Seeking revenge, she searched the Multiverse for creatures with the strength to help her challenge the elder dragon. On Ixalan, she was shocked at the cruelty of the Dusk Legion's menagerie and freed the creatures to run rampant through their corrupt city of Luneau. When she was lured to Ravnica with the rest of the planeswalkers during the War of the Spark, she fought alongside the Gatewatch to defeat Nicol Bolas.

With Bolas gone, Vivien needed a new driving purpose. On Ikoria, she found an intriguing balance between civilization and nature with the Bonders and their monsters. But there, too, she found betrayal, when her supposed ally Lukka turned on her to dominate the monsters as a weapon rather than live in harmony with them. After stopping Lukka, she saw firsthand that civilizations could change to embrace nature as the city of Drannith opened its gates to bonders. Heartened, she continued her travels, only to be dragged into the New Phyrexian conflict on New Capenna. Tezzeret and the Phyrexian Praetor Urabrask approached her, providing her with intelligence that the Gatewatch needed. After helping Elspeth Tirel finish her work on New Capenna, the two traveled to Dominaria to join the fight.

"Tread too hard in the forest and it will tread on you in return."

AMINATOU

Aminatou is a mercurial young planeswalker with power over fate. As a young girl, she foresaw that she would one day be a planeswalker and decided to simply become one early. She weaves fates by wielding her magic, expressed as intangible moths, to shift people's destiny. These changes are often subtle and could be as simple as someone stubbing their toe on a rock and avoiding certain death years later as a consequence. Aminatou's own future is constantly shifting as she decides what she wants to be.

KEY DATA

SPECIES Human

STATUS Planeswalker

SIGNATURE MAGIC
Manipulating fate

AGE Preteen

HAIR Black

EYES Black

HEIGHT 4 ft

ALLIES None

FOES None

ESTRID

Constantly striving for self-perfection, Estrid fashions magical masks that imbue her with the strengths and skills of the creatures they represent. Calm and collected in times of danger, Estrid takes pride in her adaptability. She is always ready with the right face—and set of talents—for whatever challenge she encounters. As Estrid journeys through the Multiverse, she seeks mighty creatures with unique fighting styles and weaves their powers into new masks.

KEY DATA

SPECIES Human

STATUS Planeswalker

SIGNATURE MAGIC Estrid enchants magical masks to imbue the wielder with powers

AGE Late 30s

HAIR None (shaved)

EYES Blue

HEIGHT 5 ft 6 in

ALLIES None

FOES None

GRIST

The being known as Grist is, in truth, a polymorphic insect swarm with a hive mind guided by a queen. The entire swarm cannot planeswalk, so when the queen travels between planes, she must create a hive in some secluded place in order to grow the swarm anew. The hive is made up of many specialized body types, each evolved for a specific task, including workers, drones, soldiers, as well as specialized riggers that can strip and animate corpses.

KEY DATA

SPECIES Insect

STATUS Planeswalker

SIGNATURE MAGIC Grist uses toxic chemicals to cause necrosis and can reanimate corpses with the hive

AGE Unknown

HAIR None

EYES Many

HEIGHT Variable (with size of the swarm)

ALLIES None

FOES None

WRENN AND SEVEN

Long ago, to protect her home forest, Wrenn absorbed a mystical inferno and her planeswalker spark ignited. She discovered that bonding to a tree helped her contain the inferno and control her spark, and so she inhabited her first companion, One. She hears the song of the trees and knows which trees are compatible with her—and desires to travel the Multiverse.

Thanks to the help of Teferi, Wrenn has now bonded with Seven, an oak Treefolk from Kessig's ancient forest Ulvenwald, and promised to aid him in his quest to restore lost Zhalfir. Wrenn has learned of New Phyrexia and finds the metal plane anathema to her. Together with Seven, Wrenn seeks to attempt the concept of heroism by aiding the Gatewatch in stopping this unnatural threat to the Multiverse.

KEY DATA

SPECIES Dryad

STATUS Planeswalker

SIGNATURE MAGIC Wrenn contains the power of an inferno while retaining her Dryad nature

AGE Unknown

HAIR White

EYES Orange glow

HEIGHT Variable (with tree height)

ALLIES Teferi, the Gatewatch

FOES New Phyrexia

ACKNOWLEDGMENTS

DK would like to thank: Jay Annelli for his text and expertise; Amazing 15 for peerless packaging; Kayla Dugger for proofreading; Helen Peters for creating the index; and everyone at Wizards of the Coast for their vital assistance and advice, including Paul Morrissey, Kara Kenna, Emily Mei, Ovidio Cartagena, Roy Graham, Emily Teng, Grace Fong, and Matt Danner.

Jay Annelli would like to thank: his amazing wife, Garima, and his children, Arjun and Diya, for their patience on the long days their father spent at the computer writing about fantasy worlds. He would also like to thank his co-hosts on The Vorthos Cast who put up with many absences from the show while he worked on this secret project.

Lastly, an epic thanks to the amazing MAGIC: THE GATHERING artists that bring the wonders of the Multiverse to life. Your work continues to inspire us all.